PRAISE FOR

ADRIATIC

"An excellent exploration of the Adriatic's intriguing geographic and intellectual landscapes . . . The historical scope of [Robert D.] Kaplan's canvas is vast, yet he works hard to bring to it the fruits of modern historical scholarship. That is rare among popular authors, and deserves much praise."

—*The New York Times*

"[An] elegantly layered exploration of Europe's past and future . . . Like the best European travelogues—the wandering, inquisitive weavings of Rebecca West's *Black Lamb and Grey Falcon* (1941) or Patrick Leigh Fermor's *Between the Woods and the Water* (1986)—*Adriatic* mimics the layered complexity of its subject. This is a multifaceted masterpiece, a glittering excavation of the glories and rubbish heaps of Europe's past, a meditation on history and the inner journey of traveling with books in mind, a traveler's elegy for paths taken and not taken, and a conditionally hopeful reflection on Europe's emerging future."

—*The Wall Street Journal*

BY ROBERT D. KAPLAN

ADRIATIC

ADRIATIC

A
Concert of
Civilizations
at the
End of the
Modern
Age

ROBERT D. KAPLAN

RANDOM HOUSE

NEW YORK

Published in the United States by Random House,
an imprint and division of Penguin Random House LLC, New York.

RANDOM HOUSE and the HOUSE colophon are registered
trademarks of Penguin Random House LLC.

Originally published in hardcover in the United States by Random House,
an imprint and division of Penguin Random House LLC, in 2022.

Brief portions of this work were originally published in *Mediterranean Winter*
by Robert D. Kaplan (New York: Random House, 2004).

Grateful acknowledgment is made to the following for
permission to reprint previously published material:

Farrar, Straus and Giroux and Carcanet Press Limited: Excerpts from "The Bust of Tiberius"
from *Collected Poems in English* by Joseph Brodsky, edited by Ann Kjellberg, translated by
Anthony Hecht, copyright © 2000 by the Estate of Joseph Brodsky. Rights in the
United Kingdom are controlled by Carcanet Press Limited. Reprinted by permission of
Farrar, Straus and Giroux and Carcanet Press Limited, Manchester, UK. All rights reserved.

Indiana University Press: Excerpts from *The Divine Comedy, Volume I: Inferno* by Dante Alighieri,
translated by Mark Musa, copyright © 1971 by Indiana University Press; excerpts from *The Divine
Comedy, Volume II: Purgatory* by Dante Alighieri, translated by Mark Musa, copyright © 1981 by
Mark Musa; excerpts from *The Divine Comedy, Volume III: Paradise* by Dante Alighieri, translated by
Mark Musa, copyright © 1984 by Mark Musa. Reprinted with permission of Indiana University Press.

New Directions Publishing Corporation and Faber and Faber Ltd.: Excerpts from "Canto I,"
"Canto IX," and "Canto XVII" from *The Cantos of Ezra Pound* by Ezra Pound, copyright © 1934 by
Ezra Pound; excerpts from "Canto LII" and "Canto LXV" from *The Cantos of Ezra Pound* by Ezra
Pound, copyright © 1940 by Ezra Pound; excerpt from "Canto LXXXI" from *The Cantos of Ezra Pound*
by Ezra Pound, copyright © 1948 by Ezra Pound. Print rights throughout the United Kingdom
excluding Canada are controlled by Faber and Faber Ltd. Reprinted by permission
of New Directions Publishing Corporation and Faber and Faber Ltd.

Princeton University Press: "Mythistorema" from *Collected Poems* by George Seferis,
translated, edited, and introduced by Edmund Keeley and Philip Sherrard, copyright © 1995
by Princeton University Press. Reprinted by permission of
Princeton University Press conveyed through Copyright Clearance Center.

Random House, an imprint and division of Penguin Random House LLC: Excerpts from
"The First Elegy" and "The Sixth Elegy" from *The Selected Poetry of Rainer Maria Rilke* by
Rainer Maria Rilke, edited and translated by Stephen Mitchell, copyright © 1982
by Stephen Mitchell. Used by permission of Random House,
an imprint and division of Penguin Random House LLC. All rights reserved.

LIBRARY OF CONGRESS CATALOGING-IN-PUBLICATION DATA
NAMES: Kaplan, Robert D., author.
TITLE: Adriatic : a concert of civilizations at the end
of the modern age / Robert D. Kaplan.
OTHER TITLES: Concert of civilizations at the end of the modern age
DESCRIPTION: New York : Random House, [2022] |
Includes bibliographical references and index.
IDENTIFIERS: LCCN 2021020803 (print) | LCCN 2021020804 (ebook) |
ISBN 9780399591051 (trade paperback) | ISBN 9780399591068 (ebook)
SUBJECTS: LCSH: Kaplan, Robert D.—Travel—Adriatic Sea Region. |
Adriatic Sea Region—Description and travel. | Adriatic Sea Region—History. |
Adriatic Sea Region—In literature.
CLASSIFICATION: LCC D971 .K37 2022 (print) | LCC D971 (ebook) |
DDC 909/.098224—dc23
LC record available at https://lccn.loc.gov/2021020803
LC ebook record available at https://lccn.loc.gov/2021020804

Printed in the United States of America on acid-free paper

randomhousebooks.com

3rd Printing

Title-page images from iStock

Book design by Barbara M. Bachman

To

David Leeming and
the late Charles Boer

Here I am at the station from which I left on my first journey, it has remained as it was then, without any change. All the lives that I could have led begin here.

—ITALO CALVINO,
*If on a Winter's Night
a Traveler* (1979)

But how can you look at something and set your own ego aside? Whose eyes are doing the looking?

—ITALO CALVINO,
Mr. Palomar (1983)

"Europe" is too large and too nebulous a concept around which to forge any convincing human community. And it is not psychologically realistic to posit, along lines favored by the German writer Jürgen Habermas, a local and supranational duality of communities around which allegiances may form, prudently shorn of the dangerous emphasis on "identity" associated with the historical national unit. It does not work. . . . "Europe" is more than a geographical notion but less than an answer.

—TONY JUDT,
A Grand Illusion? (1996)

CONTENTS

—

The Globe in Miniature

—

The real adventure of travel is intellectual, because the most profound journeys are interior in nature. That is why travel at its most useful creates a bibliography. For the most affecting of landscapes invite research into their history and material culture, so that the result of a journey is that books pile up in one's library: everything from poetry to history to philosophy to geopolitics and the legacies of empires and civilizations. For they all (and much more) flow together. Because such a bibliography knows no categories, it is a rebuke to academic specialization, even as the greatest of academic specialists build out from a narrow base to uncover a universe. It is the books of those particular specialists that guide me: they are characters in this journey as much as the landscapes I encounter. For it is the books you have read, as much as the people you have met, that constitute autobiography.

Because travel is a journey of the mind, the scope of the journey is limitless, encompassing all manner of introspection and concerned with the great debates and issues of our age. The glossy travel magazines, selling pure fantasy as they often do—with photo spreads of delectable fashion models set against backgrounds of Third World splendor—manifest nothing so much as a profound boredom. This has nothing to do with travel.

Travel is psychoanalysis that starts in a specific moment of time and space. And everything about that moment is both unique and sacred—everything. As Borges writes, "The moon of Bengal is not the same as the moon of Yemen."[1] Because you stand fully conscious before a moon and a sky that are not exactly like they are in any other place, in any other time, travel is an intensified form of consciousness, and therefore an affirmation of individual existence: that you have an identity even beyond that which the world, your family, and your friends have given you. And because no one has the right to know you as you know yourself, you must seek to become more than what you are by exposing yourself to different lands, and the history and architecture that go with them.

And you must do so alone! No one should get between you and a distant shore: not even a loved one. Originality emanates from solitude: from letting your thoughts wander in alien terrain. I boarded a ferry from Pescara to Split a half century ago to feel alive thus. For this reason I am alone now in a church in Rimini in winter. The lonelier the setting, the crueler the weather, the greater the possibilities for beauty, I tell myself. Great poetry is not purple; it is severe.

Seeking out the strange and unfamiliar does not confer wisdom, of course. To see the differences between peoples and cultures is not the same as to find some of them, as they say, "exotic"—a word that should itself be exiled. Exoticism arose as an escape from the mass society, where everyday life is full of banality and boredom. But as industrialization and post-industrialization seep everywhere on the planet, differences between places and peoples must be teased out of an acquired familiarity, not an unfamiliarity. The mystery of travel involves the layers revealed about yourself as you devour such knowledge. Thus, travel must lead to self-doubt. And I am full of doubts. The more I am praised in some quarters, the more I find fault with much of what I've done. With doubts come guilt and self-recrimination. Now that I am old, I realize that the differences between the groups and the peoples about which I once reported—in specific places, in specific moments in time—are transforming and evaporating before my eyes, as humanity strives towards a synthesis.

———

But these are all things that I have discovered in the course of this journey: a journey that originated with the desire for solitude and introspection, but which turned out—stage by stage—as I covered more miles, and headed into more politically fragile terrain, to be a work of reporting; where I was, in the end, talking to all manner of Slovenian and Croatian thinkers and Montenegrin and Albanian strongmen. I failed my vow of silence at some geographical point where Italy merges into the Slavic world, discovering that my questions about Europe at the end of the modern age brought back the relevance of early modernism (between the Renaissance and the Industrial Revolution) to our own times, in which identities have once again become fluid and multiple. These questions were too urgent to be left only to books and my private thoughts. The Adriatic was an obvious place to look for answers: though overlooked by journalists and professional strategists, the Adriatic defines Central and Eastern Europe as much as the Baltic and Black Seas do.

And the further I progressed in my journey, what became obvious was this:

The dichotomy between Occident and Orient, always fragile on these shores, always interwoven, registers less and less: rather than a "clash," there is a "concert." Catholicism and Orthodoxy, Orthodoxy and Islam, Western Rome and Eastern Rome, the Mediterranean and the Balkans, achieve a stirring fusion on the Adriatic. All of Europe is distilled here, within a geography that one can actually comprehend and therefore grasp. It is the globe in miniature. Indeed, the civilizational subtleties of the Adriatic now encompass the world. The age of populism that the media declares is merely an epiphenomenon: a swan song for the age of nationalism itself. The Adriatic, consequently, constitutes an elegy to a category of distinctions that I spent my life observing. I am certain only in my loss of certainty. It is in this way that I deconstruct myself—in the course of a journey, obviously.

My journey culminates in Corfu, where I confront through Greece's own past the ultimate human and historical drama: that of the refugee experience. Migration is the story of humanity. It will continue to define Europe in the twenty-first century: the influx of Arabs and Africans that we have seen so far is merely the beginning. And few migrations have been as heartrending and instructive as that of over a million ethnic Greeks from Asia Minor to Greece itself in the early 1920s. More of that later, though. First, there is much ground to cover and much to build upon.

Finally, I write at the edge of a precipice. A precious, eclectic seascape that encompasses the whole of Europe—including its Orthodox and Muslim aspects—is about to become planetary, as the new and vast maritime empire of China threatens to overwhelm all of these European associations that I have sketched herein, making this journey a mere period piece, a tour-ender in old foreign correspondents' lingo. For the Adriatic is about to be linked with the South China Sea and the Indian Ocean as key elements of a burgeoning global trade, from Hong Kong to Trieste by way of Hambantota, Gwadar, and other Indian Ocean ports.

Then there is the battle over new natural gas discoveries in the eastern Mediterranean, and the struggle over oil in war-torn Libya. More than half a dozen littoral countries are involved in both intense negotiations and military positioning to see which consortium controls these envisioned pipelines, some of which may enter Europe through the Adriatic. Truly, the Adriatic is becoming a choke point of international trade and geopolitical interests.

But how to grapple with such an overwhelming vision?

By going local, rather than global. By boring deep into the historical and aesthetic peculiarities of each place, rather than losing the texture through some bland and abstract, formulaic global approach. In the early years of the twenty-first century I traveled throughout the greater Indian Ocean, in anticipation of its christening as the "Indo-Pacific" by the Pentagon. At the beginning of the second decade of the twenty-first century I journeyed through the South China Sea, in anticipation of that region's future in news headlines. And in the middle of that second de-

cade, in 2016, I began traveling throughout the Adriatic, in anticipation of its possible destiny as the western maritime terminus of China's Belt and Road.

But my aim has not been to theorize on global geopolitics in light of China's and Russia's return to great power status. Rather, the reverse: for the macro view requires a base of granular knowledge. And thus, just as the Adriatic is about to realize a new global significance, I have decided to employ it as a geographical metaphor for an age that is passing: the modern age itself in Europe. Only by appreciating what is passing can we better analyze what is about to come.

I begin here, in this Italian church, a refuge from the wind and lashing rain, conscious of the beating of my own pulse. Is there a better way to measure time?

I begin, as I have said, in solitude, in this case with a contemplation of a failed modernist poet. But journeys like this one, however grand in design, often begin in narrow obscurity.

ADRIATIC

RIMINI

—

*Europe in
Limestone*

THE GEOPOLITICAL MAP OF EUROPE HAS MOVED SOUTH, back to the Mediterranean, where Europe borders Africa and the Middle East. The Mediterranean has now begun to achieve a fluid classical coherence, uniting continents. But explaining this will take time. It involves philosophy, poetry, and landscape before I get to international relations.

So bear with me.

NEVER DOES EUROPE'S PAGAN inheritance seem so sure of itself as at the entrance to this Christian church. The piazza, polished and lonely in the downpour, is dramatically reduced by a line of other buildings directly at my back. The longer I look, the more extraordinary the church becomes. Between the massive columns mounted on a high stylobate ledge are blind arcades guarding, in turn, a confidently deep triangular pediment. And within that triangular pediment is a lintel that anchors the whole facade. Form and proportion take over. In classical architecture, beauty is mathematical and equates with perfection.

Passing through the door, rather than a warm and embracing candlelit darkness, there is a shivery, pounding silence and the perpetual late afternoon light of an overcast day. I feel like ducking under the clouds. The loud echo of another pair of footsteps every few minutes reinforces my loneliness. A yawning marble floor overwhelms the meager rows of benches approaching the apse (rebuilt after the World War II bombing). The longer I sit here, the more vast and spare the marble becomes. The iron cold begins its assault.

Instead of experiencing the splendor of egg tempera and oil, I am aware of the white limestone clarity of an archaeological ruin: one reconstructed by the early Renaissance. Rather than color, force and volume emanate from the flattened and compressed reliefs. The feast of limestone sculptures in the side chapels takes possession of me. Because of the limestone, these crowded and intricate figures, despite their energy, expressiveness, and flowing movement, achieve an abstract and theoretical intensity. This is art that makes you think as well as feel. I am not seeing just the art—I am seeing a path back to antiquity by way of late medieval city-states, in which communal survival left little room for conventional morality. For beauty can often emerge from the celebration of power, making it a register of Europe's past, present, and future.

The fat, swollen putti are all in a frenzy to no purpose: they celebrate the primal urge to life. The sculptor has represented them as sexuality incarnate. The reliefs emerge out of the gloom, all the more extraordinary because of the inadequate lighting in the side chapels. Though the figures are pressed into the wall, their partially robed musculatures burst forth in three dimensions with only minimal carving by the sculptor, like poems that reveal whole universes with only a few words. Between the pilasters, along with the angels there are the Roman gods, the signs of the zodiac, and the exalted humanized symbols of the arts: philosophy, history, rhetoric, and music. Here Christianity is merely the final element of an accrued and vibrant civilization.

Nothing concentrates the mind like semi-darkness and cold. These monastic surroundings give me much to think about, and the memory of many books to consider before I begin my journey in earnest. Outside, the sky is slammed shut, as rain hammers the seaboard and clouds almost touch the water, like ink streaking down a canvas.

MY PATH TO THIS CHURCH—this temple, really—has been labyrinthine, in which memorable landscapes have led me to various historians and writers, and those historians and writers to more such. I must reference them all because they are part of the story, as well as beautiful in their own right.

IT ALL BEGAN OVER four decades ago at Mistra, a ruined medieval city located on a spur of the Taygetus at the edge of the Eurotas Valley, in Greece's southern Peloponnese. It was at Mistra where Byzantium finally expired. In Mistra, because of political unrest in far-off Constantinople, the Serbo-Greek Constantine XI Dragases was crowned in 1449, last of the eighty-eight Byzantine emperors and last heir to Caesar Augustus in Rome.

Mistra, on that first visit of mine in 1978, though it was spring, seemed arrested in late autumn, its broken walls and vegetation reduced to every brown and ocher shade. The most exquisite landscapes are the subtlest: they drain you, fatigue you utterly, rather than overwhelm. And thus I became obsessed with Mistra's ruins and its history. Its beauty was such that I thought everything about the place was worth knowing about.

My obsession with Mistra led to an enduring interest in its most important figure, the Neoplatonist philosopher who lived in the fourteenth and fifteenth centuries, Georgios Gemistos Plethon. Plethon was a kindler of the Italian Renaissance because of his scholarly dedication to classical antiquity, something much in evidence during an extended visit he made to Florence in 1439, when he impressed none other than Cosimo de' Medici. As the late British philosopher and translator Philip Sherrard explains, whereas Aristotle had already been assimilated into (or at least neutralized by) a "universal Christian consciousness," Plato's beliefs lay outside the Orthodox Christian establishment of the day, and thus Plato was seen by Plethon and others as the more pagan of the two philosophers. As the Byzantine world was dying, Plethon knew that Byzantium's "one great asset," in the words of another late Briton, the medievalist Steven Runciman, was how it "had preserved unadulterated the learning and literature of ancient Greece." Plethon carried that preserved wisdom with him to Italy. Thus, Plethon helped foment a Greek national resurgence, built on this classical legacy of pantheism embedded in Byzantium, in the face of a political and religious assault from the Latin West. Incorporating Plato, as the quintessence of ancient Greece, into the world of the Greek Orthodox Church enabled this process.[1]

This had all remained deeply embedded in my memory for decades on end when, in 2002, almost a quarter century after I first visited Mistra, I found myself in another part of the Peloponnese, at the villa of the British travel writer Patrick Leigh Fermor—the thrilling prospect of the Messinian Gulf and gnarled olive groves available through the arched windows as we talked. It was a cold spring day and Leigh Fermor's clothes reeked deliciously of smoking logs. We had been drinking a decanted liter of homemade retsina when I happened to mention Gemistos Plethon. Leigh Fermor's eyes flashed and he regaled me with a low-voiced disquisition, barely rising above a mumble, of how Plethon's remains had been exhumed in 1465, thirteen years after his death, when Sigismondo Malatesta, the ancestral ruler of Rimini and mercenary commander of a Venetian expeditionary force, held the lower town of Mistra and refused to withdraw ahead of an advancing Ottoman army without first claiming the body of his favorite philosopher. Leigh Fermor's voice was about to expire when he explained that Malatesta, a discriminating patron of the arts and philosophy, reburied Plethon in a sarcophagus in an outer wall of his Tempio Malatestiano in Rimini: the temple where I now sit.[2]

Sigismondo Pandolfo Malatesta (1417–1468) was the scion of a feudal family that ruled over the city-state of Rimini from the late thirteenth century to the beginning of the sixteenth. Malatesta was a condottiere, that is, a mercenary captain, because he operated according to a contract, a *condotta*. The ultimate man of action, he literally lived for years on end under a sentence of death in one form or another, as he sold his truly remarkable military skills to one city-state after the next, and in the end lost most of his own city-state of Rimini in the bargain. His image was publicly burnt in Rome. The popes were after his lands, the Medici bank after his money, and yet in spite of his constantly changing alliances and his weakness against the great powers of the papacy, Venice, and Milan—despite defeat, disgrace, and betrayals (as well as triumphs)—Malatesta managed to transform this Franciscan Gothic church into one of the most arresting of Renaissance temples, filled with bas-reliefs of pagan gods, in order only to glorify himself and his longtime mistress and later wife, Isotta degli Atti. Malatesta was an eruption of life in its most elemental and primitive form: someone who, as several historians have suggested, was without conventional morals, yet came armed with unlimited supplies of energy and heroism.[3] I think of the portrait of Malatesta executed by Piero della Francesca in 1450, which hangs in the Louvre: with the amazingly aquiline nose, the stingy lips, and the implacable and contemptuous eyes.

IT WAS NOT ONLY Mistra and Patrick Leigh Fermor that led me here to the Tempio Malatestiano: there was also *The Cantos* of Ezra Pound. Pound's poetry, much of which is not very good, is like an obscure tunnel that leads into the daylight to offer nothing less than a larger contemplation of Europe.

For Ezra Pound, Sigismondo Malatesta was the perfect "factive" personality, that is, a symbol of manhood in its entirety, a figure both brutal and treacherous, even as he was supremely cultivated in the arts. Malatesta, in Pound's formation, represents a harmonious whole created from dissident elements: a personality "imprinting itself on its time, its mark surviving all expropriation," writes Hugh Kenner, the late Pound scholar and interpreter of his poetry. In Pound's rendering, Malatesta is a man of *virtù*—manly virtue— much less because of his swashbuckling derring-do than because of the very fact that he actually restored and decorated this temple, making it such a perfect work of art. (Bernard Berenson, perhaps the greatest art connoisseur of the twentieth century, fully agreeing with Pound, writes that the building of such a monument gave Malatesta the reputation he "wished posterity to believe" he deserved.)

Why are some figures remembered, and others forgotten? For it is the Tempio Malatestiano itself—an epic in its own right—and an act of sheer will that raises Malatesta above all the other rogues and fighting men of his time. Malatesta's military exploits would have been wasted, pointless, were it not for the work of art that emerged from them: this Tempio. Imperialism and war, in Pound's view, can only be justified by art. For it is the artistic epic that permits civilization to both endure and begin anew.[4]

Pound devotes several of his early and most well-known Cantos to Sigismondo Malatesta, whom he idealizes with so much biographical detail that the poems (and this is a serious issue with *The Cantos* in general) "decline into catalogue" in places, in the estimation of another Pound biographer. Pound in "Canto IX" calls Malatesta "POLUMETIS," a Homeric adjective meaning "many-minded," a reference to the adaptability and resourcefulness of Odysseus himself. Pound is simply infatuated with Malatesta: the toughened warrior he both critiques and identifies with. Just as

Malatesta was a patron of the arts and of philosophy, Pound, consciously modeling himself after his hero, was likewise philanthropic to other writers and artists in the course of his own life in Europe. There was clearly a Malatesta-like gallantry to Pound's own efforts. Pound famously tried to help James Joyce find a publisher for *Dubliners* and *A Portrait of the Artist as a Young Man*, and later to find a magazine to serialize *Ulysses*. This was at a time when Joyce was living in exile in near poverty in Trieste. Pound also helped T. S. Eliot publish "The Love Song of J. Alfred Prufrock." It was Pound who helped discover Eliot, in fact, and who, as we all know, edited *The Waste Land*. Pound grasped early on both the artistic potential and the *epic* quality of the work of both writers. For Pound, manly risk was almost inseparable from the creation of the artistic tour de force: so that the image of the larger-than-life violence of Malatesta, which helped produce this masterpiece of a temple, where I now ache in the cold, would ironically become central to Pound's own nascent fascism. In fact, Pound's infatuation with Mussolini, another Italian man of action, can be traced directly to his infatuation with Malatesta.[5]

Pound's writing in the Malatesta Cantos is superficially infectious. It is just so relentlessly obscure and panoramic, sending you constantly to the encyclopedia. I'll never forget reading "Canto IX" for the first time as a young person, and coming back to it periodically over the years. It begins in wide-screen mid-gallop:

> One year floods rose,
> One year they fought in the snows . . .
>
> And he stood in the water up to his neck
> to keep the hounds off him . . .
>
> And he fought in Fano, in a street fight,
> and that was nearly the end of him . . .

And he talked down the anti-Hellene,
And there was an heir male to the seignor,
And Madame Ginevra died.

And he, Sigismundo, was Capitan for the Venetians.
And he had sold off small castles
and built the great Rocca to his plan,

And he fought like ten devils at Monteluro
and got nothing but the victory

And old Sforza bitched us at Pesaro ...
And he, Sigismundo, spoke his mind to Francesco
and we drove them out of the Marches.[6]

I am quoting but fragments of a Canto that goes on for eight long pages, assaulting the reader with a deluge of factual minutiae that, however admirably researched, sometimes border on the incomprehensible (at least for the layman) because they often lack the proper context, yet are at once both aromatic and cinematic, even as they express within Malatesta's own person the evil, wasteful forces of an entire age.[7] Though, whether this makes for good, that is, disciplined, poetry, I am not sure. There is an air of dilettantism about it. Hugh Kenner rises to Pound's defense: "This was a poetic of fact, not of mood or response, or of disembodied Overwhelming Questions."[8]

I have grown out of much in life, but never out of what I consider the very best of Ezra Pound's sometimes very bad poetry—which is evident in his early Cantos, before he lost his way. Here is Pound's own justification:

The only way to escape from rhetoric and frilled paper decoration is through beauty. ... I mean by that that one must call a spade a spade in form so exactly adjusted, in a metric in itself so seductive, that the statement will not bore the auditor. . . . There are few fallacies more common than the opinion that poetry should mimic the daily speech. . . . Colloquial poetry is to the real art as the barber's wax dummy is to sculpture.[9]

Indeed, everywhere there is the poet's granular infatuation with the pre-industrial world, attesting to what James Laughlin, the founder of New Directions publishing house, calls Pound's "ideogrammatic" method,[10] in which the poet, according to his own words, is "bottling" history, shifting from one image to another, "ply over ply." In "Canto III" we meet El Cid at Burgos. In "Canto IV" we are at Troy, which is "but a heap of smouldering boundary stones." There are the Plantagenets in "Canto VI" and Dante in "Canto VII," followed by Malatesta and it would seem everything about his times in the next Cantos, complete with references to Classe, Ravenna, and San Vitale: places where I will go next following Rimini, after I leave Pound as a subject far behind in my travels.

Inside the Tempio Malatestiano, my mind wanders to the Chinese landscape in "Canto LII":

> This month are trees in full sap
> Rain has now drenched all the earth
>   dead weeds enrich it, as if boil'd in a bouillon.[11]

And then to the famous—infamous actually—"Canto XLV":

> Usura is a murrain, usura
> blunteth the needle in the maid's hand
> and stoppeth the spinner's cunning. Pietro Lombardo
> came not by usura . . .
> nor Pier della Francesca . . .[12]

Pound had an obsession with everything that is old to a naive, ideological, and therefore dangerous purpose. Usury, lending money, was associated with the Jews, and certainly there is overt anti-Semitism in "Canto LII" and covert anti-Semitism here in "Canto XLV." The overt anti-Semitism of "Canto LII" quotes a statement by Benjamin Franklin about keeping the Jews out of the New World, a statement that in fact was forged: so that Pound's history is sometimes—often, according to his critics—very bad history. For Pound, usury functions as nothing less than the original sin that prevents man from creating a paradise on earth. Pound, in other words, decidedly harbors a utopian streak, which almost always is perilous. Pound's fascism and anti-Semitism are more than well known—they are one of the first organizing principles one discovers about him. And this does—must, in fact—undermine his poetry. There are, for example, no mitigating circumstances to Pound's World War II radio broadcasts in defense of Mussolini. Indeed, he even praised *Mein Kampf.* Still, as William Carlos Williams once said about Pound's work: "It's the best damned ear ever born to listen to this language!" Or as Kenner writes at the beginning of his book *The Poetry of Ezra Pound,* in an obvious reference to Pound's moral disrepute: "I have had to choose, and I have chosen rather to reveal the work than to present the man."[13]

But the demolition of Pound has gone on. Such literary and intellectual personages as George Orwell, Robert Graves, Randall Jarrell, Joseph Brodsky, Clive James, and others—Robert Conquest most notably—have all eviscerated Pound both as a person and as a poet, and in some cases convincingly refute Kenner's implication that the two can be disentangled. Pound's Cantos are too often unreadable and make no sense, these poets and critics say, and even some of his translations are bad: Pound, as one critic has said, is like an incoherent blogger many decades before his time. And always there is his hate.

Pound hated more than just Jews. He was deeply estranged from the United States and any place, in fact, where "his family belonged and [he] had a personal history," writes biographer Humphrey Carpenter. This is very much in line with what the Yale professor

Langdon Hammer observes about Pound's friend and modernist contemporary T. S. Eliot:

> Modernism meant *de-naturalization* for Eliot: only a se-
> ries of intimate estrangements—from his place of origin, his
> family, his "native" language, his early self—could have made
> Eliot the particular poet he was. In this respect, Eliot never
> changed nationality; he gave up nationality in order to enter
> an international community, a community unified not by its
> use of a specific language, but by its relation to language as
> such.[14]

Indeed, both Eliot and Pound go quite a bit further than mixing foreign words, foreign place-names, and whole foreign-language passages into their English-language poems. Inspired by European and world literature more than by American literature, they aim to deeply enrich the English language with other traditions, leaving it immeasurably altered. (*The Waste Land,* for instance, which Eliot dedicates to Pound, has passages from six foreign languages, including Sanskrit.)[15] Of course, these men are not really American poets at all, and to consider them as such is to diminish them. The fact that they were expatriates is obviously not coincidental. They are cosmopolitan poets, erasing the distinctions between East and West. The poet Charles Olson mused that Pound, with his nostalgia for civilizations and his philosophical and moral decadence, may have become "the ultimate image of the end of the West," something that warns of our own time.[16]

KEEP BEARING WITH ME.

Pound, like Eliot and Joyce—again, as we all know—helped to define literary modernism. And literary modernism, according to the critic Edmund Wilson, arose in part out of the French Symbolist movement—this is where the obscure tunnel I mentioned earlier begins to open into daylight. As Wilson explains, the starting point of Symbolism is this: "Every feeling or sensation we have, every moment of consciousness, is different from every other," and therefore it is "impossible to render our sensations as we actually experience them through . . . ordinary literature." Consequently, each poet or writer must invent a language of his own, in which, rather than use direct statements and descriptions, he conveys images and metaphors that suggest his personal experience of consciousness to the reader. Pound, along with Eliot and Joyce, all write in symbols, and for Pound these symbols have their essences in obscure historical facts. While both Pound and Eliot are nominally American and write in English, they base their work on a revolution that occurred outside English literature—in French and European literature. This is yet another layer of their cosmopolitanism, and relatedly of the collapse of the East and West into each other, of which their poetry is a portent, and which is ultimately part of today's European crisis.[7]

Moreover, with Pound there is this intoxicating, lava-coated aura to his historical references that once appealed to my youthful sensibility: a heady element of his granular attention to distant epochs in both Europe *and* Asia. And, as I matured and became more interested in abstract matters rather than in atmospherics—in Confucian philosophy itself rather than in merely the setting for it, in the geopolitics of Italian city-states rather than in the art they produced—Pound's evocative allusions to such matters, idiosyncratic as they might be, arguably nutty and crackpot for significant stretches, kept me from altogether deserting him.

But what had ignited my interest in him? I ask myself, as the January cold subjugates this church.

It began at the beginning, with "Canto I," published in 1925. I still remember reading it for the first time as a nineteen-year-old:

> And then went down to the ship,
> Set keel to breakers, forth on the godly sea, and

> We set up mast and sail on that swart ship,
> Bore sheep aboard her, and our bodies also
> Heavy with weeping, and winds from sternward
> Bore us out onward with bellying canvas,
> Circe's this craft, the trim-coifed goddess.
> Then sat we amidships, wind jamming the tiller. . . .
> Sun to his slumber, shadows o'er all the ocean,
> Came we then to the bounds of deepest water,
> To the Kimmerian lands, and peopled cities
> Covered with close-webbed mist. . . .
> came we then to the place
> Aforesaid by Circe.
> Here did they rites, Perimedes and Eurylochus . . .
> Poured we libations unto each the dead. . . .
> Dark blood flowed in the fosse,
> Souls out of Erebus . . . of brides
> Of youths and of the old who had borne much . . .
> *A man of no fortune, and with a name to come. . . .*"[18]

Here is the ultimate adventure, in which the hero Odysseus is steeled by the memory of the Trojan War, just as the poet Pound is steeled by the memory of World War I. The preparations to sail out of the Underworld, the start of an epic journey, the dramatic sense of discovery in the obscure, fog-wrapped far shore of the Black Sea, where the barbarian Cimmerians lived; the very act of leaving, once again, with no respite, for the unknown; the wisdom that can come from war and desolation, and the triumph that may follow in the course of a long and painful life. *Damn Pound.* Yes, his worst critics make a good case. *The Cantos* are in large measure an incoherent failure, a "rag-bag faking of the extraordinary," in the words of the late Robert Conquest.[19] And yet there are a few Cantos, as well as fragments of others, that linger beautifully in the ear.

My original attraction to the poem was narcissistic. I was young and imagined my own heroic life story ahead of me. But as I accu-

mulated my own disappointments, and my own guilt-laden professional and personal burdens that have nearly immobilized me at
times, the poem's depths that I had previously skimmed over shone
through. Thus, I have spent my life with it.

Pound had found the medieval Latin version of the *Odyssey* by
Andreas Divus in a Left Bank bookstall. He immediately became
attracted to the "Nekyia," often considered the most "pervasively
archaic" part of the *Odyssey,* about Odysseus's journey to the Underworld on the goddess Circe's instructions.[20] Just as Divus translated the *Odyssey* from ancient Greek into medieval Latin, Pound
translated the medieval Latin into English, employing the rhythm
of the Old English "Seafarer." That was the basis of what would
eventually become the first Canto. Conquest disparages Pound's
knowledge as "adventitious."[21] But isn't so much of the most useful,
satisfying knowledge explained and discovered that way? Wasn't the
philosopher Walter Benjamin's ragpicker, in fact, a finder of useful
things in the course of haphazard searches?[22]

Travel leads to books, and good books lead you to other good
books. And thus, I have become an obsessive reader of bibliographies. It was a similar method that led Pound on an intellectual and
artistic journey to *The Cantos,* which audaciously evoke history and
landscape in a way that even Robert Conquest, with all of his classical erudition, and with all of his incisiveness, cannot quite take
away from him.

A YOUNG ENGLISHMAN, Adrian Stokes, discovered the beauty of
Pound's Malatesta Cantos in 1926. The consequence was a book
that Stokes himself authored in 1934, *Stones of Rimini,* about his
own aesthetic passion for the Tempio Malatestiano.* I now hold my

---

*   Stokes's book is in style and themes replete with Poundian spirit. Donald Davie,
Ezra Pound: Poet as Sculptor (Oxford: Oxford University Press, [1964] 1968), pp. 127–31 and
155–56.

yellowy and dog-eared 1969 paperback edition of Stokes's book on my lap inside the Tempio.

"I write of stone. I write of Italy," Stokes begins. In particular, the entire 264 pages are an ode to limestone. "Of all weathering, that of limestone . . . is the most vivid. It is limestone that combines with gases in the air, that is carved by the very breath we breathe out. It is limestone that forms new skins and poetic efflorescence: above all, limestone is sensitive to the most apparent of sculptural agencies, the rain." The entire Mediterranean ambience, Stokes goes on, is based on limestone. "Those inlets and harbours, dear to commerce, are mostly of limestone formation. . . . Vine, olive and fig flourish on limestone soils. . . . In the Tempio reliefs Mediterranean life has complete expression: there, water is stone."

Many of the Tempio reliefs, Stokes goes on, "have the appearance of marble limbs seen in water," even as there is "the delicious torture of hair and clothing by an unseen, evocative wind." There is such a ferment of movement everywhere here that it is almost as if "the figures were conceived in the round and were then pressed into low relief." The sculptor responsible for all this—and the hero of Stokes's book, in fact—was one Agostino di Duccio of Florence, who was in the service of Malatesta and who lived in Rimini between 1449 and 1457.[23]

This flawless and obscure volume has been my guide here. Patrick Leigh Fermor, Ezra Pound, Edmund Wilson, Bernard Berenson, the clashing criticisms of Hugh Kenner and Robert Conquest, the rich and tapestried histories on Eastern Orthodoxy and Gemistos Plethon by Philip Sherrard, Steven Runciman, and C. M. Woodhouse, and so many other disparate books—they led me to this one by Adrian Stokes. In this way, travel is the ultimate rebuke to the servitude of what the Spanish philosopher José Ortega y Gasset calls the "mass-man," who in this technological era of ever-intensifying specialization knows nothing beyond his own narrow cubicle of existence.[24] It is my own form of revolt as an individual.

For the bibliography I have begun to assemble must be vast in
scope—and I am only at the beginning. My aim is to use a linear
geographical journey as a method of orienting my reading, with
each place and book building on the ones before, with contemporary people and voices ultimately coming into the picture. And it all
must start and end with Greece, Europe's rear door: with Mistra
and with Corfu. It is only in this way that Europe—what it has
been, and what it might still be—may reveal itself better to me.

THE THIRD CHAPEL TO my right is where Agostino di Duccio
carved the pagan gods and signs of the zodiac—Diana, Saturn,
Mercury, Ganymede, and so on: as if, like Ezra Pound, Agostino
were obsessed with cataloguing through his own art the full extent
of classical knowledge. It being shortly after Christmas, this pagan-
ized chapel has been taken over by a Nativity scene, with straw
completely covering the floor as in a manger, and tawdry makeshift
statues of the Wise Men around the plastic infant Jesus. I glance
for a moment toward the renovated apse where a magnificent
fourteenth-century crucifix by Giotto hangs. Here in this semi-
darkness is Europe, where the Greek and Roman world gave birth
to Christendom. And Christendom in diluted and affectingly naive
and gaudy form—as demonstrated by this Nativity scene—still anchors these deeply insecure, secular societies. Secularism, rather
than contradict a Christian inheritance, offers resistance against
Muslim immigrants who openly and understandably practice their
religion. In other words, Pound's own moral decadence—his dedication to aesthetics often to no higher purpose—need not signal an
end to religious values in the land of his exile. Europe, buffeted by
demographic and cultural winds coming from Afro-Eurasia, of
which the cosmopolitanism of the literary moderns was a forerunner, may still require an anchoring belief that is less restrictive than
old-fashioned nationalism.

———

I FIND ANOTHER BOOK in my day pack, also battered and a half century old. *Europe: The Emergence of an Idea* is an extended essay by a British scholar at the University of Edinburgh who died in the mid-1990s, Denys Hay. It was originally published in 1957. Because comparison is the register of all serious scholarship, the only way to escape the deafening monotone of the commentariat is to compare and contrast it with the writing of those who asked similar questions at an earlier historical juncture. Thus, I find freshness in what is old and forgotten, even as later generations of academics have usefully modified and in some cases disproved some of these ideas. After all, ruins are so much more interesting than what is above ground and obvious. Only ruins can put what is above ground into perspective. So I reread parts of Hay's small gem of a book inside this church.

European unity (that is, the very concept of identifying oneself as a "European"), Hay writes, had its rudimentary beginning with the notion of medieval *Christendom*, embodied in the eleventh-century *Song of Roland*, which was in "inevitable opposition" to Islam and would soon culminate in the Crusades. This foreshadowed the religious and cultural tensions in Europe, and particularly in France, today. Christendom, though it indicated a "totality," a complete civilization almost, and therefore a psychological unity, was also a very "insecure" idea, since it clarified the difference with—and the perceived danger of—a nearby Muslim world. (Thus was Edward Said's concept of Orientalism born.)

Later on, explains Hay, because of Church schisms—political and otherwise—that religious unity would be lost. But it didn't matter really, since in a larger sense the very idea of being Christian had already become geographically identified with the European subcontinent itself, especially after the Orthodox Christian empire of Byzantium lost Asia Minor to the Muslim Turks in the fourteenth and fifteenth centuries, bringing the so-called Islamic threat even closer. The Ottoman Empire would go on to conquer much of the Balkans, which lies just inside the European subcontinent. Yet this only advanced the concept of European identity, since the Ottoman advance contributed to a feeling of siege and dread among Europeans:* a word that was now used interchangeably with Christians, for to be one meant to be the other, even without the religious unity once associated with the popes of the early Middle Ages. The contrast with their neighbors to the east made the continent see its commonality. "The papacy might temporize with the Ottoman Turk, Francis I might seek the Sultan as an ally," Hay writes, "but the universal cry of despair at the loss of Rhodes in 1522 and the general rejoicing over the victory of Don John of Austria at Lepanto in 1571 [against the Ottoman Sultanate] indicate a profound consciousness of the unity and function of Christendom."[25]

Beyond fear of the Turks and Saracens, the Renaissance would bring with it greater awareness of other continents (particularly Asia and Africa, as demonstrated in the poetry of Ronsard and the great novel of Cervantes), which by virtue of comparison vivified the whole idea of Europe. So while the "vitality of Christendom . . . extended well into the seventeenth century," Hay goes on, it would slowly enter "the limbo of archaic words," and instead Europe would emerge as "the unchallenged symbol of the largest human loyalty." To wit, the very secularism of the late Renaissance and early modern republics would be an excuse for philosophers like Machiavelli, Montesquieu, and Voltaire to extol Europe's superiority over other continents at the time. Europe also would come to be seen as the bastion against the despotism best exemplified by Russia.[26]

Christendom, it was once hoped, would extend throughout the world, whereas Europe, geographically circumscribed, came to

---

*   Some chroniclers believed that it was only the threat from Persia against the Ottoman Empire that saved Europe from the Ottomans. Bernard Lewis, *What Went Wrong? The Clash Between Islam and Modernity in the Middle East* (New York: Oxford University Press, 2002), p. 9.

mean "a region rather than a programme," writes Hay.[27] And yet as the early modern era gave way to the modern one—the cataclysmic Long European War of 1914–1989 notwithstanding—Europe would emerge at the very beginning of the twenty-first century as the exemplar of human rights and *the good life*, achieving for a short moment in time a universal deference that Christendom never did or could have had.

Hay's book poses this question:

Europe evolved out of Christianity and into secularism while never losing its perceived sense of superiority. But as the European crisis—debt, migrants, pandemic—has deepened in our own postmodern era, threatening that very self-esteem, Europeans may have to confront inertia and even decline relative to other continents. Could the soul-searching that will emanate from this decline lead them back, over time at least, to a fervent conviction in Christianity, a faith that is their ultimate inheritance from Greece and Rome? Might the art inside the Tempio Malatestiano represent the future as well as the past?

These are big questions that will require layer upon layer of more reading, in turn leading to deeper considerations. In order to have meaning, a journey that is horizontal, from one city to another, must also be vertical, from one idea to another. Such explorations tell us not only about the past—and the future, as it emerges out of the past—but about ourselves too. In this way, loneliness can be a revelation.

HAY'S WORN AND TATTERED paperback feels good between my fingers. It is like a talisman almost. What is obscure represents a self-discovery: something the crowd has yet to lay its hands on. Yet there is vanity itself in the pride of discovering an old book. For to accept Hay as the last word is to reject decades of more recent scholarship that have complexified Hay's vision, showing, for example, how prodigious commercial ties between Muslims and

Christians continued and even advanced following the Islamic conquest of North Africa, and so the separation of Christendom and Islam was not nearly as final as Hay suggests, his own nuances and qualifications notwithstanding.

My day pack is filled to excess: containing, too, my notes of other books read, relevant to my thoughts and to where I am at the moment. And so before leaving this church, I consider one more book—my notes of Henri Pirenne's *Mohammed & Charlemagne*, the work of the great Belgian historian published in 1937, two years after his death. Pirenne tells a parallel story to Hay's, who no doubt was influenced by him. "Of all the features of that wonderful human structure, the Roman Empire," Pirenne begins his great thesis, "the most striking . . . was its Mediterranean character." And, as Pirenne goes on, even after the collapse of Rome in the West, Rome in the East (Byzantium) still managed to hold sway over the Mediterranean into the early seventh century. But the Arab conquest, which would replace Latin with Arabic in North Africa—with the southern shore of the Mediterranean gravitating over time toward Baghdad—brought an end to this classical world. Germanism and the empire of Charlemagne would emerge in Europe's north as a consequence of the division of the Mediterranean, even as the "ever-increasing prosperity of the Musulman countries . . . benefited the maritime cities of Italy," and even as communities of Greeks, Coptic Christians, Nestorians, and Jews survived and prospered in this new Muslim civilization.[28] *Europe*, in sum, did not only create itself, but was created by other peoples as well as by historical migrations.

Pirenne chronicles in delicious depth not only the erosion of Byzantine sea power, but the very exceptions to the division of the Mediterranean that serve as the theme of his book: as when the Venetians sold Slavic-speaking slaves to the Arabs as part of a larger commerce. Like all bold theories in history and the social sciences, Hay's and Pirenne's have served as markers for later scholars to attack, in the course of erecting new theories of their own: this is how knowledge advances. Hay's and Pirenne's visions, it turns out, were too stark, especially as it was Muslim civilization itself that helped keep the classical heritage of the Greeks and Romans alive in the Middle Ages, another example of the interweaving of civilizations that erodes the barrier between East and West. And yet the literary, somewhat eccentric quality of these academics from now-bygone ages, which only accentuates their brilliance, remains something to behold. They are closer in spirit perhaps to the consummately erudite travel writing of Patrick Leigh Fermor in *Mani* (1958) and *Roumeli* (1966) than to the generally specialized class of many of today's academics.

I LEAVE THE CHURCH and walk around the building to my left. There it is, just where Leigh Fermor had once told me it would be, completely exposed to the street under an arch of the outer retaining wall: the sarcophagus of the Neoplatonist Greek philosopher Georgios Gemistos Plethon. A bus now passes within a few feet of this slice of long-ago history. The cobblestones with their mournful hues glisten in the rain. Across the narrow street from the church and the sarcophagus are accessory and apparel shops whose display windows are like museum art, with silk scarves or leather boots on mannequins. Men and women pass by holding umbrellas. They wear tight-fitting winter coats in sumptuous earthen shades that open to flaring collars, reminding me of the figures in John Singer Sargent's paintings of Venice from the early 1880s, whose dress, even in near poverty, evokes Renaissance courtiers. You have to dress seriously when you come to Italy, especially in the off-season.

I enter a simple café. There are masses of fine liquors reflecting against stage-lit mirrors, which are mounted behind gleaming wooden shelves. Beyond the marble bar are a few round tables covered in brocaded cloth. Evocative black-and-white photos of postwar movies decorate the walls. The intense, vitalizing aromas of coffee and pastry declare civilization as much as any museum does. Two elderly ladies with canes get up and pay for their drinks. They, too, wear tight-fitting black pants, black fedoras over their hair, and look beautiful. A couple enters. They are very old. The woman wears a fur coat over her dress and the man a smart gray sports jacket with a pink tie and scarf. They order double espressos and slowly go through the newspapers. They have dressed up to do this. This is a culture deeply evolved through history, and it emerged from the same stem as the carved limestone inside the church. To leave the Tempio is not to lose the thread of my story.

I stay at the Grand Hotel. It is nearly empty in January and therefore all the more revealing (and inexpensive, too). Built in 1908, the brilliant lights from its chandeliers refract off the white marble, the fleshy columns, and the burnt-orange upholstery. The bedroom decor suggests an abundance of perfume. The cramped elevator with the rusted dials only adds to the illusion of Old World luxury. "Rimini," says the 1909 Baedeker, "the ancient *Ariminum,* a town of the Umbrians, became a Roman colony in 268 B.C., and was the frontier fortress of Italy in the direction of Gaul, and the termination of the *Via Flaminia.* The town was extended and embellished by Julius Caesar and Augustus. During the [Byzantine] Exarchate it was the northernmost of the 'Five Maritime Cities'... and in 359 a council against Arianism was held there."[29] Rimini, a road junction between northern and southern Italy, was a crossroads of armies from ancient Rome through the Gothic Wars, all the way up to World War II. The film director Federico Fellini was born in this Adriatic resort and pictures of him line the walls of the hotel lobby.* To the northeast are the Julian Alps through whose many passes the Visigoths, Huns, and Lombards came; whereas from the sea the Levant beckoned. Rimini was contested between the Papal States to the south and the Germanic cities to the north. This is as much the heart of Europe as anywhere, a logical place to begin my journey.

Now, beyond the wide French doors of the lobby, waves crawl

---

* The Grand Hotel is a backdrop for a few scenes in Fellini's masterpiece *Amarcord.*

out of the mist and the sea crashes within earshot of the café tables under the rain. Nothing evokes desolation and rouses your memory like empty café tables in the off-season.

Forty years ago to the day, I suddenly realize, January 2, 1976, I was in Sfax, traveling south along Tunisia's coast en route to the border of the Sahara desert, walking through the local market located inside the medieval Aghlabid walls. I recall from my diary large, dense packs of young men with "hungry eyes" and "sweaty upper lips," jostling people aside and crowding the cafés, with nothing to do during working hours, and without a woman their age in sight. I felt so far from Europe at that moment, in a sexually repressed society ravaged by unemployment, kept quiet by a dictator's subjugation. The Mediterranean was then like a vast no-man's-land between its northern and southern shores. Today the dictator's hand is gone and Europe is a destination for the youth of North Africa and the Levant. Sfax, over six hundred miles due south from Rimini, no longer seems far away. The Mediterranean has now begun to achieve a fluid classical coherence at the expense of Europe.

Forty years ago, I was seeing Europe's future, though I didn't know it. At the time, in my early twenties, I was unable to process what I saw and experienced. Those young men, in shabby Western dress, breaking loose from one culture and unable to enter another—and thus forged by anger and frustration—fit into no prepared category that I could identify based on history, political science, and travel books. And so, I told myself then, what I was seeing was unimportant, a matter of my own hypersensitivity, even as such youths were preparing the destiny for a tumultuous Middle East: a Middle East that, in turn, would be reintegrated with Europe through migration and terrorism perpetrated by extremists. But never having had the benefit of the professional instruction and conditioning offered by graduate school, I would have to find my way alone on such matters, assembling these and other images, one after the other, over the years. The more I learned, the more aware I became of my own ignorance and autodidacticism. Only in late middle age would

I become intellectually comfortable in my own skin, confident that the truest and most revealing insights sometimes involve seeing what was right in front of your eyes as you traveled. The future, I have learned, is often prepared by what cannot be mentioned or admitted to in fine company. The future lies inside the silences.

I SEE VAST STORES of disposable wealth everywhere in Rimini, and yet the headlines about Europe's economic and political crisis spell doom, soon to be accentuated by the coronavirus. Even the headlines, moreover, obscure a difficult historical truth to which few will admit, but which I know from my memories of Sfax and the rest of southern Tunisia.

What the headlines will not say is that Europe's stability and consequent prosperity for almost two-thirds of a century following World War II required, in part, isolation from its own near-abroad. The door to Europe from the Middle East was virtually shut for decades by prison states whose dictator-wardens kept their people in order. In particular, the rules of various Iraqi strongmen culminating in Saddam Hussein, the Assad family in Syria (particularly the elder Assad), and Muammar Gaddafi in Libya were correlated with Europe's happy decades. The great twentieth-century French geographer Fernand Braudel wrote that the Mediterranean was not Europe's southern border: the border, in his view, was the fringe of the Sahara desert, where migrant caravans now assemble for the long-term demographic influx into Europe proper, and where forty years ago I saw groups of young men like those in Sfax.

Yes, everything here in Rimini—the café, the accessory and apparel shops, the general opulence right down to the ubiquitous fur coats and cutting-edge designer eyeglass frames worn by so many of the women, the luxurious fleece and plaid comforting for their dogs—was all, in some part, a product of Europe's relative cultural and demographic separation from the adjacent Muslim Middle East: something that, in turn, went back to the emergence of Christendom itself, and that through a centuries-long and tortuous historical process, with all of its contradictions and subtleties, achieved a formal geopolitical basis during the Cold War and its aftermath. Yes, there were the guest workers, from Algeria and Turkey especially, and the barely manageable social tensions that they caused. But the near-abroad in North Africa and the Levant was still further away than it is now.

Throughout history, the coherence of Christian Europe was a partial product of its opposition to the Islamic world, however hypocritical that opposition was in the face of ongoing commercial contacts and a false sense of superiority. But alongside that opposition came Europe's relative physical separation from Muslim societies, a separation that has been dissolving for years now through globalization and state collapse.

Would the Renaissance have happened as it did if Islam had seeped farther north than Spain and Sicily? Medieval Muslim civilization, while brilliant beyond imagining, would have changed irrevocably the course of Europe's cultural and political development, perhaps even for the better. Then again, it might all have been different. Machiavelli's *Prince*, which proclaimed the invention of secular politics untethered from the fatalism of the Roman Catholic Church—and which was a foundational element of Richelieu's *raison d'état*—could not have been conceived except in a Europe moving beyond feudalism and continuing to rediscover in full the pagan-cum-secular values of Greece and Rome. Indeed, the Italian city-states were themselves ruthless incubators of excellence—political, military, and artistic—illustrated by Machiavelli himself, Sigismondo Malatesta, and Agostino di Duccio.

Of course, there were many other factors to consider besides Christendom's development and articulation in opposition to Islam. Throughout the Cold War, for example, America had paid the security bill so that European societies could afford generous social welfare states. America also protected Europe from the Soviet Union, whose internal chaos for a decade after its demise did not much affect Europe either. But now, along with the millions of migrants from the Middle East and Africa, quasi-Asiatic Russia threatens to slowly undermine Europe, just as some of the early modern philosophers feared.

Everything I see here is so beautiful, I realize—erotic even. It is like paradise.

But there is a sense of poignancy, even before the outbreak of Covid-19. It is as though what I am seeing in the streets and the cafés is already being consigned to the past.

What is Europe? I ask myself. Where does it begin and end? And what will it become?

THE QUESTIONS ARE BECOMING clear now. Rimini has started me on an inner journey whose terminus I cannot yet foresee.

RAVENNA

—

*How Theodoric
and Dante
Shaped the West*

HEADING NORTH FROM RIMINI, I LOOK OUT THE TRAIN window at nondescript and tacky seaside towns, each one merging into another, all partially deserted in the off-season. It continues to rain heavily. Like the semi-darkness of the churches, the weather lends an interiority to one's thoughts. It is a landscape given to abstraction, as if even the sky has moved indoors under museum light. So much of the postmodern world is neither urban nor rural, but an erasure of both.

The train is Europe's crowd symbol, like the *"sea"* is for the English and the *"marching forest"* for the Germans, to quote Elias Canetti.[1] The train is modernism writ large: it completes the logistical unity of the continent that began with the to-ing and fro-ing of Napoleon's army. The train is the moving café, defined during my travels as a young man by those jerking old compartments where six strangers used to cram together: three sitting across from three, their knees almost touching as in old movies. The travelers came from different countries, different cities, different age groups, and different circumstances. The temporary intimacy forced a leisurely, timeless conversation in the era before smartphones. The train, by conquering distance, creates the illusion of possibilities. The soaring, iron-columned stations with their particle-laden air have been the archetypal backdrop for assignations and separations amid the rivers of steam rising from the undercarriages. Trains witnessed history. Jews went to death camps on trains. Aren't converging railway tracks a shorthand symbol of the Holocaust? European armies traveled to the front on trains; Lenin returned from exile on one. The train is the point of concision for the most unimaginable horrors as well as for *the good life*. The train has united the European state system, utilized even by Muslim migrants through their own, desperate journeys. The train remains the icon of state power, the way that the car in America signals the autonomy and loneliness of the individual. The rush, the bustle, and the anxieties of departure vanish the moment the wheels slide forward. The train is the perfect place to think and read.

EVEN JUST ONE DAY of travel constitutes a moment of lucidity that breaks through the grinding gears of daily habit, so that it becomes a bit more difficult to lie to oneself. I travel in order not to be deceived. Camus writes, "I realized . . . that a man who'd only lived for a day could easily live for a hundred years in a prison. He'd have enough memories not to get bored."[2] Very overstated perhaps, but not if that one day was a day of travel.

What is a human life, really? Years of toil and production, overshadowed by a few accidents or actions you didn't intend, but which, nevertheless, you must take moral responsibility for, and which define you? And if that is so, such accidents define you because they seize you in a moment of time that revealed your worst, or at least your unluckiest, inclinations. I think of Henri Pirenne's understated and elegant assessment of Boetius:

Boetius, born in Rome in 480, belonged to the distinguished family of the Anicii. Consul in 510, he became Theodoric's minister, and was entrusted with the duty of reforming the monetary system. He was executed in 525 for intriguing with Byzantium. He translated Aristotle, and his commentaries influenced the thought of the Middle Ages; he also translated the Isagogue of Porphyry, and the works of Greek musicians and mathematicians. Finally, in prison, he wrote *De consolatione philosophiae,* in which Christianity is blended with a stoico-Roman morality. He was a man of spiritual distinction, and a thinker.[3]

Yet, for just one case of bad judgment Boetius was tortured and executed, his life a misfortune. Gibbon lavishes several thousand words on him, extolling his erudition and literary gifts, yet uses Boetius as an example to show how the word "happy," as applied to a man's life, is a "precarious epithet," unless one knows how it will all end.[4]

What is sin? I ask myself. (Travel is like lying awake in the dark, when such questions assault you.) Sin can be not living up to your own standards. If you must reach old age before you feel comfortable and fulfilled, it may mean you regret your youth and middle age: not all of it necessarily, not even most of it, but some of it. You regret being the person you were. Certainly you have had accomplishments, and you have stood up for your beliefs, however unpopular they may have been, but to yourself you have been a failure. There is no solution; no redemption. You want what everyone wants, to have been as wise and mature earlier in life as you think you are now. You want to be like Chekhov, who as a twenty-nine-year-old writer could deeply imagine the nostalgia of an old man nearing death, observing his "flabby," "clumsy," and "brooding" wife—and realize in a moment of revelation all the transitions his wife has made from the once slender and passionate young woman he had fallen in love with.[5] But it was only in my mid-sixties that I came to know about growing old what Chekhov knew at twenty-nine (even as his artistry obviously remains unattainable). And because there is no redemption, there is only confession.

"Do not take opium, but put salt and vinegar in the soul's wound," in order to attain a higher level of awareness, writes the early-twentieth-century Spanish philosopher Miguel de Unamuno. Indeed, "suffering is the substance of life and the root of personality."[6]

Travel should cultivate an awareness that makes you a better person, and hence in my own case a better writer: perhaps a writer that can do more good, by showing a way forward out of a seemingly intractable darkness. Maturity means to distrust oneself, while at the same time holding on to your fundamental beliefs, which are the product of decades of experience.

A FEW BLOCKS REMOVED from the railway station, the spell of this city descends on you like strong incense. Ravenna, the very sound of the name—the three fluid, understated syllables—evokes a dusty ruby. Ravenna, to the degree of perhaps no other city, constitutes an ideogram of Late Antiquity. Here, between A.D. 400 and A.D. 751, the city moved from Roman emperors, to Ostrogothic kings, to Byzantine governors. The very word Ravenna is like a sound from one of Ezra Pound's most aromatic Cantos. T. S. Eliot wrote a French poem about it, "Lune de Miel," or "Honeymoon." It describes two midwestern travelers being devoured by bedbugs while they lie awake in their hotel in the city, suffering in the summer heat, completely ignorant of such a "precise" Byzantine gem as Saint Apollinare in Classe, less than a mile away: a basilica known for "its acanthus columns which the wind batters."[7] I think of the Lombard warrior in the story of Jorge Luis Borges, who deserted his own army to defend Ravenna, the city he had just been besieging—because of the sight of "cypresses and marble," as well as of "statues, temples, gardens . . . capitals and pediments," all of which to him manifested *order*, a city, an organism, thus constituting a revelation of something higher than he had ever before experienced; for there is spirituality in the triumph of civilization.[8]

In Baghdad, in Tehran, in Kolkata, in Hanoi, places that over the years and decades I reported from as a journalist and which all held their own allure, I always daydreamed of one day visiting Ravenna: the writings of Princeton historian Peter Brown, for one, had inspired me to savor the fusion of art and mysticism before I was completely devoured by age.

Ravenna, which actually ruled Venice for a few short years in the eighth century, today lies some miles inland from the Adriatic; though in Roman and Byzantine times it was on the coast, at the southern edge of the Po River delta. In fact, it was an "island-studded lagoon on the Venetian pattern," making it "virtually impregnable," in the words of historian John Julius Norwich.[9] Ravenna may have been officially founded in the first century B.C. by the emperor Augustus, who enlarged the harbor as a base against piracy. Julius Caesar stayed in the area the night before crossing the Rubicon and beginning the civil war. Ravenna moves in stages into the hinge of history as Western Rome collapses and the barbarian Odoacer—and especially the Ostrogoth Theodoric—deliver a measure of order. But the key date is March, 540, when Belisarius's Byzantine army captured the city from the Ostrogoths, though the pretext for this westward expansion had been the murder of Theodoric's own daughter Amalasuintha, who had appealed to the Byzantine emperor Justinian for help. The Byzantines—Greeks who called themselves Romans—took over a city that had never known the plague and devastation that the Gothic War had been wreaking on so much of the Italian peninsula. This set the stage for the building and elaboration of Ravenna's great monuments: the purpose of my journey.

Ravenna is a Byzantine jewel of barrel-vaulted brick bearing all the subtle and complex hues of a dying autumn leaf. With its elegant shops, its pencil-thin stone and marble columns under archways, inside yellowing brick walls—with its bone-darkened clay tiles, its fossilizing campaniles with their round and shallow domes, its moss-splashed sarcophagi under cypress trees, Ravenna is a great solace because of the way it shows the refinement that comes with age and discoloration.

The streets in the winter rain are empty. They induce meditation. Ravenna is the next best thing to a monastery. The Byzantine mausoleums and churches are like a concentrated version of Athens or Istanbul, but located in a manicured, Italianate setting, adjusted to scale, instead of lost in a noisy and vast urban morass. I feel, too, like I am in the heart of Sofia, which during the Communist ice age constituted another Byzantine jewel of eerie silences.

Outside my hotel window, I see a roof of rust-red, conical clay tiles, beautiful with time and mold. Atop the roof is a small oblong chimney of wafer-thin brick culminating in three arches, decked by a triangular roof of its own, made of the same aging clay tiles. Modern architecture, with its use of metals and plastics that come from everywhere and nowhere, indicates no locality and no identity. But staring at this little chimney, I know where I am. This chimney is a perfect signature of both Byzantium and the Mediterranean. Chimneys like this, commonplace in Ravenna, educe the very process of history.

I LOOK AT A MAP of Europe in A.D. 69 from *The Oxford Anthology of Roman Literature*.[10] This map inspires, with its depiction of a unifying seaboard and the related suggestion of peace. Italy and Dalmatia are part of the same political world as Carthage and Cyrenaica; as are, going clockwise, the Aegean Islands, Phoenicia, and the Nile Delta. For the Roman Empire at this historical juncture encompasses the entire Mediterranean basin, as well as Yugoslavia, France, the Low Countries, England, and Iberia: all of Europe, in other words, with the exceptions of Central-Eastern Europe and Scandinavia, which are consequently revealed, spatially at least, as part of the barbarian penumbrae of deeper Eurasia. The Mediterranean, under Roman dominance, again appears as the great twentieth-century French geographer Fernand Braudel intimated it always was: a connector rather than a divider, with the Sahara desert functioning as the true southern border of Europe. Braudel's concept, as I have previously indicated, is both ancient and postmodern, given the crisis of seaborne migrants in the second decade of the twenty-first century. For too long Europe deceived itself, believing it was protected from upheavals in the developing world by the so-called barrier of the Mediterranean.

The Pax Romana, which this map clarifies, was a period of relative calm and stability throughout the greater Mediterranean. Even as late as A.D. 200, the Roman Empire still existed in the generous shadow of the recently deceased emperor and philosopher Marcus Aurelius: a time when, according to historian Peter Brown, "a charmed circle of unquestioning conservatives" gave order to the world.[11] But over the next five hundred years, everything would change.

By A.D. 700, the Roman Empire had disappeared from the map of the West, the Sassanid Persian Empire had vanished from the Near East, Europe had become Christian, and the Near East and most of North Africa had become Muslim. Poor, uneducated, and extremist Christian heretics and sectarians—Donatists, Pelagians, Manicheans, rabble-rousing monks, and so on—had dispersed around the Mediterranean, often burning and terrorizing synagogues and pagan temples, before they themselves were overtaken in North Africa by Arab armies proselytizing a new and austere faith.* Meanwhile, Gothic tribes ravaged Europe, and Asia Minor was on the brink of an epic conflict between Christians who venerated icons and other holy images and Christians who glorified in their destruction. Brown, in the course of a lifetime of scholarly work, has given a name to this pungent epoch in which the world

---

* These are, perforce, generalizations. For example, despite the Arab conquest of North Africa, commercial links among Christians, Muslims, and Jews continued.

gradually turned upside down and conservatives were disarmed by radicals: Late Antiquity.

Late Antiquity, between A.D. 150 and 750, was dominated by vast civilizational changes, though many were not marked or even noticed at the time.* Writing similarly about the Middle Ages that followed, the late Oxford historian R. W. Southern notes, "This silence in the great changes of history is something which meets us everywhere."[12] The Adriatic in this period is both an emblem and a concentrated reduction of this vast, albeit silent, historical transition: it is full of constant tumult, yet one must take a step or two backward in order to observe the pivotal shifts. The greater Adriatic offers, in a word, a scaled-down version of a crumbling, classical world, complete with riches to ponder for both the antiquarian and the geopolitical analyst, even as it is embedded with meaning for a twenty-first-century Europe that is internally fracturing and externally disintegrating into the wider cosmopolitan civilization of Afro-Eurasia, with its own Chinese overlay.

This is why by focusing on the Adriatic, I can better appreciate what has been happening in Europe as a whole, without becoming too overwhelmed. My journey is like an extended seminar, where books and the landscape itself are the teacher. (My greatest regret is that I did not have the advantage of Judith Herrin's exhaustive *Ravenna: Capital of Empire, Crucible of Europe*, because it was published several years after my journey.)

I look at more maps in my hotel room in Ravenna: those of the greater Adriatic. Rome is eventually replaced by Western Rome and Eastern Rome; then by the Visigoths, the Ostrogoths, the kingdom of Odoacer, and Eastern Rome, all elbowing for territory; then, in turn, by the Arians and the papacy, though by the sixth century the Adriatic is all Eastern Rome. In the early eighth century the division is between the Lombards and Eastern Rome, in the early ninth between the Franks and Byzantium. In the Middle Ages the Nor-

---

* The phrase and dates were coined by Peter Brown.

mans, Hungarians, and Serbs, as well as the German Empire, Salerno, Naples, and Venice, all gain prominence; until by the late fifteenth century, as the Renaissance reaches full flower, it is Venice facing off against the Ottoman Empire, even as northern Italy is divided among Savoy, Milan, Genoa, Mantua, Florence, and Siena, and southern Italy between the Papal States and the kingdom of Naples.

Later on, all of these polities, too, will become shades: disappearing, literally, into the past. Voltaire said Rome fell "because all things fall."[13] Indeed, empires are not illegitimate simply because they eventually collapse: the wonder is that so many have lasted as long as they did. Rome's universal civilization, with its cruel yet rational, i.e., *charmed-conservative* paganism, ultimately became impossible to sustain in the hinterlands; and Rome's breakup led to the panoramic migrations, coupled with the religious passions and particularism, that we associate with Late Antiquity and the Dark and Middle Ages, with all of their attendant political-territorial complexity. Still, the geographic breadth of Rome, lasting as it did for so many centuries, remains an astonishment: an imperial domain impossible to imagine reassembled in any form. Only world governance could equal or surpass it.

In sum, the passage from antiquity to Late Antiquity registers a more confused ethnic and territorial map, with the big shifts that merit chapter breaks in history books barely noticed at the time. For example, the deposition in A.D. 476 of Romulus Augustulus by the barbarian Odoacer—an Arian Christian soldier of vague Germanic and Hunnish descent—is commonly marked as the endpoint of the Roman Empire in the West, though the event elicits little mention by any chronicler of the era: its significance becomes apparent only much later in hindsight. After all, Odoacer, rather than eviscerate what remained of the empire, actually restored some facade of order and stability to it, even as he reconquered Sicily from the Vandals in A.D. 477 and annexed Dalmatia in A.D. 480. The real break with the classical past occurs only later with the Gothic

War of A.D. 535–554, which devastated much of Italy with famine and chaos, and was quickly followed in 568 by the Lombard invasion, so that Italy was at war for more or less seventy years until 605. Italy would never again be united until modern times. The Lombards, a Germanic confederation with a strong Arian element that included Saxons, Gepids, Bulgars, Sueves, and others—a fascinating horde first recorded by Tacitus—truly herald the passage of Late Antiquity into the so-called Dark Ages.

By this time the drama has shifted noticeably from Rome to Ravenna, that seaport on the Adriatic protected by swamps, which, at the beginning of the fifth century, had replaced Milan as the center of Roman civil administration. Rome and Ravenna would come to represent antiquity and Late Antiquity respectively: the pragmatic, secular regime embodied in the Roman eagle and the incense-wrapped, otherworldly faith embodied in the Byzantine icon; the past and the present, that is; the official authority and the emerging, actual power; one city and historical epoch in opposition to the other, even as the culture and values of one epoch were quietly giving way to—as well as deeply influencing—those of the other. To rule from Ravenna was to consciously resist the Senate and the popes in Rome; and to build monuments in Ravenna was to challenge the very symbolic authority of Rome.

But it is the Gothic War that concomitantly seized my interest as I was planning this journey, with those affectingly small, deliciously green-covered volumes of the Loeb Classical Library that hold the pages of the eyewitness historian Procopius's account of it, as well as the accounts of the Persian and Vandal campaigns. The smoky art and architecture of Ravenna had at first led me to the city's Byzantine foundations, and thus to the very miracle of Byzantium's considerable perch here, so far westward from Constantinople, on the Adriatic. And Ravenna, in turn, led me to Late Antiquity in Italy in the larger sense, and eventually to the Gothic War as recorded in Procopius's eyewitness recollection, as an advisor to the Byzantine general Belisarius. The centuries and ages literally fell away as I immersed myself in the vivid narrative clarity and almost modern sensibility of lengthy sections of Procopius's text. While the differences between then and now are immense beyond measure, the similarities are arresting. I recall looking at an inset of a fourth-century-A.D. gold cross—holding a portrait of three members of a family, whose expressions and bearing are strikingly contemporary, timeless.[14] Their eyes and features come alive. I can almost imagine talking to them. As I read Procopius, it was as if I were looking at that family.

To wit, Procopius documents the capture of Naples in A.D. 536, quoting Belisarius's lament at the cruelty suffered by civilians in war, something to which we can all relate:

> Many times have I witnessed the capture of cities. . . . For they slay all the men of every age, and as for the women, though they beg to die, they are not granted the boon of death, but are carried off for outrage and are made to suffer treatment that is abominable and most pitiable. And the children, who are thus deprived of their proper maintenance and education, are forced to be slaves, and that, too, of the men who are the most odious of all—those on whose hands they see the blood of their fathers.[15]

And there is this warning about overconfidence after the Ostrogoths desert Rimini in A.D. 537:

> For those who, accounting themselves victorious, are lifted up by their achievements are more readily destroyed than those who have indeed suffered an unexpected reverse, but thereafter are actuated by fear and abundant respect of their enemy.[16]

Fate, too, is reflected upon: how despite the "wisdom" and "excellence" of men, "there is some divine power which is ever warping their purposes."[17] To this day, questions of fate, determinism, and human agency dominate military and foreign policy discussions. The lessons of the Gothic War are forever relevant. While the Byzantines triumphed in the battles of the mid-sixth century, they lost money and lives and eventually strategic control over Italy, having to resign themselves to the presence of the Lombards here before the dawn of the seventh. How many examples are there in modern history of something similar, of a tactical and operational victory enhancing a strategic defeat!

Of course, forming the heart of Procopius's drama are the Goths, or more properly the Ostrogoths: that is, the eastern Goths whose origins lie in the region north of the Black Sea in today's Ukraine, which was or had been a rather well-developed entrepôt for various peoples, including the Scythians, Sarmatians, and Cimmerians of Ezra Pound's first Canto.

Ostrogothic rule during the long reign of Theodoric (A.D. 471–526) saw the last flowering of secular Roman letters in the West. Theodoric's respect for law and land ownership and support of the arts created a degree of freedom unique for the era that attracted Christian and pagan religious exiles from the east, and Jews from Naples and Genoa. Theodoric, who was moderate in his Arian beliefs, wrote thus to the Jews of Genoa: "I cannot command your faith, for no one is forced to believe against his will." And so he imposed harsh penalties for anti-Semitism.[18]

Theodoric's rule served to more firmly establish Ravenna and the Adriatic Sea as the political-cultural axis of Italy. He built towns and fortresses between Ravenna and the Alps, even as he restored the city of Rome. Theodoric repaired and erected a mass of new structures in Ravenna, including churches for Arian Christians and Orthodox both. Despite the paranoia of his last years, Theodoric in his very person constitutes proof that the official termination of Rome in the West in A.D. 476 carried little actual significance, as the state of order and culture was higher under him than under quite a number of late Roman emperors. Rome's fall in the West was a subtle gradation, an arbitrary marker only.

Pannonia-born Theodoric, probably educated in Greek and Latin in Constantinople, had taken power in a typically brutal fashion. After signing a peace treaty with Odoacer in A.D. 493, Theodoric invited him to a banquet, where he drew a sword across his collarbone and slew him. Thereafter he was called *rex*, the title to which the barbarians were accustomed. "Theodoric was a usurper, yet in fact he was as truly an emperor as any who have distinguished themselves in this office from the beginning; and love for him among both Goths and Italians grew to be great," says Procopius, the Byzantine chronicler.[19] Machiavelli, in his *History of Florence: And of the Affairs of Italy*, tells us that Theodoric was one of those rare rulers whose talents were exceptional in both war and peace. "No other Germanic ruler, setting up his throne on the ruins of the Western Empire, possessed a fraction of his statesmanship," writes the historian John Julius Norwich.[20] And here is Gibbon: "The reputation of Theodoric may repose with more confidence on the visible peace and prosperity of a reign of thirty-three years, the unanimous esteem of his own times, and the memory of his wisdom and courage, his justice and humanity, which was deeply impressed on the minds of the Goths and Italians." Gibbon devotes many pages of *The Decline and Fall of the Roman Empire* to Theodoric, saying "he might have deserved a statue among the best and bravest of the ancient Romans."[21]

THEODORIC'S MAUSOLEUM, BUILT OF limestone ashlars while he was alive, sits alone and worn away by the centuries amid vast fields of stunted, seaweed-dark grass. The monument hypnotizes by stages. I felt fastened in place despite the rain. It is not particularly high, but like a short person radiating charisma its effect is that of a giant. If Ravenna is a city that best represents Late Antiquity, then

Theodoric's tomb draws all the civilizational elements of that wondrous transitional period into one thickset monument. The lower
level, with its heavy, ungraceful arches, signifies late Rome. The
upper level, with its astonishingly flattened, mold-darkened dome,
bordered by a circular band of armor-like tongs in bas-relief—and
spurs on the capstone monolith that appear like hideous clamps—
screams *Gothic* and *medieval*. The mausoleum's interior, with its
cracked and open porphyry vessel—where Theodoric's remains may
once have been placed—holds the ghosts of dying soldiers' shouts
and voices. In the winter cold and drizzle, with the faint rumor of
lignite fumes, you know that the past, however distant, is real and
defined by transformations so subtle and yet so substantial that they
cannot be encompassed by a mere human lifetime.

That singular roof holds within its blunt design all the centuries
between antiquity and the Renaissance: a period at once uncouth
and frightening, yet containing in its flexible, feudal obligations the
faintest germ of the modern West to come. In no cloister have I
felt the medieval world so condensed and Germanic—so brutal
and romantic—as I do here: the more powerful because it sits atop
a Roman base. The linkages are all apparent in the architecture:
from Rome to the various rites and sects and heresies that gave
birth to a monolithic early Christendom. History means narrative,
and narrative requires transitions and revelations—comprehended
in a nanosecond as the eye unconsciously moves from the lower
level to the upper level of this mausoleum.

Theodoric was an Arian Christian, a member of a sect founded
by an Alexandrian priest, Arius, who lived between A.D. 256 and 336.
It denied Christ's full divinity and believed that Jesus was only the
Son of God, and therefore subordinate to him, as if a great and holy
man, but little more. At the end of the fifth century and at the beginning of the sixth, Theodoric built the Arian Baptistery in
Ravenna, where I go next. Inside this sunk-in-the-ground, small,
and immortal brick monument, I stare in amazement at the mosaic
dome—a version of time travel, a veritable window into the Chris-

tianity of Ostrogothic Ravenna in Late Antiquity. In the center a boyish Christ, chubby and nude, is being baptized by John the Baptist, who stands on a rocky prominence and wields a shepherd's crook. On Jesus' other side is the personification of the Jordan River, in the form of an old man with a beard and horns. The entire background is brilliant gold tesserae. This central medallion is surrounded by the twelve apostles wearing white tunics, *clavi*, and mantles, themselves set against a gold background. Deborah Mauskopf Deliyannis of Indiana University, whose background is in archaeology, architecture, and medieval history, notes that it is not altogether clear what separates the iconography here from that in Ravenna's traditional Orthodox churches, and in any case these mosaics were not destroyed upon the Baptistery's rededication as an Orthodox church later on, which means that the art was acceptable to the larger Christian faith.[22] Yet what touches me about the iconography here is its apparent naivete, reflecting an early and barely articulated belief without any previous tradition—since paganism had been consciously rejected by the Arians. The figures here lack the stern and imposing elaboration of traditional Orthodox iconography. I thought of the affecting Nativity scene in the Tempio Malatestiano in Rimini, for that was also so cheap and naive. In both cases, people must have felt deeply, even if their artistic values were lacking or not fully developed. After all, strong faith and good taste in aesthetics often do not fit well together.

Arianism, founded in Egypt by a man who was born in Libya and died in Constantinople, was part of the process by which the East shaped Europe. It would later be engulfed by a Byzantine Orthodoxy based on the frontier of Asia Minor, which was challenging the papacy in Rome. European Christianity, though a bulwark against Islam, had its early political development influenced by Eastern roots. Arianism, Donatism, Monophysitism, and so forth were part of the swirling tapestry of doctrinal disputes that defined the Mediterranean basin when both its northern and southern shores were still part of a unified world in the weakening shadow of

Rome. Theodoric's mausoleum and his Arian Baptistery are, while built to last the ages, examples of a Europe in constant, tumultuous evolution: from antiquity to Late Antiquity; from an Italian peninsula ascending through stages of early popes, through various warrior sects, through the challenge of Byzantium, and hence to a unified Christendom, itself to be transformed almost beyond recognition. The only stable element in all of this was the partial barrier erected by the Muslim advance across the Levant and North Africa.* Why shouldn't such transformations continue, I ask myself, with the European Union merely an interregnum, especially as the Mediterranean is less and less a barrier?

TO MY MIND, the most wondrous aspect of Late Antiquity and the Dark Ages in Italy is Byzantium itself, for which Ravenna serves not merely as an outpost on the western shore of the Adriatic, but as a full-fledged second Constantinople in its own right, despite being geographically separate from the principal Byzantine homelands of Asia Minor and the Balkan peninsula. Byzantium was the heir to Rome, and thus to the classical world and its Mediterranean *oikumene*—the inhabited or civilized portion of the earth. Byzantium, moreover, would continue to prove itself deep into the Middle Ages with its signal capacity for political regeneration in Constantinople. Despite the cleavage wrought between East and West by the Avar and Slav invasions of the Balkans, and by the gradual loss of the Greek language in the West, Byzantine Ravenna survived into the mid-eighth century, a spiritual and cultural redoubt of ancient Rome, more than Rome itself by that time.

Byzantium was critical to the emergence, survival, and definition of the Western world. At the height of the Islamic expansion, it was Constantinople that did the most to block the Muslim advance,

---

* The Muslim advance did not completely eliminate Christianity from North Africa; pockets remained, especially that of the Coptic community in the Nile Valley.

even while Byzantine sea power preserved Italy. The Oxford scholar John Darwin observes that "Byzantine models of centralized, autocratic government, and of military and naval organization, inspired the post-Roman states in the European West."[23] The rise of Venice was integrally connected with the continued economic vitality of Constantinople and the East–West trade it generated. And by the time the Muslim Ottoman Turks finally did capture Constantinople in 1453, the balance of power in Europe had already shifted to the Latin West.

Furthermore, it was Near Eastern monasticism—a Byzantine cultural achievement—with its "simplicity and grassroots popularity" and doughty survival against Arab invasions, that helped shape devotional practices in medieval Western Europe.[24] This is how the physical edifice of the church itself was less crucial than human institutions. Princeton's Peter Brown notes that "the emergence of the holy man at the expense of the temple marks the end of the classical world."[25] The holy man was the Orthodox anchorite in the Near Eastern desert, as well as the less-isolated monk and devout man of purity, residing on a column, perhaps, who dispensed wisdom and advice to those who came to visit him. The temple, meanwhile, though a place of pagan worship, was symbolic of the secular power of the Roman state. The holy man represented the quest for individual denial and perfection (what the Middle Ages were, at root, largely about), while the temple stood for the compromise with the material world as it was: the essence of the classical past. Byzantium constituted both: the holy man of the otherworldly Eastern Church and the physicality of the church edifice itself, an architectural descendant of the pagan Roman temple. The Italian Renaissance united these two worlds by helping to recover the learning of the ancient Greeks and Romans and leavening it with the moral purpose of the medieval Church—a step towards the emergence of the modern West as we know it. The philosopher Gemistos Plethon, whose sarcophagus I saw in Rimini, one of the last intellectual flowers of Byzantium, helped stir the Italian Renaissance by bringing knowledge of classical antiquity to fifteenth-century Florence. Byzantium, thus, was a critical conduit of knowledge and tradition, for it encompassed the journey from ancient Greece to the European West.

GREAT ART SHOULD AFFECT you physically, it should "tune us like instruments," because painting is an intensification rather than a distortion of the material world. "We must look and look and look till we live the painting and for a fleeting moment become identified with it," writes Bernard Berenson. "A good rough test is whether we feel that it is reconciling us with life." Berenson, in yet another battered, age-old paperback I own, called this "the aesthetic moment," which is "that flitting instant, so brief as to be almost timeless, when the spectator is at one with the work of art," so that he "ceases to be his ordinary self."

I feel this with Byzantine art: an art that Berenson called, in order to be exact, "medieval Hellenistic art," that is, a remnant of ancient Greece. To him, this art is "precious, refulgent, monotonous," and ends around 1200 "as a gorgeous mummy case."[26] I don't mind the monotony, and yes, there is the touch of beauty-in-death about it. But Byzantine art to me, exactly as Berenson suggests, has always been classical, in the sense that it evokes its forebears in ancient Greece. Thus, it is a fusion of East and West, and what the Adriatic is all about—a guidepost in my journey. I keep Berenson's thoughts in mind as I enter San Vitale.

THE CONSTRUCTION OF SAN VITALE, which began after A.D. 540, established Saint Vitalis—the slave of Saint Agricola—as Ravenna's chief martyr. This may have had something to do with the rivalry between Ravenna and other Italian cities (Milan, Bologna, and Florence), which housed the relics of the two saints who had died in Diocletian's persecutions of the early fourth century. I had known for years of the fame of San Vitale's mosaics, but it was only upon reading Deborah Deliyannis's book *Ravenna in Late Antiquity* that I understood it as the very embodiment and summation of Byzantine aesthetics. Here is the feast of iconography that must have graced Hagia Sophia in Constantinople before the invading Turks in the mid-fifteenth century destroyed it.

Let's start with the architecture. San Vitale, Deliyannis writes, "is a double-shell octagon, that is, a building with a domed octagonal core surrounded by a passageway." She then describes how that octagon and passageway—complete with a second-story gallery—open on one side into a high-vaulted presbytery and polygonal apse. The chambers flanking the apse feature brick barrel vaults, domes, and half domes. As for the veined lotus and acanthus columns, they appear even more formidable because of the pyramidal impost blocks placed between the capitals and the arches, which in effect raise the height of the arches and the building in general.[27] It is a world of curves and spheres evoking the mathematical beauty of the universe, one that would become even further advanced in the great mosques of the early Islamic centuries. Such a well-socketed and completely evolved certainty, I thought, manifesting both strength and beauty, political power and lavish imperial budgets.* The Byzantine iconography of Constantinople and the Balkans is about the worship of God through painted and mosaic images; this same iconography in Ravenna, so far west in geographical terms, is also about empire.

But rarely have I seen Orthodox iconography more piercing than in San Vitale's presbytery and apse, with their mosaics of stone and glass tesserae depicting imperial figures, Church figures, and Old and New Testament saints caught in freeze-frame, in an imperishable moment in time. They are haunting precisely because of

---

* Judith Herrin, professor emeritus at King's College, London, writes that the mosaics and their royal depictions at San Vitale "played a shaping role in the imagination of power ever since." *Ravenna: Capital of Empire, Crucible of Europe* (Princeton, NJ: Princeton University Press, 2020), p. 167.

their lack of expressions, all surrounded in gold and swimming, earthy greens. The art here is a historical and geopolitical document. There is the emperor Justinian in his most arresting pose, arrayed in his white tunic, purple chlamys, and bejeweled crown inside a halo: he is resolved, eternal, enigmatic. This San Vitale portrait of him is reproduced in art and history books everywhere. But here he is no larger than any of the other personages on either side of him on the north apse wall. You could almost miss Justinian if you didn't know where to look, such is the vast array of images here.

Justinian tried to expand the eastern empire deep inside the West. Without him there might have been no Ravenna as we know it in history. He never visited Ravenna, but the Byzantine Exarchate (viceroyalty) of Ravenna was established in his name. He was more famously the builder of Hagia Sophia in Constantinople, and gave his name to a civil code still relevant in the West. Justinian was a political giant, who in his very person represents the influence of the East in the Western Europe of Late Antiquity, and he towers over San Vitale, although his portrait is barely life-sized.

Opposite Justinian on the south apse wall is his politically powerful wife and empress, Theodora, also in a halo. This former actress, dancer, and single mother is swathed in jewelry, especially emerald earrings that reach down the length of her neck. Her sharp and angular features evince a frightening, otherworldly beauty. She, too, is one figure among many in her retinue. The mosaic work is so fine that it appears from a distance like an exquisite oriental rug. In the empress's crown, near her hands, and elsewhere, the most vivid color is ocher—the color of Ravenna, really—that reddish-brown pigment with a measure of iron ore that equates with the earth itself. The link between Justinian, Theodora, and the beardless Christ, flanked by winged angels and Saint Vitalis in the vault of the apse, is so intense as to be almost seamless. Rarely has there been such a fusion of heaven and worldly power.

This is religious art, and realism is eschewed. The facial features are all two-dimensional and distorted. The eyes are too large, the noses too long—so that even the emperor and empress on earth are depicted as saints. Dematerialized, they are presented as abstract symbols for veneration. We look at them and see God.

Empire, to be successful, requires unquestioned moral legitimacy. America has failed at this, and this is something for the emerging Chinese to keep in mind. In Byzantium (Eastern Rome) that moral legitimacy rested inside the Church itself because the Church and the state were nearly one. Christ was close to being both the state and the imperial ideology. Thus, Christendom, as a political concept, was more deeply felt in the East than even in the West. And when Byzantium fell to the Ottoman sultanate, Europe saw itself as being even more exposed to Islam, despite all the bloody conflicts that had gone on between the two branches of Christianity.

Lingering in San Vitale for hours, literally, I realize that although the Byzantines left behind no universal moral achievement that reached beyond Christianity itself, they did leave us a deliberately completed and spiritually assured beauty, which perfectly united religion with aesthetics: a finished world, in other words, what Berenson lightly derided as a "gorgeous mummy case." We in modern and postmodern times may do no such thing, though. Milan Kundera, in *The Unbearable Lightness of Being*, takes possession of the subject:

> Beauty in the European sense has always had a premeditated quality to it. We've always had an aesthetic intention and a long-range plan. That's what enabled Western man to spend decades building a Gothic cathedral or a Renaissance piazza. The beauty of New York rests on a completely different base. It's unintentional. It arose independent of human design, like a stalagmitic cavern. . . . Another way of putting it might be "beauty by mistake." Before beauty disappears entirely from the earth, it will go on existing for a while by mistake . . . the final phase in the history of beauty.[28]

San Vitale—like old Ravenna—is intentional beauty, like Kundera's Gothic cathedral or Renaissance piazza. It is not beauty by mistake. So its effect will go on and on.

ELIOT WAS RIGHT IN his description. Saint Apollinare in Classe is a "precise" Byzantine gem of Julian brick and Marmara marble, its column capitals shaped like acanthus leaves blowing in the wind. The nave is so vast it evokes the great Gothic cathedrals of Northern Europe, but here there is a *plein air* sensation, owing to the high wooden roof, as if truly the whole structure were open to the sky, creating the grandeur and solemnity of a pilgrimage site it would be a sin not to see. Andreas Agnellus, the ninth-century historian to whom we are indebted for so much of our knowledge of late antique Ravenna, writes of this sixth-century edifice and the light hitting the marble columns: "No church in any part of Italy is similar to this one in precious stones, since they glow at night almost as much as they do during the day."[29] The mosaics in the apse vault and triumphal arch—depicting a jeweled gold cross and a bearded, haloed Christ dressed in purple like an emperor—are, with their intense splashes of gold and other colors, like a break in a prison wall that reveals the heavens at their most turbulent. These are scenes that liberate and overwhelm, without the viewer ever being conscious of the artistic technique behind them.

Once again, like at the Arian Baptistery, I am struck by the fluid geography and geopolitics of Europe, North Africa, and the Levant that produced this artwork: artwork originating in the East and finding expression here in the West, so that the very terms East and West—and the dichotomy they represent—may be less secure than we have often been led to believe. For variations of this iconography can be found not only around the Mediterranean littoral, but in the Nile Valley and Abyssinia, and as far east as the Caucasus in Georgia and Armenia, wherever Orthodoxy in one form or another took hold. In the Roman Catholic churches of Poland, amid the bloodied intimacy of the crucifixes and the forests of flickering candles, you feel—amid frenzied, pressing bodies and ostentatious metalwork—that you are on a fault line, in which Western Christianity must be defended by sympathetic magic against onslaughts from the East. But here the East is nevertheless dominant, and fits precisely with the designer sleekness of one of Western Europe's great café cultures.

Ravenna leads to counterfactuals. Ravenna shows the idea of Europe, both political and aesthetic, as greater and lesser than the European subcontinent, with all the possibilities of different interactions around the Mediterranean that might have occurred had the Arabs, carrying the banner of Islam, displayed any less martial vigor than they did across North Africa; or had the Byzantine and Sassanid Persian empires not clashed as *they* did, weakening them both and helping to allow for the Arab conquest of much of the Mediterranean basin in the first place. (Muslim raiders, in fact, pillaged Classe in the mid-ninth century.) And because the past is so contingent not just upon overwhelming cultural and geographical forces but also upon the merest of individual circumstances, so, too, is the future. Despite the mummified nature of this art, it is gravid with possibilities. Ravenna, though a time capsule, is about change. Thus, it is a perfect backdrop to the encroachment of China and the weakening of America in the Mediterranean, as China develops ports in Italy and Greece, as well as becoming a regional trading behemoth.

Alas, Byzantium gradually lost interest in its Italian colony. As we know, the invasions of Slavs, Avars, Bulgars, and Persians in the Balkans and Near East not only cut land routes to the west and reduced the number of ships plying the Mediterranean, but caused a financial crisis at home in Constantinople. Then there was the aggression of not only the Persians but the Arabs, too, so that migrations and military movements originating almost in Central Asia

had a direct effect on Europe. But it had been Byzantium in the
many decades before Charlemagne, when the West was weak militarily, that helped wall off Europe itself (north of the Mediterranean) from seventh- and eighth-century Arab invaders.[30] Ravenna
is also about these other linkages.

And nobody organizes this concept—that of Europe's fate interwoven with that of Eurasia—better than Gibbon. His *Decline
and Fall* is mainly known on account of the first three volumes,
which conclude with the end of Rome in the West in A.D. 476. But
it is in the last three volumes when Gibbon—continuing the story
right up to the capture of Rome in the East by the Ottoman Turks
in 1453—majestically unfurls his narrative, revealing, among so
much else, how Islam was erected on the ruins of Sassanid Persia
and Rome, how the Crusades lightened the burden of feudalism,
how Bulgaria owed its origins to the Volga region in Russia, and
how the Mongols and the Turks, originating from deep in Central
Asia, shaped both the eastern boundaries of Europe and the western boundaries of China. The late Hugh Trevor-Roper, quoting the
Chinese historian C. S. Ch'ien, writes that "from the Pisgah height
of his universal . . . learning, Gibbon could clearly see how the East
and West affect each other and co-relate in a causal way events apparently unrelated."[31]

ON A RAINY WINTER morning the tomb of Dante Alighieri in
Ravenna has just opened, and I walk inside to the precious light of
an airy, classical marble enclosure. A lamp from the vaulted ceiling
burns olive oil from the Tuscan hills. In a bas-relief executed in 1483
by Pietro Lombardo, the poet, who died on the night of September
13–14, 1321, is depicted facing a book. He is lost in both concentration and contemplation, emanating a formidable and suffering elegance. Outside, just beyond the white and roseate marble, are laurel
and cypress trees.

I close my eyes and recite the first three stanzas of *Inferno*, volume 1 of *The Divine Comedy:*

> Midway along the journey of our life
>   I woke to find myself in a dark wood,
>   for I had wandered off from the straight path.
>
> How hard it is to tell what it was like,
>   this wood of wilderness, savage and stubborn
>   (the thought of it brings back all my old fears),
>
> a bitter place! Death could scarce be bitterer.
>   But if I would show the good that came of it
>   I must talk about things other than the good.[32]

How many people, far across the ages, have profoundly related to—have been immeasurably helped by—those lines, lines so simple and yet so abundant and compressed, written in the early years of the fourteenth century! To find oneself "in a dark wood," suddenly in the midst of a deep and painful crisis—whether moral, spiritual, psychological, professional, political, even, or a combination of such—facing it as "one man alone,"[33] no less, when you no longer have the resiliency of youth and are already burdened by commitments and bad choices made along the way, so that it constitutes a seemingly unalterable fate; and yet in spite of all that, to willingly descend into the fearful abyss and acknowledge the most humiliating—the most personal—of flaws, in order, as Dante says at the end of the poem, "to see once more the stars:"[34] that is the ultimate journey and the ultimate epic.

Dante, in truth, has spoken to me. I remain on my knees before the tomb of the poet, who was banished here to Ravenna from his native Florence because his White Guelf faction was put out of favor—so many intrigues and complications, now virtually forgotten, but which once dominated life at the time. Dante gives us a path out of the "dark wood," even as all of his characters have been judged, and have been held accountable, before God in the afterlife. For the acknowledgment of sin can be the greatest and most necessary of teachers. Guilty introspection is hard on one, especially if it goes on for months and years—as it sometimes must. But there can be relief at the end, with years of life still to live, if one is fortunate. (I can attest to that.) And just as the truth about someone's character can be known and judged (by oneself, and by God), there is no such thing as an unyielding fate about which we are powerless to do anything. We are all granted free will in order to forge better and worse outcomes in life, from which our true natures are then revealed. Dante calls to account those in politics who have brought medieval Italy to such a moral abyss precisely because he believes that even such a thing as a poem can right the world, and change the fate of individuals in the process.

The Divine Comedy was always more than a work of philosophy for me: it was also a historical and geographical adventure, befitting an epic. For an epic at root is about the hunger for knowledge played out against a specific landscape.

In the first Canto, Virgil appears as the pilgrim's guide to Hell, and we learn that the pagan world of Virgil's *Aeneid* and the City of God offered up by Saint Augustine's Roman Catholic Church are not really in conflict, for both exist in parallel, intertwining with each other, seeking a form of moral and spiritual perfection that can guide the politics of Dante's own city-state toward a better outcome. In Canto IV, in the realm of Limbo, we encounter Homer, Horace, and Ovid, and soon Avicenna and Averroes: for as Jacob Burckhardt wrote, Dante brought classical antiquity (and the Golden Age of Islam) back "into the foreground" of medieval European culture, where they belonged.[35] He also, in Walter Pater's words, helped "reestablish a continuity" with the original, "primitive church."[36] With Dante, the past always works inside the present.

And given the constant classical references in *The Divine Comedy,* it becomes obvious that neither Eliot's nor Pound's poetry would have been possible without Dante, who, with all of his literary allusions, is arguably the most European of poets. Eliot, in a small book about Dante, even suggests that modern verse in general requires knowledge of Homer, Dante, and Shakespeare. "I love Dante almost as much as the Bible," Joyce said. "He is my spiritual food, the rest is ballast."[37]

All of Dante's personages are anchored in physical territory. Hell in Dante's telling is a wondrous, tactile geographical space, with the vastness and intricacies of a continent. There is "the filthy mess of muddy shades and slush," the swamps, the boiling springs, the flaming towers, the burning sands and ditches and sarcophagi, immersed in a "prodigious stink." There are the holes where evil churchmen are buried headfirst; "the crowds, the countless, different mutilations"; the throng of souls stuck in ice, their teeth clicking from the cold "like storks' beaks snapping shut."[38] And by climbing down through the ice along Lucifer's hairy, three-headed body, the pilgrim, as we know, finds a path that leads back to the surface where shine the stars above.

And with the worst left behind, there is hope:

> For better waters, now, the little bark
> of my poetic powers hoists its sails,
> and leaves behind that cruelest of the seas.

> And I shall sing about that second realm
> where man's soul goes to purify itself
> and becomes worthy to ascend to Heaven.[39]

There is no time to linger, for as Virgil tells the pilgrim, "the more one learns, the more one comes to hate the waste of time." We struggle and strive through life, even as we despair, but as Dante

advises, "a backward glance"—to survey all that we have scaled—
"can often lift the heart."[40] Meanwhile,

> Keep up with me and let the people talk!
>   Be like a solid tower whose brave height
>   remains unmoved by all the winds that blow . . .[41]

In other words, never be distracted—the curse of our age, and of
our time on earth. For "if the world today has gone astray, the cause
lies in yourselves and only there!" Thus, we must not only never give
in to fate, but through it all, we should be careful to judge everything and everybody always by its truth, not by its reputation.[42]

The adventure is nearing its climax. Dante invokes Apollo to
guide him through the Christian Heaven.[43] And so:

> I set my course for waters never travelled;
>   Minerva fills my sails, Apollo steers,
>   and all nine Muses point the Bears to me.[44]

In Paradise, as in Purgatory, as in the Inferno, in every realm that
Dante explores, the indispensable combinations never cease, whether
it is the pagan and the Christian; or the Greek, the Roman, and the
Byzantine; since all true wisdom flows together, for wisdom itself is
about seeing the similarities and the parallels between all things
and cultures and religions. (I am thinking of the entirety of Canto
VI in *Paradise*, which is reserved for the wise counsel of Justinian.)
Dante's Heaven, with its various spheres and "lofty wheels" where
one so admires the work of "that great Artist," makes me think of
nothing so much as Einstein's famous description of Spinoza's God,
who reveals himself in the harmony of all that exists. It is "fusion of
all things" that stuns, like Neptune gazing upon the *Argo*'s keel.[45]

Dante, like Gemistos Plethon, helped reintroduce more of the
philosophical and aesthetic riches of classical Greece and Rome to
late medieval Europe, allowing it to evolve further out of Christen-

dom and the Middle Ages. He thus summoned forth the universal civilization celebrated by Sigismondo Malatesta and Agostino di Duccio in the church in Rimini—the same civilization that inspired the modernist poets and writers of the early twentieth century. As Europe now struggles to find its way, Dante still has more lives to live.

CHAPTER

3

VENICE

—

Frazer's
Golden Bough *and the*
Defeat of Fate

TURNS OF GOOD FORTUNE ARE OFTEN ASSOCIATED WITH people you meet, who henceforth change your life. I associate the phenomenon as much with books I have run across. At the gift shop of the Clark Art Institute, in Williamstown, Massachusetts, some time ago, I noticed the third volume of a trilogy called *The Emergence of Western Political Thought in the Latin Middle Ages*. It was an academic text written by a retired Williams College professor, Francis Oakley, and despite its slim size, the retail price was over $70, owing no doubt to a limited print run.

I ended up buying and reading this and the first two volumes. The books are not readable in a popular sense, owing to the highly abstract nature of the subject and the intricate and capacious scholarly detail. But, as with the best of academic writing, I find, if one can truly concentrate and read slowly, a few pages at a time, the riches gained are beyond measure. While the bulk of output in the humanities is notoriously spoiled by jargon, the mark of the high academy (which Oakley represents) is exquisite subtlety, literary precision, and vast documentation. Sitting on the train from Ravenna to Venice on a cold January day seems to me like the perfect juncture to go through the pages of notes I have made on Oakley's three books: for these books restore an edifice of understanding regarding the origin of Europe and the West, only a few fragments of which I was able to reassemble in Rimini and Ravenna.

Oakley, trained at Oxford and Yale, begins the first volume in ancient Greece and ends the third volume in early modern Europe: in between, the West, as an idea, is imperceptibly invented. He starts by quoting the late Romanian intellectual Mircea Eliade, who remarked that the Greek philosophers were actually the summation of the primitive mentality. This was because in archaic times, nature was perceived as alive and the individual inseparable from it, even as the king or ruler was quasi-divine and thus an intermediary between man and nature. In not only Greece, but also ancient Egypt, Persia, and Mesopotamia, the space between gods and men was so much narrower than what we can ever perceive. The kingdom was nothing less than an "analogue" of the divine universe, and this was true of even the "more consciously philosophical" Greek city-states, as well as, later, of imperial Rome. Nevertheless, Christianity, as a more elaborate successor to Judaism, would destabilize this entire structure of what Oakley calls "sacral monarchy," that is, a monarchy dependent on sacred rites.[1]

It was the Hebrew conception of God that had first undermined the transactional relationship between archaic man and nature. But when Jesus instructed that his kingdom was "not of this world," he implied an "altogether novel separation of 'religious' from 'political' loyalties," the forerunner of the separation of church and state. Oakley quotes the nineteenth-century French historian Numa Denis Fustel de Coulanges as explaining that Christianity "separates what antiquity had confounded," or confused. And yet, as this story has so many more twists and turns and subtleties than my brief notes can suggest, Christianity, by way of Byzantium, would accommodate itself to sacral kingship, with the imperial authority in harmony with the clerical priesthood: a concept that I witnessed firsthand in the mosaics of San Vitale, where biblical figures like David and Melchizedek are depicted in imperial regalia. Of course, Saint Augustine would delegitimize the whole concept with his writings after the Visigothic sack of Rome, seeing political authority as real yet separate from his "City of God," and existing only as a "punishment" that must be endured following Adam's fall from grace.[2]

The Christianized Celtic and Germanic tribes in the north, meanwhile, were also evolving a model of sacral kingship, but one limited and restrained by rudimentary forms of tribal consent. Indeed, the king and his people, by Merovingian and Carolingian times in the late fifth through tenth centuries, consisted of something like a "united church-kingdom," in which a webwork of relationships between the king and his nobles defined governance. Those relationships, along with the pressures of invasions from without—Viking, Magyar, Arab—and the disintegration of the Carolingian Empire from within, not to mention the legacy of a boisterous Germanic past, all worked decidedly against absolutism. Feudalism, therefore—a catch-all phrase as Oakley demonstrates for the "fragmentation of political power," the placement of "public power in private hands," and armed units secured partly through "individual and private agreements"—became an organic element in the development of Western constitutionalism: after all, the Magna Carta was "essentially a feudal document."[3]

The West was an exceedingly gradual and contingent creation, in other words, in which the medieval centuries played as large and estimable a role as ancient Greece and Rome and the Renaissance (to say nothing of the role played by the clash of empires in the Near East and North Africa, which in effect moved *Europe* northward away from the Mediterranean basin). As Oakley points out, the very term "Middle Age" was invented by Renaissance humanists in order to denigrate the long interregnum between themselves and the glories of the classical age that they so much revered. But such "periodization" of European history (into ancient, medieval, and modern) is obviously inaccurate. To wit, Locke's Enlightenment philosophy of government was "based on feudal law," which developed in the Middle Ages, and it was the medieval Carolingians who preserved much of the classic literature of antiquity.*

In short, Europe did not just take a detour of a thousand years between Late Antiquity and the Renaissance. The Renaissance did not simply pick up where Rome left off. It was a lot more complicated than that. Without the medieval centuries, there would have been no *West* as we know it.

In the second volume, Oakley elaborates on the transition from sacral kingship to oligarchy and consensualism, and finally to national monarchy and individualism: a transition that, for the most part, happened during the course of the Middle Ages, again in Europe's north. In the eleventh century, disputes between the papal authority and the Holy Roman Empire, between king and priests, that is, "can best be understood on the analogy of the different branches of government in a modern political system committed constitutionally to the separation of powers." By the end of the twelfth century, the pope himself was "bound 'by the norms of faith and order' which emanated from the consensus of the Christian community." At the same time, a juristic culture was "nurturing among its many other seedlings the notion of the natural subjective rights of individuals" that would find full flower in the early modern philosophers. This is a story that, in a larger sense, is about the papacy challenging the holiness of kings, even as the pope's own powers become more constrained; so that Oakley's saga about the development of Europe and the West is really about the fragmentation of authority.[4]

---

* Francis Oakley, *Empty Bottles of Gentilism: Kingship and the Divine in Late Antiquity and the Early Middle Ages (to 1050)* (New Haven, CT: Yale University Press, 2010), p. 200. Francis Oakley, *The Mortgage of the Past: Reshaping the Ancient Political Inheritance (1050–1300)* (New Haven, CT: Yale University Press, 2012), pp. 45–46 and 140. Classical writers like Aristotle were also translated in the Arab world and through Jewish thinkers like Moses Maimonides found their way into Europe.

Whereas from the mid-eleventh to the early fourteenth centuries the "driving [historical] forces" were the conflict between the papal and temporal powers and "the renewed familiarity with the Greek and Roman cultural legacy," by the late fourteenth and fifteenth centuries the Vatican's power was itself partially delegitimized by the rival claimants to the papacy—with Latin Christendom's subsequent division into feuding camps. And then, in the early sixteenth century, you have the challenge to the whole ecclesiastical structure by Martin Luther. This breaking apart of Christendom, because it forced a public recognition of different ideals and viewpoints, would lead ultimately and somewhat ironically to toleration, and the consequent removal of religious concerns from the public domain to the "private conscience." Oakley ends the third volume with the execution of Louis XVI of France in 1793, which, because of a still-remaining sacral tie to kingship, constituted a direct assault on Christianity itself, symbolizing, in Albert Camus's words, "the secularization of our history and the disincarnation of the Christian God."[5] Thus, the modern secular West comes into existence mainly in northern Europe, directly from obscure feudal beginnings.

How I regret not continuing my formal education beyond college and toward a PhD. I am now at the age when it is common to fantasize about having lived other lives. I would have become, say, a scholar of medieval China, writing about the Central Asian trade routes of the Tang Dynasty; or a scholar of Romanian studies specializing in the imperial conflicts of the Balkans; or a scholar of the Latin Middle Ages like Francis Oakley himself. Instead of poring through grammars and acquiring a familiarity with many languages, many gradually forgotten, I would have perfected one or perhaps two of them. I would have wanted to dig deep and narrowly like an archaeologist, in order to illuminate something both profound and panoramic. But the best that I can do now is to continue as a writer who reports on such scholarship, making it accessible to a wider audience.

Truly, I travel in order to read. I cannot do one without the other. The weight of clothes in my gear is constraining, the weight of books liberating.

I THINK THAT IF you live long enough, the process of memory ruthlessly condenses your experiences, consigning much to oblivion. My memories of a few days spent in Venice nearly half a century ago consist of occasional flashes, seconds of recollection really, little more: massive time-blackened arcades, where on the other side of the windows lay sumptuous interiors of shops, cafés, and restaurants, filled with men and women whose clothing intimidated me with its elegance; the luxury granted by the absence of automobiles in the midst of a great city, as I dashed over one canal after another; entering the sprawling and cavernous wonder-house of Saint Mark's, where I was brought face-to-face with my ignorance of art and history. Venice was a delicious put-down, and still is.

The older I get, the more out of reach it seems, though for different reasons. And yet, while my memory of that earlier trip has nearly vanished, I do remember distinctly being generally happy: that is, I was consumed by *presentness*. I was living in the moment. Now, arriving in Venice's Santa Lucia station, despite successes, I am consumed by the usual worries and fears of late adulthood, tied to the world beyond Venice as I am by electronic communications, and by so much else that accumulates in the course of one's life and from which I feel increasingly estranged. Despite my ignorance, I *knew* Venice back then: I was less lonely. Yes, it is the common problem of too much thinking. Now I must consciously construct an *idea* of Venice in order to move beyond my inner demons.

I do not recall being oppressed by tourist throngs, though it was September, almost five decades ago. Nowhere were there lines, like at the present. Now it is the end of October, I am with my wife of nearly four decades—*yes, I am not that much of a recluse!*—and there seems to be no one here except tourists. Venice is the apotheosis of globalization, which along with its cruelties, has also created upper-middle classes in Asia as well as in Europe, which for the first time in their families' collective histories have the means to travel. If Europe is one big outdoor museum as they say, then Venice is a cross between an amusement park and an archaeological site, with the visitors poking all around at the maze of walls and churches, and the indigenous inhabitants seeming almost to vanish, in places, into the ether of time. Venice today is partly an illusion. It represents the legacy of high civilization, which is increasingly global, and which is therefore the ultimate threat and counterpoint to those all over Europe still stuck in the nation-state. The right-wing nationalists want pure ethnic nations, but the metamorphosis of Venice works against that notion.

And yet I must be careful about all this. For I have only my own life span as a means of comparison. As the late Cambridge University scholar Tony Tanner noted, it was "between Byron's time and Ruskin's, between the early nineteenth century and the mid-nineteenth century," that Venice actually became a tourist city, as opposed to an occasional stop on the Grand Tour.* So what I notice is not really a new development.

AT THE END OF OCTOBER, the rainy sky and the time-battered buildings of Venice appear streaked and blackened by smoke.

---

* Tony Tanner, *Venice Desired* (Cambridge, MA: Harvard University Press, 1992), p. 75. It was during this period, in the early and mid-nineteenth century, when the English painter J. M. W. Turner made three trips to Venice. The result was a series of paintings, some of which now hang in the Tate Britain in London, that the critic John Ruskin particularly adored. They depict Venetian light as if it were a strong lamp filtered through a veil—further refracted by the water itself. There is the aura of the soon-to-be-born impressionism about these absolutely remarkable paintings, which a Turner biographer, Franny Moyle, says (regarding the earlier ones) harbor "a uniquely quiet and ghostly sensibility," in which the artist captures "everything other than the tangible." About the later ones, which made such a strong impression on me at the Tate, she says they depict "not the firm stuff of the physical world, but the far more elusive reflection of it captured in particles of light." Franny Moyle, *Turner: The Extraordinary Life & Momentous Times of J. M. W. Turner* (New York: Penguin Press, 2016), pp. 310 and 395–96.

Weather imprints on brick, plaster, and stone, like time itself, further darkening the Gothic and Renaissance facades into a banquet of ocher and ash. Without the sun, the lagoon and canals are opaque, gaseous, something more introspective and mysterious than color itself. And they are silent, as if you are sliding across them. Even in the most claustrophobic alleys you are uplifted by the briny sea air. I take a private boat around the lagoon. I am struck by the vast and limitless horizontality of madder walls and low domes coming at you from different angles, barely peeking above the dirty pearl waves. I think of the low walls of Constantinople as seen from the sea. The rugged silver dome of Santa Maria della Salute, like that of Hagia Sophia in Istanbul, is like a half planet visible from space as the boat slips into the Grand Canal—with each brush of a wave there is the intimation of another faraway conquest. Empire: that all-encompassing and boundless ambition. Water is space incarnate, more expansive and limitless than flagstones. Indeed, there are few more arresting sites than the classical, Istrian stone facade of San Giorgio Maggiore, jutting out as it does at a slant across the water from Saint Mark's Square. There is the outer world and the intimation of travel every time you glimpse a canal joining the sea. And because the sea indicates the great highways of civilization more than any land route does, the visual logic of Venice is imperial. City and empire have been nearly eternal in the story of humanity, even if the state has dominated in recent centuries. Venice fuses these two older historical constructions, and metaphorically welcomes the Chinese, who are now constructing their own seaborne empire stretching from Asia to the ports of Italy.

I AM BUT A tourist in Venice. My whole experience has been prepared for me by the holiday industry. I pass miles of high-end international boutiques, seeing merely what millions have already seen, doing the things that millions already have done. Tourists have the illusion of feeling special, of having moved up a peg or two in the social and economic ladder from their workaday existence. But we are still on the assembly line. It is as if I am being led along by a rope. Venice, I feel, has an element of tackiness reminiscent of Las Vegas. And yet, because I am consciously aware of this, rather than be depressed I believe I can, at least to some degree, counterintuitively render invisible all the other tourists from my mental world. Yes, I can take an interior journey as brilliantly colored as an external one. And I can take this journey only because of the books I have read—another case where books liberate. Travel, as opposed to tourism, is only made possible by literature. A landscape must be anchored in books during this time in history when globalization has obliterated much of what is distinctive.

So let me explore Venice, or more properly the idea of Venice, based on the books I have read. I am certainly not special in this regard. Other tourists have done something similar. We appear undistinguished on the outside, but it is our inner lives and thoughts that provide us with the sanctity of individuality.

"PASSION IS LIKE CRIME," writes Thomas Mann in *Death in Venice:* "it does not thrive on the established order and the common round; it welcomes every blow dealt the bourgeois structure, every weakening of the social fabric." And so Mann's aged protagonist, however distinguished in his professional life, pursues, as we all know, the young Polish boy Tadzio, with the "head of Eros" and the "bloom of Parian marble," even as the city falls victim to disease and subsequent chaos.[6] Passion contradicts realism and materialism, ironically the very operating principles of this medieval and early modern city-state. Great art and literature, which are passion incarnate, aspire toward moral significance. (This, after all, is the great theme of Bernard Berenson's *Aesthetics and History*.)

And yet the medieval Venetian mindset was a very hard kind, cultivating as it did communal survival, as well as political and economic moderation and realpolitik, through such devices as a determined emphasis on diplomacy, extreme secrecy, and one of history's greatest intelligence services (Venice just avoided being a police state). An "aristocratic oligarchy" that perfected the various techniques of torture and assumed "the worst in everyone," Venice lifted cynicism onto a pedestal, observes the historian James (Jan) Morris.[7] The Venetians, somewhat like the present-day Chinese about to commercially invade these waters, had no ideology or universal values to export to the world. They had no missionary impulse like the Americans; nor were they fanatics like the Spaniards.[8] The result was well over a millennium of independence and, more pertinently, extraordinary wealth, which, grafted upon a constricted real estate veined and crisscrossed by water, made for an overwhelming pre-industrial architectural beauty. Jacob Burckhardt and Marco Antonio Sabellico described Venice as the "jewel-casket of the world," which, with its cupolas, towers, and marble fantasies is the ultimate compression of splendor.[9] But because art must, in any case, seek out the higher ideal, one that does not actually exist and for which this city's singular beauty and elegance may qualify as a metaphor, perhaps there is no contradiction with the artists' love for Venice, after all.

And not to love it is perverse. The artistic style of Venice, exemplified by its greatest painters, is about illusion and execution rather than construction and analysis: thus it appeals more to one's taste than to one's intellect.[10] Venice is layer upon layer of pigments, as rich and reddish and decisive as in the work of Titian.

The Venetian aesthetic extends to sound even. Is there any sensation more perfect and refined—a consummate intermingling of faith and sensuality—than the music of Monteverdi, who is associated more with Venice than with any other city? Monteverdi's music is like the most expensive lace against one's skin. And then of course there is Vivaldi, another Venetian, which no amount of elevator music can diminish the sheer buoyant delight of. The sound of Venice may all begin with the sound of the bells issuing from the campaniles. This is the only city where the soft slapping of the water in the canals is the replacement for the painful racket of cars. In how many other cities can you hear the sound of your own footsteps?

In the early autumn of 1888, the twenty-three-year-old Bernard Berenson crossed the Alps and saw Venice for the first time: "the campanile and S. Marco I thought they would fall on me. I have read since that blind people suddenly restored to sight feel just so about their first glimpse of the world."[11] His ensuing book, *The Venetian Painters of the Renaissance,* published in 1894, helped launch this Jewish American's career as arguably the most storied art connoisseur of the twentieth century. Berenson's nineteenth-century British counterpart, John Ruskin, was so inspired by Venice and its monuments that he wrote perhaps the most famous treatise on Gothic architecture ever published, celebrating "this magnificence of sturdy power, put forth only the more energetically because the fine finger-touch was chilled away by the frosty wind" of the north where Gothic architecture had originated. Ruskin, observing the Doge's Palace (1320–1350), arguably the greatest Gothic building in Europe, saw "the peculiar energy which gives tension to movement; and stiffness to resistance, which makes the fiercest lightning forked rather than curved, and the stoutest oak-branch angular rather than bending, and is as much seen in the quivering of the lance as in the glittering of the icicle."[12] For Ruskin, Venice was not just a blend of the Christian West and the Islamic East, but as the Ducal Palace demonstrated, a blend of the Lombard North and the Arab South.[13]

The historian Morris lists close to fifty universally renowned artists and writers over several centuries given to such romantically inspired, analytic raptures about Venice. Take your pick from Goethe to Proust to Rossetti to Petrarch to Hemingway, to Rilke to Dickens to Browning, to Freya Stark and Oskar Kokoschka. Henry James, who, with his cosmopolitanism and explication of the minutiae of consciousness, is a bridge to the modernism of Joyce and Eliot, sees Venice in *The Wings of the Dove* as a place where you want to die in order first to *live*—to live amid the "half-lighted beauty" of palatial rooms in "crumbling" palaces, and to see through "the old columns . . . open to the storm."[14] Whether carnality, deception, or redemption: no backdrop is more dramatic than Venice. In the Venice of *The Aspern Papers*, James talks of "a mystic companionship, a moral fraternity with all those who in the past had been in the service of art."[15]

Yet, it is possible that the most unsurpassable description of Venice appeared more than three decades after Morris's book: the late Russian-American poet Joseph Brodsky's *Watermark*, which at a slender 135 pages can count as an epic, for so powerful and devastating are its metaphors and asides that while technically a work of prose, it is like a long poem. It is the inverse of Pound's *Cantos*. Whereas that work seeks sprawling greatness and erudition and for the most part fails, Brodsky's little book effortlessly produces perfection, even as it is clearly intended to be a minor effort. Of course, the brilliance of metaphor is usually a matter of sheer artistry, not hard labor. Just listen to Brodsky reduce the visitor's Venice to its essentials. True happiness is "the smell of freezing seaweed" at night along "the black oilcloth of the water's surface"; "beauty at low temperatures *is* beauty"; "water is the image of time," and since music evokes time, "water, too, is choral." On the boat from the *stazione*, "the overall feeling was mythological, cyclopic," the Gothic and Renaissance buildings a "bevy of dormant cyclopses reclining in black water, now and then raising and lowering an eyelid." Marble inlays, capitals, cornices, pediments, balconies "turn you vain. For this is the city of the eye; your other faculties play a faint second fiddle."[16] Ergo, Venice is materialism and superficiality writ large. Physical beauty is everything here. Venice tempts idolatry.

Brodsky puts you in your place; he exposes your inadequacies by his own metaphorical brilliance, which is so austere and mathematical almost. (He hates writers and academics with "too many tidy bookshelves and African trinkets." I am partially guilty on that score.) For Brodsky is the pinnacle; you are a dozen levels below him, at the very least. And because he is such a genius, every off-hand remark he makes carries weight. No doubt, he would quietly sneer at my own work ethic, my neat desk, my endnotes, my anxious indulgence in analytical categories and organization, for people of his caliber simply don't require any of it. Their genius can handle disorganization and rise above any system. They can afford to be lazy even (though he certainly wasn't). They may publish sparingly, in small amounts, and leave a deeper, more lasting imprint than any of us (though, again, in Brodsky's case his production was prodigious). As for the hardworking, incessantly striving Ezra Pound, in Brodsky's eyes he is beneath contempt. From the viewpoint of any Russian, Pound's "wartime radio spiels" in service to the Axis Powers should have earned him "nine grams of lead."

The Cantos, Brodsky goes on, "too, left me cold; the main error was an old one: questing after beauty." Beauty "is always a by-product of other, often very ordinary pursuits."[17] Yet, here I would like to argue a bit. Despite the ordinary workings of time and geography that help make Venice what it is, isn't Venetian architecture itself premeditated beauty?

For the rest of us, if not for Brodsky, Venice is a city of "trite" associations, "a series of souvenirs and 'views,'" writes Mary McCarthy: "no word can be spoken in this city that is not an echo of something said before. *Mais c'est aussi cher que Paris!*' exclaims a Frenchman in a restaurant, unaware that he repeats Montaigne." Truly, there is nothing new that can be said or even thought about Venice. "'I envy you, writing about Venice,' says the newcomer. 'I pity you,' says the old hand." McCarthy, a novelist, critic, and towering American intellectual of the mid-twentieth century, also has the enviable and lapidary gift of metaphor that routs mere hard work. "No one would complain of Canalettos that they are 'all alike.' That is precisely their point. They please us by repeating, just as a mirror does." That is why the eye never tires of Venice.[18] In this sense, Venice depresses me, for I know that when I write about it I am competing badly with the greats. "So much has been said and written about Venice already," writes Goethe—and this was in 1786![19] And yet how can I avoid it, as it is in the path of my journey?

I cannot sidestep Venice for yet another reason: it is basic to what I believe about history, culture, and international relations. Mary McCarthy, in her shrewd and incisive—in its own way unequaled—little book about Venice, *Venice Observed*, published in 1956, introduces the matter.[20] "Booty and trade concessions were extorted by the Venetians impartially from Christian and heathen. This impartiality . . . was what caused them to be hated, as sometimes the Jews have been." To wit, "the Crusades were a bonanza for Venice, which . . . treated the whole affair as a business operation."

Venice offered its troops at a steep price, transported a Crusader army to *Outremer* ("overseas," or the Holy Land), and "when the Crusaders did not pay up," proceeded to use the Crusading spirit as an excuse to capture Adriatic ports in which it had a commercial interest. The Venetians signed a treaty with the Muslim Turks in order to deal in "goods forbidden to Christians," and sacked the capital of Constantinople in 1204, which involved three days of murder, rape, and plunder. This is realpolitik to no purpose except enrichment, and it is through such crass and pitiless deeds that Venice became the fantasy city for artists and writers to admire. For Venice's foreign policy and its very political system were built exclusively on principles designed for business, and conducting *business as usual*. "Departure. Risk. Profit. Glory" is how historian Roger Crowley describes the pattern of Venetian sea voyages, with "profit" the singular important element. Because Venice had no agricultural land, it had no feudalism. Its barter was money, not crops.[21] "A wholly materialist city is nothing but a dream incarnate," McCarthy writes of the result. "Venice is the world's unconscious: a miser's glittering hoard, guarded by a Beast whose eyes are made of white agate."[22]

Pragmatism, of both the ruthless and the enlightened variety, was the guiding spirit of medieval Venice. The Venetian government was a bureaucratic machine "in which the wills and passions of men would have no part," constituting, in McCarthy's words, "an invention in the field of political science, a patented device" with each branch of power holding the other in check, making for an early variant of the American system. The Venetian clergy encapsulated the spirit of the Most Serene Republic, or *La Serenissima*. "There were no martyrs, no Thomas à Beckets or Thomas Mores," as she says. "Like all true Venetians," the clergy "lived in the here-and-now." This meant not only no heroes, but also no inquisitions. Pragmatism meant no fervor, which in turn meant no fanaticism. And so unlike the other states of Catholic Europe, points out the historian John Julius Norwich, Venice never burnt a heretic at the stake. Venice, in its love of statecraft and its disdain for moral perfection, was an eminently practical place—a secret of its interminable survival from the close of the Dark Ages to the first drumbeats of modern times. McCarthy here makes a telling comparison with that other city-state, Florence. Florence, incapable of ruling itself well, nevertheless produced a great abstract theorist of government, Machiavelli. Venice had no such theorists, yet evolved a "model Republic." For in everything about Venice, there is this reverence for the "concrete."[23] Religious disputes did not interest Venetians; only political ones did. They practiced Machiavellianism better than the Florentines. The Venetians were doers, not thinkers.

A HALF CENTURY AGO I may have had more peace of mind in Venice, but I hadn't yet discovered McCarthy and so many other authors, enriching my experience on this return visit.

Of all the brilliant descriptions of Venice written by artists and intellectuals over the centuries, I'll never forget McCarthy's first words about Saint Mark's, that dusky shell of sprawling gold leaf and Byzantine iconography, whose catacomb-like darkness I associate with the colder climate of Constantinople:

From the outside, it "looks like an Oriental pavilion—half

pleasure-house, half war-tent, belonging to some great satrap. Inside, glittering with jewels and gold, faced with precious Eastern marbles, jasper and alabaster, porphyry and verd-antique, sustained by Byzantine columns ... scarcely a pair alike, this dark cruciform cave has the look of a robber's den." The purpose of all this practicality and materialism throughout history, it turns out, was luxury, of a very refined and sensuous kind that emanated from the East, from Byzantium. Even the Gothic influences that infiltrated Venice from places like Avignon and Flanders had not been sufficient to displace Venice's essentially Byzantine artistic character. Venetians, McCarthy says, remained in their hearts "icon-makers and mosaicists ... "arrested in a motionless magnificence."[24] And yet, as the dependably revealing British historian John Julius Norwich notes, what helps make it all work is the "'Gothic Crown' of marble pinnacles and crockets that so entranced Ruskin."[25]

It isn't that the East in a cultural and artistic sense began in Venice as it did at Ravenna, for such a statement accepts an inflexible, artificial division. It is just that in Venice, as elsewhere on the Adriatic, East and West first met, and still to this day collapse and disappear into each other, even as they re-emerge everywhere on stone and tempera as distinct elements of their former selves. In these medieval and early modern port cities, fortified by the cosmopolitanism that comes via the sea, the dispersal of Eastern and Western sensibilities allows us to steal glimpses of our future world. The East stands out in Venice particularly because it is framed and highlighted by the Gothic and Renaissance influences of the West. As Ruskin notes, in Venice, Gothic architecture "superseded" Byzantine and was in turn superseded, if only partially, by Renaissance, which, as it happens, owes its grand effect to the vaporous, bottle-green water lapping at its foundations.[26] The result overall is a unique aesthetic sensibility that we can delight in.

Medieval Venice was so drenched in trade with the Levant that, more than any other city or power in Europe, Venice both comprehended and summarized Eurasia. "It was the central cog that meshed two economic systems—Europe and the Orient," writes Crowley.[27] Of course, Venice's Easternness is also a cliché. "In Venice, as any gilded cockatrice will tell you, the East begins," writes Jan Morris, whose own book, which describes Venice literally down to its vast population of alley cats, is yet another example of why there may be nothing original to say about the city anymore.

What do I believe is so important about the story of Venice that makes me go on, though? That culture rules all, even while culture is constantly evolving and combining with other cultures. That geography matters. That geopolitics—the battle for space and power—is eternal. That states built on realist and pragmatic principles survive longer than states built on idealistic and moralistic ones. Thus, we must think tragically in order to avoid tragedy. This, in turn, means that order comes before freedom and interests come before values, because without order there is no freedom for anybody, and without interests our values cannot follow and operate. And yet realism requires beauty or else it slips into coarseness and vulgarity: this, too, is the genius of Venice.

NORWICH WRITES:

"Venice, alone of all the still-great cities of Italy, was born and brought up Greek.... Long after she shed her dependence on Constantinople, she continued to turn her back on Italy and to look resolutely eastward; the nightmare tangle of medieval Italian politics, of Guelf and Ghibelline, Emperor and Pope ... none of this was for her." Doges used Byzantine honorifics. The Venetian ruler's dress was modeled on that of the Byzantine exarch. Byzantine girls were sent to Venice to marry; Venetians sent their sons to finish their education in Constantinople. Venice's political links with Byzantium helped shield it from the quarrels among the other city-states of Italy, with their rapidly shifting tactical alliances that were the epitome of amorality. Because a rival commercial system, run by Arabs, stretched across North Africa and the Middle East, Venice became crucial to Constantinople as a Byzantine outlet to Europe. The Venetian model of beauty, as exemplified by the low domes and small windows of Saint Mark's, recalling Hagia Sophia in Constantinople, was mainly Eastern.[28]

Of course, the underpinning of Venice's fortuitous separation from the rest of Italy was at root geographical. That great lagoon, the few miles of shallow water that protected Venice from the mainland in all its aspects, allowed it to focus eastward toward Byzantium, and, in addition, was the savior against Saracens, Magyars, and other invaders in the early centuries of Venetian independence. The lagoon, by confining Venetians to so restricted a space, also fostered internal cohesion. "Among Venice's rich merchant aristocracy," Norwich explains, "everyone knew everyone else, and close acquaintance led to mutual trust of a kind that in other cities seldom extended far outside the family circle." The result was efficient administration by which risky trading ventures, involving vast outlays of capital, "could be arranged on the Rialto in a matter of hours." Neither utopian nor egalitarian, Venice represented the triumph of a closed elite. Optimism was banned, unless it could be grounded in facts and percentages.[29] (It was from such a tightly woven merchant aristocracy that Marco Polo, the late-thirteenth-century Venetian explorer of China and Central Asia, originated— of whom more later.)

Without the lagoon and the canals—without the presence of water, that is—Venice simply would not have had the beauty that endowed its population with such love of their city-state: it was a love of the polity, rather than that of one man or king. This, and the internal peace they enjoyed, fostered a "humaneness of feeling" that, as Berenson suggests, made Venetians "the first really modern people in Europe."[30]

For the "myth of Venice" is that of an exemplary structure— "monarchy, oligarchy, and democracy" in a thoroughly fluid combination, rising, perfectly formed, from the waters. It was Petrarch who equated Venice with "justice" itself. The sixteenth-century canvases of Paolo Veronese in the Doge's Palace show the city-state's moral progress from militarism to imperialism to peace. Another painting in the Doge's Palace, by Domenico Tintoretto (early seventeenth century), has Venice receiving blood from Christ's side, manifesting a "direct rapport with the Eucharist," according to the Columbia University art historian David Rosand.[31] Supreme aesthetic beauty is here bound up with the utmost spiritual self-confidence, which, in turn, was built on realistic principles of governance.

What ensues, with its succession of eighty-four doges from 726 to 1797, is a thousand-year history as long, intricate, dense, intoxicating, and overwhelming as that of Byzantium itself, mind-numbing in its constant intrigues and periodic insurrections. It is a comparatively dim and opaque canvas that produced few giants and larger-than-life heroes (Pietro II Orseolo, who governed toward the end of the tenth century, being one exception to this rule), for trade and commerce, dull as these things are, reduce the long-term impact of bloodshed and its accomplice, glory. Because it is so thematically uninspiring, Venetian history is generally hard to remember, and for the literate, non-expert public is known best through the works of Shakespeare—who uses Venice as a somewhat shameless and cynical backdrop to reveal vulnerability and passion contained in everyone, Moor and Jew alike, people otherwise depicted as one-dimensional and therefore uninteresting in his day.

Mary McCarthy writes: "those hale old doges . . . seem to us a strange breed of sea-animal, who left behind them the pink, convoluted shell they grew to protect them, which is Venice."[32] The supreme calculation encouraged by this ducal system resulted in, as Norwich tells us, only three strategic blows in the course of almost 1,100 years of dogeship: the discovery of the Cape route to the Indies in 1499, which overshadowed Venice's own trade routes to the Levant and Central Asia; the gradual spread of Ottoman power in the eastern Mediterranean following the fall of Byzantium in 1453;

and the onslaught of the League of Cambrai against Venice in the early sixteenth century—none being Venice's fault. Realism worked wonders and was the one true religion of Venice, a place and a system that worshipped Byzantium, but besieged it when it suited her, and gave the Byzantine emperors only limited help later on, in order not to antagonize the Ottomans who loomed as the successor power in Constantinople.[33] Venetian doges always had one eye cocked over the horizon.

Venice was an independent republic built on separation of powers (especially between church and state, as Oakley's history sets up) and an empire at the same time: enlightened at home and rapacious abroad. The idea that empire arises from tyrannical foundations is only partially borne out by history. Venice was a cross between a "theoretical democracy," in that the dogeship was an elected office, and an "oligarchy," in that power resided within a constellation of wealthy families. And as the late Johns Hopkins University historian Frederic C. Lane has intimated, Venice was aristocratic through and through.[34] Yet, as Lane goes on to say: "Nearly everywhere [else in sixteenth-century Italy] the republican principles, derived from the communes and extolled by civic humanists, were abandoned, if not completely in theory, at least in practice. Venice alone survived with independence while perpetuating republican institutions."[35]

Venice was ruled by the Council of Ten: the doge, the ducal councilors, and the Heads of the Forty (a high constitutional body), which together constituted the *Signoria*, the government executive. Burckhardt in *The Civilization of the Renaissance in Italy*, published in 1860, provides the best description of it:

> The Council of Ten, which had a hand in everything, which disposed without appeal of life and death, of financial affairs and military appointments . . . was yearly chosen afresh from the whole governing body, the Gran Consiglio, and was

consequently the most direct expression of its will. It is not probable that serious intrigues occurred at these elections, as the short duration of the office and the accountability which followed rendered it an object of no great desire. . . . it acted from rational motives and not from a thirst for blood. No State, indeed, has ever exercised a greater moral influence over its subjects.[36]

Surrounded by gold leaf, luxurious dark wood, and, in the final centuries, masses of Tintorettos and Veroneses, all celebrating God and military conquest, the rulers of Venice imbibed a certainty of mission that bordered on magical thinking. A world without the Republic simply could not be imagined.

Efficient governance combined with economic dynamism leads to trade and interests far and beyond, so that imperialism naturally follows. Empire does not begin with a group of men plotting in a high chamber. It happens organically, in a nation's sleep, as it were. For as a state expands commercially, it finds that it has newly wrought security concerns abroad. The Venetian empire may arguably have begun in the year 1000 with an anti-pirate expedition along the Adriatic's Dalmatian coast (the pirates being Croats). As a city-state of no more than 100,000 inhabitants, Venice would eventually acquire great naval power "in the medieval age of sprawling, loosely jointed empires," Lane writes. By the end of the fourteenth century, in order to check the steady westward movement of the Ottomans in the eastern Mediterranean (as well as that of the rival city-state Genoa, as Fernand Braudel reminds us), Venice, for reasons both commercial and strategic, would acquire southern Dalmatia and many Aegean outposts in the Morea, Crete, the Cyclades, and the Dodecanese. Farther east, in the late fifteenth and sixteenth centuries, Venice also took Cyprus, which it corruptly misgoverned.

Like the United States, though in a very different way, of course,

Venice was a republic with a seaborne empire of sorts, the eastern Mediterranean constituting as far-flung a domain in the late Renaissance and early modern periods as the whole globe itself today. The Venetian Republic, when Napoleon finally brought it down with a coup d'état in 1797, had lasted well over four times as many years as the current United States. It did so in part by the shrewdest of foreign policies. For example, it performed what Lane calls the "double balancing act" of playing France off against Spain, and Spain off against the Ottoman Empire. Even though Venice shared in the Christian League's great victory against the Ottoman Empire in 1571 at the naval battle of Lepanto, off western Greece, Venice mainly gained peace by concessions in the aftermath.[37] The United States would do well to emulate the pragmatic spirit of Venice, which was enlightened by the standards of its day.

Of course, the evolution of European power politics in the early modern and modern eras gradually caught up with Venice. When Spain and France became united kingdoms, as Lane explains, "the Italian balance of power was submerged into the European state system."[38] Thus, Venice was besieged both by rivals in western Europe and at sea by the Ottoman Empire. Furthermore, as the Industrial Revolution appeared with the emergence of modern capitalism, the Venetian ruling class was insufficiently flexible to admit new wealth and talent into its ranks. The Venetian Republic, as enlightened as it was in earlier ages, could not cope with the new democratic spirit. And so, as all empires do, Venice declined.

IN *THE ASPERN PAPERS*, Henry James writes:

I was standing before the church of Saints John and Paul and looking up at the small square-jawed face of Bartolommeo Colleoni, the terrible *condottiere* who sits so sturdily astride of his huge bronze horse, on the high pedestal on which Venetian gratitude maintains him. The statue is incomparable, the finest of all mounted figures, unless that of Marcus Aurelius, who rides benignant before the Roman Capitol, be finer.[39]

I am now standing at the same spot. The statue of the helmeted Colleoni, his sword at the ready, is a perfect summation of action and aggression. Every muscle of man and horse appears flexed. Even the towering and peeling Gothic brick walls of Saints John and Paul do not diminish the sculpture. I think of how the person of Colleoni, a ruthless soldier of fortune like Malatesta, who fought for different sides in the course of a lifetime according to who paid him the most, and yet who also found time for good works, represents an intermediary step between the barbarism and darkness of early man and the fragile light of beauty and civilization of which this cityscape remains the supreme emblem.

The passage from the former barbaric state to the exalted latter one is told most effectively through literature, and thus my eyes retreat from the statue and café table where I am sitting nearby, and recall my almost visual memory of the famous opening text of Sir James George Frazer's *The Golden Bough*, which influenced Eliot's *The Waste Land*.

> Who does not know Turner's picture of the Golden Bough? The scene, suffused with the golden glow of imagination in which the divine mind of Turner steeped and transfigured even the fairest natural landscape, is a dream-like vision of the little woodland lake of Nemi—"Diana's Mirror," as it was called by the ancients.... In antiquity this sylvan landscape was the scene of a strange and recurring tragedy.[40]

In the midst of this sacred grove, as Frazer tells us, "a grim figure might be seen to prowl," deep into the night around a certain tree, armed with a sword. For he held the priesthood up until the moment when another man would set upon and murder him; a man who then, in turn, prowled around and near the same tree, sword drawn, until he, too, was murdered. And on it went. "Such was the rule of the sanctuary. . . . For year in, year out, in summer and winter, in fair weather and in foul, he had to keep his lonely watch, and whenever he snatched a troubled slumber it was at the peril of his life."

There is no parallel in classical antiquity, with its civilized cities and empires, for such a rude and barbarous custom. "It must have been handed down from a time beyond the memory of man," Frazer writes, with the custom eventually emerging into literature as the forerunner to the so-called King of the Wood, an armed priest who protected a sacred beech or oak tree and served under the Roman god Diana (the Greek Artemis). According to the logic of this fable, the violent early death of the priest protects him from the bodily decay of age, with his youthful spirit transferred in all its vitality to his stronger successor. Human life is secondary in this dark fantasy, as long as the sacred tree, upon which grew a mistletoe (the "Golden Bough"), is protected. This is the violent state of nature at the beginning of time.[41]

Yet Frazer's tome is not just a recounting of barbarism, though that is how his story begins. It is also about how sympathetic magic—the erection of taboos, the transference of evil, the use of fire to defeat the darkness, and so forth—all constitute attempts and pathways that begin the journey towards challenging the impersonal forces of nature and defeating fate: these are the first steps, in other words, however primitive, towards constructing a moral and ethical world. It starts with fear and ends with beauty: that is, it begins with "beast-gods" and human sacrifice and advances to Doric pillars and the redeeming epics of Homer and Virgil (and to the architecture of Venice), to paraphrase the classicist Edith Hamilton.[42]

We know where all this should lead—to the individual declaring his or her own agency, learning how to master nature itself, and, having done that, working over time and the vicissitudes towards a more humane world. It begins with the crudest form of politics and dominance, demonstrated by the King of the Wood, then passes through the terrible *condottieri* Colleoni and Malatesta, and ends with parliamentary systems, or with the most liberal and benign of autocracies. In political science terms, it means, again, that order comes before freedom, but once order is established the task begins to make order itself by stages less tyrannical.

This monumental journey, to repeat, originates in darkness: with the bloody rite around the Golden Bough at Nemi, with its stark deterministic outcome of violent death and its depiction of a lonely man literally trapped in the state of nature. This is why Machiavelli's *Prince,* for its time at least, was not a cynical work of political philosophy but rather an instructional guide about how to overcome fate. And because fate can be so overpowering, the individual practitioner of politics has to be especially devious. Indeed, Plutarch wrote his *Lives* for the moral instruction they offered: of great men using every instrument at their disposal to turn the direction of history. In speaking of Alexander, Plutarch notes that "an expression or jest" may inform us better of his character and inclination than his most glorious exploits—even the crossing of the Granicus—such is the Shakespearean dimension of history.[43]

Yet, no matter how devious or determined or heroic an individual may be, there will always be limits, and thus the truly evolved political man of action will know how to work inside those limits. Here is Fernand Braudel, the great French geographer, who had perhaps the finest grasp of what could and could not be accomplished in the natural world:

> By stating the narrowness of the limits of action, is one denying the role of the individual in history? I think not. . . . the true man of action is he who can measure most nearly the constraints upon him, who chooses to remain within them and even to take advantage of the weight of the inevitable,

exerting his own pressure in the same direction. All efforts against the prevailing tide of history—which is not always obvious—are doomed to failure.[44]

The key phrase here is "not always obvious." Therefore, we cannot give in to fate, precisely because the historical outcome is often unknowable: so it is individual struggle itself, often multiplied in great numbers, that creates "the prevailing tide of history" in the first place. The King of the Wood never gave up in his struggle for survival, for every extra day he survived was a triumph; neither did Colleoni and Malatesta give up: by their very unrelenting energy and ambition and deviousness they came to define a whole era. It was Ezra Pound's tragedy that he never moved intellectually and morally beyond their example.

EZRA POUND WAS BESOTTED with Venice. In "Canto XVII," written in 1924, he writes about

> ... the waters richer than glass,
> Bronze gold, the blaze over the silver,
> Dye-pots in the torch-light ... [45]

It was this poem, in which Venice appears as "the white forest of marble, bent bough over bough"—a triumph of nature and of the gods[46]—that initially introduced Pound to Adrian Stokes, before Stokes had even read the Malatesta Cantos and contemplated a book about the church in Rimini.

Now I am sailing to the island of San Michele, the municipal cemetery less than half a mile out in the lagoon, where Pound is buried in the small Protestant section. San Michele is inlaid in the water: almost a perfect square of land bordered by brick walls punctuated by white arches, with cypresses everywhere dignifying the prospect.

What thou lovest well remains,
the rest is dross

What thou lov'st well shall not be reft from thee
What thou lov'st well is thy true heritage . . .[47]

Those memorable lines, so intoxicating when first encountered—
so appealing to many a young person with a falsely imagined sense
of nostalgia—are from the libretto of "Canto LXXXI." They form
part of Pound's "Pisan Cantos," written while he was interned by
the U.S. Army as an enemy combatant and propagandist outside
Pisa at the conclusion of World War II. Pound's world—that of the
Axis Powers and the Fascist cause—has just collapsed. He is a ruin,
and rich memories of an epic life, it appears, are all he has left. Living in a cold and rainy tent after a life of aesthetic elegance in Rapallo, near Genoa, he tells himself to

Pull down thy vanity
Thou art a beaten dog beneath the hail,
A swollen magpie in a fitful sun . . . [48]

The poet Robert Lowell, who had distinctly mixed feelings
about the "Pisan Cantos," did in fact compliment them on their
"loveliness."[49] Yet, they are all so interminably self-centered. This is
a world where tens of millions have just died in excruciating circumstances in history's most violent cataclysm, a cataclysm directly
caused by the ideology Pound very publicly espoused. True, he does
write,

How mean thy hates
Fostered in falsity . . . [50]

But that, along with some moving passages about regret that
come much later in "Canto CXVI," is almost all there is, when it

comes to genuine remorse or empathy. Pound ends this libretto with more rhythmic, graceful lines, this time about how his real error might have been insufficient inspiration, and insufficient determination, as a poet. Here is John Ruskin: "to carve our own work, and set it up for admiration, is a miserable self-complacency, a contentment in our own wretched doings, when we might have been looking at God's doings. And all noble ornament," Ruskin goes on, is about concentrating on God's world.[51] The corollary of this, in Pound's case, would have been for him to contemplate the suffering and wreckage of Europe, as overwhelming as it was, and investigate his own moral responsibility for it. That, given "the best damned ear ever born," in the words of William Carlos Williams, might have made for some very good poetry indeed. Pound, as the critic Tony Tanner says, was a poet who truly grasped paradise—spending his life in places like Venice—and ended up contributing to hell.[52]

Toward the end of his life, upon hearing a story about Bernard Berenson's Jewishness, Pound's face reportedly "collapsed into a mask of abject misery, shame and guilt." Later, Pound admitted that his "worst mistake" was his "stupid, suburban prejudice of anti-Semitism [which] all along . . . spoiled everything."[53] One must give him a little credit for that, but he was never to internalize enough of it within *The Cantos*.

And yet, and yet . . . it never ends with Pound. There is, as the critic Michael Dirda points out, Pound's simple unrivaled energy and infectious enthusiasm for literature itself, which leaves us with such hard truths as "More writers fail from lack of character than from lack of intelligence," and "One definition of beauty is: aptness to purpose."[54] Then, of course, one cannot forget that famous, truly awe-inspiring imagist poem of 1913 he wrote, "In a Station of the Metro."

> The apparition of these faces in the crowd;
> Petals on a wet, black bough.[55]

He really could be a great poet when he aimed for less.

Pound's grave on San Michele is a simple slab lying in the ground, with only his name in the Latin style on it. An overgrown bush and a vine nest almost hide the slab, even from a short distance. I stumbled around for a quarter of an hour before my wife, Maria, located it. A gravestone can be a person's final signature. This grave has the air of partial abandonment: symbolic for a poet so often disparaged. I move to another grave only about twenty feet away: that of Joseph Brodsky. Brodsky's upright slab, with his name carved in both Russian and English, is exquisitely tended, with tiny, neatly arranged potted plants, roses, and a rose bush, all recently clipped. It is clearly a beloved and much-visited site.

Whereas Pound consciously set out to be great, Brodsky, with more talent, set out merely to record his emotions and the material world as it appeared before his eyes. Whereas Pound was full of ideology, theories, and grand schemes, Brodsky, who served eighteen months of hard labor in internal exile in the far north of European Russia—before being forcibly expelled from his homeland—had only contempt for such abstract things. Whereas Pound's pungent historical panoramas, despite their emphasis on great heroic figures, leave little room for intimacy—for the personal life, that is—Brodsky's inner lives and loves, so agonizingly personal, attain almost a numinous state in his poetry. Brodsky cares about the individual, not merely archetypes as Pound does. With Brodsky, a lover's embrace is holy; with Pound sometimes only a bloody battle seems to be. (And yet Brodsky is deeply interested in history. In the space of only three lines in a poem about the Russian military hero Zhukov, the names of Hannibal, Pompey, and Belisarius pop up. Then there is his famous poem about Tiberius, his essay on Byzantium, and so much more.)

But Brodsky is great simply because no other poet, perhaps, has his unstoppable gift for the most surprising and revealing of metaphors. "Dust is the flesh of time"...the dental cavities of an old man "rival old Troy on a rainy day"...a dense garden is like "jewels closely set" . . . "darkness restores what light cannot repair."[56] Trying to explain his technique, Brodsky said that a poem "should be dark with nouns" on the page.[57] Additionally, Brodsky can "see analogies where others do not suspect them," writes the poet Charles Simic, and this is inextricable from his humanity. Brodsky, "the great poet of travel . . . wanted to be a universal poet, someone at home everywhere, and he largely succeeded."[58] This is precisely why Brodsky is so crucial to Europe now: to what Europe at this perilous moment should yearn for . . . and that is an acceptance of some universality, of some cosmopolitanism, to ease the transition to more diverse societies.

Brodsky, obsessed with universalism and the personal life of the individual, represents a Europe of legal states over ethnic nations, and the rule of law over arbitrary fiat. Pound, with his obsession with the strong man of action and manly *virtù*, now represents the dark, populist forces that have been gathering for years in Europe. Here in this Venetian cemetery are the two paths that Europe can tread. May it choose the right one.

If only I had appreciated all this sooner, as a younger man. For me it came too late. The benefit has only been in the journey, the covering of the vast distance from one level of awareness to another. The looking back while moving forward is replete with self-recrimination. But what more can the inner life offer than the broadening of one's perspective, rather than the narrowing? Still, to have known more about Brodsky earlier, to have been instructed in his significance, that could have helped. Yet his poetry was there all along for me, if only I had looked.

I now stand over Brodsky's grave and read "The Bust of Tiberius," written in 1981, nine years after Pound's death in this city.

> . . . All
> that lies below the massive jawbone—Rome:
> the provinces, the latifundists, the cohorts,
> plus swarms of infants bubbling at your ripe

stiff sausage. . . .
What does it matter what Suetonius
cum Tacitus still mutter, seeking causes
for your great cruelty? . . .
you seem a man more capable of drowning
in your piscina than in some deep thought. . . .
Ah, Tiberius!

And such as we presume to judge you? You
were surely a monster. . . . [59]

Pound would have been jealous. Imagine, beaten at his own game of rendering the earthen texture of history. For there is so much in this poem that I haven't quoted. The allusion to Stalin, without even mentioning his name, putting the poet on firm moral ground: again, *beaten*. Nevertheless, Tiberius's obscene cruelty was specific to the second half of his reign, from A.D. 23 until his death in A.D. 37, when the aged emperor—perhaps suffering from mental disease—delegated power to the Praetorian Guard. From A.D. 14 to A.D. 23, he had been a model of caution who abandoned gladiatorial games, built few cities, annexed few territories, and used diplomacy against the German tribes. [60] Of course, this does not weaken Brodsky's employment of symbols to evoke unbridled power.

I SEE THE PINKISH Gothic facade of the Danieli Royal Excelsior Hotel and recall the most moving pages from John Julius Norwich's magisterial *A History of Venice*. On this spot, now cluttered with kiosks selling T-shirts, postcards, and cheap carnival masks, a member of a mob stabbed Doge Vitale II Michiel to death in 1172. For fifteen of his sixteen years in power the doge had directed the affairs of Venice brilliantly, besieged as he was by Frederick Barbarossa in one direction and Manuel Comnenus in the other, with northern Italy unified by the Lombard League and southern Italy unified by an alliance between Norman Sicily and the greatest of twelfth-century popes, Alexander III. But in his final year, meaning only to do well by his city-state and not shrinking from moral responsibility, Vitale Michiel raised a fleet of 120 ships and set out south along the Adriatic for the east, on a peace mission to Constantinople. Yet the negotiations with Byzantine officials proved inconclusive, even as plague broke out on the overcrowded ships while his fleet awaited developments on the eastern Aegean island of Chios. Then his emissaries returned from Constantinople reporting complete diplomatic failure.

Doge Michiel returned to Venice having been humiliated by the Byzantines, while much of his navy had been lost to disease, and those that did not perish were close to mutiny. In addition, the doge was seen in Venice to have introduced the plague into the city. Thus was he set upon by the mob. As Machiavelli emphasizes in his *Prince*, you can advise a leader in *virtù*, the manly vigor associated with human agency; but as to the other half of the equation, *fortuna*, luck or fortune, you cannot help him. So we are left with this tragic conundrum: that while man does not have to give in to fate (indeed, must not) and human progress itself depends on such risk-taking, those that do take such risks—and are, therefore, in our eyes quite estimable—are often destined to fail. Venice, besides so much else, teaches us that life is hard.

BEAUTY IS A FORM of truth, as the poet says. One of the great assemblages of modern art is here, in the late Peggy Guggenheim's palace on the Grand Canal, near where the canal meets the lagoon, not far from where Henry James resided at the Palazzo Barbaro. This prodigious collection, encompassing everything in the field from Picasso and Brancusi to Max Ernst—from Klee and Kandinsky to Andy Warhol—manifests the power and, yes, vitality, of introspection, fear, juxtaposition, decomposition, analysis, and above all abstraction in all its forms. Indeed, because cubism, surrealism, and the like are all so intensely cerebral, and the graceful and sensuous Venetian aesthetic is its very opposite, the relief that Venice offers the eye puts a viewer in a suitably calm state of mind to do the work of contemplating and appreciating modern art.

From the rooted-in-place, Italianate perfection of the Grand Canal as seen from Peggy Guggenheim's terrace, you turn to admire the cold, universalist abstraction of twentieth-century painters and sculptors, who owe their own inspiration as much to Africa and America—to Freud and the unconscious, even—as to Europe. You can see why she required a villa on this spot to amass such a collection. Her life as a connoisseur of the abstract—even as Bernard Berenson was exclusively preoccupied with the painting of the Renaissance—demonstrates why Venice provides such an inspiration for every kind of aesthetic. This is ultimately why the Biennale for contemporary art finds a natural home here.

LEAVING VENICE: NO ONE has described such a departure better than Lawrence Durrell, at the beginning of his travel memoir, *Bitter Lemons*, the finest book he ever wrote—greater than all the volumes of *The Alexandria Quartet*. For his obsession with aesthetics does not deter him from political and moral analysis of the waning British Empire in the eastern Mediterranean in the 1950s.

> Journeys, like artists, are born and not made. A thousand differing circumstances contribute to them. . . . They flower spontaneously out of the demands of our natures—and the best of them lead us not only outwards in space, but inwards as well. . . .
>
> These thoughts belong to Venice at dawn, seen from the deck of the ship which is to carry me down the islands to Cyprus; a Venice wobbling in a thousand fresh-water reflections, cool as a jelly. It was as if some great master, stricken by dementia, had burst his whole colour-box against the sky. . . .

Fragments of history touched with the colours of wine, tar, ochre, blood, fire-opal. . . . The whole at the same time being rinsed softly back at the edges into a dawn sky as softly as circumspectly blue as a pigeon's egg.[61]

Durrell, a close friend of Patrick Leigh Fermor and a fellow aficionado of Greece and its shadowlands—who doesn't even make it onto James (Jan) Morris's voluminous list of writers who have described Venice—is himself, as one is preparing to say goodbye to this city, difficult to match.

TRIESTE

—

*Italy's Geographic
Complexity*

Leaving Venice by road and heading east toward Trieste across the top of the Adriatic littoral, the landscape has the spare power of an engraving. The ruler-flat fields of vine cultivation, sectioned by poplars, carry the soaked density of color common to mineral-rich soils, as if everything here has instantly begun to rust. Each farmhouse has the beauty and character of a ruin.

Such an Italianate landscape! And yet the problem with geographic determinism is that geography tells many contradictory stories. What seems obvious in one age of technology may indicate its opposite in another age. For example, in the early twenty-first century there appears to be no more natural geographic and political unit than the Italian peninsula, extending so dramatically as it does some seven hundred miles south from the body of Europe, and consequently providing definition to the two halves of the Mediterranean. There seems to be no ambiguity about it. What could be more natural than Italy! But it wasn't always so. It wasn't unified until the mid-nineteenth century. A closer look is required.

The Apennine Mountains bisect the Italian peninsula from north to south, separating the two coasts, with the eastern coast influenced throughout history by Eastern Orthodoxy, Islam, and the Levant, and the western coast influenced by the Renaissance and northern Carolingian Europe. Moreover, these two gently sloping coasts with their many natural harbors were both easily *invadable* and thus subject to a plethora of influences from around the Mediterranean.[1] This only worsened the peninsula's fragmentation. The drive for empire under the Romans, and for Italian colonies in Africa and Dalmatia in the nineteenth and early twentieth centuries, ultimately originates from the need to overcome the peninsula's exposed position at the heart of the Mediterranean Sea.

Italy's geographical fragmentation is further exacerbated by Sicily and Sardinia, the two largest islands in the Mediterranean. Then there is the peninsula's vastly unequal economic development, itself a creature of geography. The Po River valley, running from the Alps to the Adriatic in northern Italy, with its navigability, rich soil, and proximity to Central Europe, comprises Italy's commercial and industrial core, while at the opposite, southern end of the peninsula is an arid climate given to agriculture and poverty.[2] Turin and Naples might as well be in two different countries, one nearly antiseptic and hard-angled, the other rather chaotic, where even the air and light are different. These and other divisions led the Austrian statesman Prince Clemens von Metternich in 1847 to famously call Italy not a country, but a mere "geographical expression." As such a consummate expert on Italy as Sir David Gilmour writes, until the end of the eighteenth century, "Italy remained [only] a literary idea, an abstract concept, an imaginary homeland or simply a sentimental urge."[3] Thus, Italian unification, or the Risorgimento, though it ended in a single state over the entire peninsula, was also a civil war among the various regions. And these differences linger still in the fragmented politics of twenty-first-century Italy.

As I travel across the corner of northeastern Italy in eastern Friuli, from Venice to Trieste, I am in the vicinity of the most fraught of Italy's struggles for geographic identity in modern times. For an important faction of Italian politicians, the country's entry on the side of the Allies in World War I was all about expanding Italy's borders into the south Tyrol, the Isonzo Valley, Trieste, Istria, and particularly Dalmatia, on the Adriatic's eastern shore, in order to safeguard Italy's western Adriatic shore. The price of this expansion was horrific. Whereas the nineteenth-century wars of unification cost fewer than 10,000 lives, the struggle to annex those final territories cost the lives of 689,000 Italian soldiers—more than the total of Austro-Hungarian dead in this theater, writes British historian Mark Thompson about World War I. This does not include the 600,000 Italian civilians who also died because of the Great War's hardships. The "enduring sense of bitterness," Thompson goes on, "was an essential ingredient in the rise of Mussolini and his Blackshirts."*

What was it that Mussolini and his supporters said? "We will carry the Roman eagle to Addis-Ababa, and civilize Ethiopia. . . . Soon we will have the entire Dalmatian coast down to Greece."[4]

To be sure, Italy's borders, which seem to us so natural, were not considered as such for generations of Italians in previous centuries, even if Mussolini went much further than anyone else. And as the European Union struggles on, giving rise not only to reinvigorated, populist nationalisms but also to region- and city-states, geography may in the future have other stories to tell as far as Italy is concerned.

SUDDENLY THE SEA APPEARS right next to the road as I near Trieste, so vast and with a blue so pale that it melds with the pallid

---

* Mark Thompson, *The White War: Life and Death on the Italian Front, 1915–1919* (New York: Basic Books, [2008] 2009), pp. 26, 28, 32, and 381–82. The Italian front against Austria-Hungary in World War I was where Ernest Hemingway, working as an ambulance driver, was badly wounded in 1918, an experience that would shape his worldview and fiction for the rest of his life. See Malcolm Bradbury's introduction to Hemingway's 1929 novel, *A Farewell to Arms* (New York: Everyman's Library, 1993).

winter sky and is like the gassy, opaque surface of a distant planet. The signature of the wind is written in the bended pines, even if the towering poplars appear stoic in their resistance.

The Mediterranean "is a complex of seas," Braudel tells us. And the Adriatic, along with the Aegean, is the most geographically definable of them, a nearly enclosed channel 480 miles long and 100 miles wide. Going in a northwest–southeast direction, it is the liquid equivalent of the long Italian peninsula to its west, also serving as the gateway to the former Ottoman Empire on its wonderfully shattered eastern shore. So "deeply crenellated" is that eastern shore with its reefs, offshore islands, and indentations that if one could stretch that seaboard into a straight line it would extend well over 2,000 miles. At the southern end, heralded by Corfu and the Strait of Otranto, the Adriatic finally empties out into the Ionian Sea and the main body of the Mediterranean.

The Adriatic was the heart of the Venetian Empire, the *Stato da Mar* or "Territory of the Sea" as it was called, for without sea control over the Adriatic, Venice could never have gained Corfu, Crete, and Cyprus, not to mention other Aegean islands, as well as anchorages in the Holy Land itself. Because of the *Stato da Mar,* the Adriatic was always strongly Italianate, even as its Roman Catholicism was back then a fighting religion because Orthodox Byzantium and the Muslim Turks were palpably here or close by. The Levant spoke everywhere in the Adriatic through the trade of Venice, while Western Europe remained proximate, by virtue of the rival city-states of Genoa and Livorno (Leghorn) on Italy's western shore. A frontier zone of races, cultures, and religions, yet intimate and homogeneous at the same time, the Adriatic basin also included, according to Gibbon, Braudel, and others, the so-called barbarians in the mountains of the adjacent Balkan peninsula. Precisely because of these contradictions, this sea guards a wild mystery all its own, helped, in the memorable words of Roger Crowley, by "the moon's tug" at its northern "cul-de-sac." Horace called the Adriatic "bad-tempered" and "unconscionable." It is also a "sea of intimacy," as enclosed as the Red Sea, and thus unlike any of the other Mediterranean seas, wrote the late Bosnian-Croat scholar Predrag Matvejević and the University of Miami academic Dominique Kirchner Reill.[5]

BEFORE TRIESTE, I STOP at the Duino Castle. All around me, sweeping down to the sea, is a pageant of joyful Mediterranean vegetation—an abundance of flowers, oak and pine scrub, and needle-like cypresses all rubbing against each other. It is the kind of landscape that only the wealthy can afford. I pass flaking statuary and ascend the winding stairs of the labyrinthine villa built within the castle. In the second-floor corridor I pass seventeenth- and eighteenth-century violas and violins resting on tapestries inside glass cases, and then continue into an airy drawing room of period furniture. I push open a door badly in need of a paint job and enter onto a terrace swathed in flowers with a trellis above. The view below is a succession of stunning bays formed by karst outcroppings and topped by ruins, where gravity itself appears to diminish, for while looking down at the sea below I might as well be looking at the sky. The Adriatic here is truly planetary, the sea like a breathing mirror. In the opposite direction, when the air is clear after a winter rainstorm, you can see the Alps.

Right here, over the winter of 1911–1912, Rainer Maria Rilke began writing the famous *Duino Elegies*, while he was staying at the castle as the guest of his friend Princess Marie von Thurn und Taxis–Hohenlohe. He would complete them only a decade later in Switzerland. The elegies were conceived in a sudden and unexpected moment of inspiration, as a sea wind raged. He actually finished the 112 lines of "The First Elegy" by evening of the same day, even though he had been distracted by a worrisome business letter. Since Rilke grew up in Prague, and then lived a life of constant movement, from one temporary home to another, mainly in Italy, France, Germany, and Scandinavia, one of his translators, Michael

Hulse, says of him that he "might plausibly be described as the first truly [modern] 'European' poet,'" as different national histories and literatures contributed to his acute sensibility.

In *The Notebooks of Malte Laurids Brigge*, Rilke's novel about the early assault on the self by a mass urban society that knows no national boundaries, he describes the act of writing as a means to "ward off fear." And the worst fear can be that of fame, Rilke goes on, "that public demolition of one who is in the making, on to whose building site the mob irrupt, knocking his stones all over the place," so, he advises, "make good use of the fact that no one knows you!" Moving closer to his target, he says that people "have never set eyes on a solitary; they have merely hated him without knowing him." They have thrown stones at him and engaged in all manners of cruelty, in order to distract him from his solitude. And when all their attempts fail, people abuse him with "their final and ultimate tactic": that of granting him "fame."[6]

Truly, anyone who has been written about by others, even quite positively, sees only a distorted measure of his true self in print. Publicity can make you go mad.

In "The First Elegy," Rilke writes:

> ... listen to the voice of the wind
> and the ceaseless message that forms itself out of silence.
> It is murmuring toward you now from those who died
>   young.[7]

And in "The Sixth Elegy":

> The hero is strangely close to those who died young. Permanence
> does not concern him. He lives in continual ascent,
> moving on into the ever-changed constellation
> of perpetual danger.... But
> Fate, which is silent about us, suddenly grows inspired

and sings him into the storm of his onrushing world.
I hear no one like *him*. All at once I am pierced
by his darkened voice, carried on the streaming air.[8]

The pleasure of these poems, for me, is not unburdened. I, too, am pierced by the hero's "darkened voice." The heroes who died young are not abstract and archetypal, not some literary heroes out of Greek and Roman myth. For me they are those Americans who died in Iraq, a war that, I realized too late, should never have happened. Because I am alive now and lived through that war first as a promoter of it and later as a war correspondent on the ground, I cannot and must not escape from it. It is with me always, marring this beautiful scene before me and every other scene that I experience, focusing my energies continually on the lessons of the past. These reflections that I have must last a lifetime. They have shaped my thinking during every day that has passed for many years now.

Poetry, like all literature, should not only inspire, but trouble. It is serious business. And it is only through guilt and shame that I have finally realized how serious poetry is. Knowledge begins with a deep wound. Only when they became blind did Teiresias and Oedipus truly see, free as they finally were from illusion.[9]

I ENTER THE CRAMPED lobby of my hotel in Trieste in what by now is the gloomy dusk of a late winter afternoon. The decor is that of a private club where the average age of the members is seventy. I am embraced by faded oriental carpets in magenta hues on parquet floors, lots of heavy upholstery and brocaded curtains, gilded picture frames, bronze sculptures and classical engravings. The walls are a lovely, dismal yellow. The tourists are gone. In 2016, Trieste has not quite yet been discovered by the travel business. I am experiencing it at a precious moment before the full onslaught of cruise ships and Chinese port building, which, in turn, will lead to even more development. I said goodbye to my wife in Venice as I continued my journey.

The hotel gives on to a vast square facing the sea and bordered by Austro-Hungarian architectural masterpieces in neoclassical styles, sand-blasted in various bright clay hues. Across this glassy well-lit expanse in the rain that has just started, I walk into a café straight out of Vienna and Budapest but with the expressive language of Rome, with a feast of rich pastries and loud, crackle-and-pop conversation, with people reading newspapers on wooden rods. An African waitress maneuvers between the massive cabinets, leather ormolu couches, and comfortable wooden tables and chairs. Lamps illuminate the heavy window curtains against the encroaching night. Trieste is Central European intimacy with an Italian-global spin.

The next morning the bora is blowing hard, furious and unrelenting. The sea has gone from the palest blue to the darkest inky color, flecked with waves. The immaculate Austrian veneer does not cease. The windows, the building facades, every single surface I see—the iconostasis inside the Serbian Orthodox Church of Saint Spyridon, or the wheel bases of the morning delivery trucks even—manifest a manic cleanliness. Graffiti is almost absent. I sense both a globe-spanning worldliness and a deep intimacy: *Mitteleuropa*.

I reach the Grand Canal. It is a close-cropped view that fits easily inside a camera frame. A narrow, straight, dazzling emerald-green panel of water, lined with small boats and stalwart nineteenth-century buildings, that begins at the sea and ends at the nineteenth-century neoclassical Church of Saint Antonio Taumaturgo ("Miracle Worker"), which evokes all the light and clarity that was the gift of Greece and Rome to the West. *The canal,* I think, *the creamy Ionic columns, the dome, the café-lined street: this is like the whole world and cosmopolitan civilization crammed inside someone's living room.* Trieste is a city that does not sprawl. It is like a salon, a place without anonymity, as if everyone knows each other. While Venice is materialism writ large, Trieste is like a distinguished old aristocrat, a city of

dark wools and shade with high bank deposits, where nothing glit-
ters except the lights on the Christmas trees punctuating the main
square: a statement of civic pride that defeats the winter darkness.

I step inside the Stella Polare café, across the narrow street from
Saint Antonio Taumaturgo, for a double espresso. This is the biggest harbor for the coffee business in the Mediterranean, I am told.
The café is bustling with chic people standing by mirrored shelves
of liquors, chocolates, and Cuban cigars. Later I learn that it was a
favorite haunt of James Joyce, who read the early pages of *A Portrait
of the Artist as a Young Man* to his brother Stanislaus here.[10]

MY JOURNEY HAS NOW begun to shift gears. In Trieste, my solitude will begin to give way to conversation, conversations that will
pick up in intensity and frequency throughout the rest of my journey. It is in the ethnic and geopolitical fault zone of Trieste that I
quietly decide that being a well-read and intelligent tourist is not
enough; I must talk to people.

That evening in my hotel a bald, gray man appears, nattily
dressed in a silk tie and pin-striped shirt, with eyes that sparkle as
if just noticing a great work of art. We sit down for coffee in a side
room with dim yellow lamps and wallpaper, where it is quiet and
you can talk in a low voice above quiet melodies from the 1950s.

Mario Nordio is a retired local journalist who covered international news for forty years. His lovely German-speaking wife, Rose-
Marie Borngasser, another retired journalist who covered the Soviet
war in Afghanistan in the 1980s, accompanies him. Mario also
worked for a time in a military intelligence unit for the Italian cav-
alry, giving briefings to his superiors in Rome about the nearby
mountains, hills, rivers, and so on, as the border with Yugoslavia
during the Cold War was only a few miles away from here. "I am a
spiritual son of Adenauer, who, ever since I was young, has harbored
a profound sympathy for the Habsburg Empire," he tells me, by
way of introduction to his political values. "Trieste gave itself to

Habsburg Austria in order to deter Venice, which was a rival." His narrative throughout is filled with a Europe of regions and empires: Lombardy-Venetia, Istria, Friuli, Styria, and Carinthia; Venetian, Habsburg, and Prussian. Yes, with Mario, I will officially break my silence: an ideal, I realize, I cannot completely live up to. I had had a desire for solitude, but as I enter politically more fragile terrain to repeat, I need to start talking to people. My journey henceforth will be very different.

Later, all three of us relocate to a nearby restaurant for Prosecco, Friuli chardonnay, and masses of shellfish.

"Trieste," he begins, "always flourished under a big project: Habsburg, of course, as Vienna saw the need of a great port for its commerce.* Then there was the Italian Ost-Politik of the 1930s, which also benefited us. That lasted until 1938, when Mussolini, in the big square right next to this hotel"—pointing his finger—"celebrated his developing alliance with Hitler and declared for the first time the laws against the Jews. If Mussolini had not tragically allied with Hitler, he would have been remembered today as no worse than Franco. After all, Mussolini was popular in the West in the 1920s—popular with Winston Churchill, no less."

"Or remembered like Salazar," I interject.

"No! Salazar was like a monk. He was a much more serious thinker than either Franco or Mussolini. Portugal's geographic isolation allowed Salazar a mystical view of empire and the corporatist state. Salazar couldn't imagine Portugal without the empire."

There is much more I could say about Mussolini and Salazar. But I just let him talk. Reporters interrogate. Travelers listen after giving away something of themselves.

"It was the Habsburgs who gave Serbs, Greeks, Jews, and others the right to settle here. When the Italian downtown merged with the new immigrant quarters just outside, well, that was the real birth of cosmopolitan Trieste. Trieste is actually less cosmopolitan

---

*   Pula, on the Istrian Peninsula to the south, would be Austria's naval base.

now, as the natives of the city slowly moved out to some extent during the Cold War and were replaced by Italians from Istria—real Venetians, of the old seaborne empire, I mean. The Serbian community here," he goes on, his eyes jumping around a bit, "was always rich and anti-Tito. It was a community of traders—just look at the fine condition of their church! Because Serbia is distant to Trieste compared to next-door Slovenia and Croatia, we always considered Serbia less of a threat. In geopolitics, of course, it is the nearby states that you have to worry about most. And Tito, as you know, always favored the Slovenes in the north and the Kosovars and Macedonians in the south, in order to balance against Serbia and therefore hold Yugoslavia together.

"We have always been the smallest province of Italy," he continues, "a true enclave, practically surrounded by the Slavs. Remember that because we were right next to Communist Yugoslavia, the Allied occupation here did not end until 1954. Yes, this was the only part of Italy where there were no anti-American demonstrations throughout the Cold War, because we felt threatened in a way that the rest of Italy did not.

"The defining ethnic tension here"—looking directly into my eyes for emphasis—"was between Italians and Slovenes, who were among us and right across the border. It was made worse by the fact that the Slavic national awakening within the Habsburg Empire occurred several decades after Italy's own national awakening, so that we Italians, having just become nationally aware, suddenly felt threatened by the Slovenes as they became nationally aware. But since Slovenia has in recent years joined NATO and the EU, normalization between the two communities has set in. The local conscience of Trieste was always European as much as Italian, and this cosmopolitan aspect of our personality has been helped by Slovenia joining the European Union," and particularly by joining the Schengen open-border system three years later, in 2007, he added.

History, in his telling, is usually a matter of nuances, fateful choices, and different directions at once, and yet always subject to the pressures of regional powers and economic forces: that elusive combination of determinism and human agency. For the port of Trieste, he goes on to mention, is where the Transalpine Pipeline, opened in 1967 by an international consortium, begins its journey, transporting oil shipped from the Middle East to Bavaria and parts of Austria. Trieste is still the port of Central Europe. And Trieste is also the main container shipment link with Turkey, whose power will likely grow in the twenty-first century. "But now I am suspicious of Germany," he says, "just like the Balts and the Poles are. Culture affects geopolitics. Prussia, yes, had its wars with Russia, but also had its common ground, with czarist commanders of ethnic-Prussian origin. So it is unclear where Germany is headed, even as the American commitment to Europe may weaken.

"*Ah*, yes." He regains his train of thought, recalling the decisive battle of the Austro-Prussian War: "If only the Habsburgs had defeated Bismarck at Koniggratz in 1866. Then Central Europe would have been ruled from Vienna, not from Berlin. And there would have been no First World War, no Hitler!"

I mention that *Rigoletto* is playing at a local theater. He tells me that the opera here was built by an Egyptian Coptic family that made its money in the Suez Canal trade, following the opening of the canal in 1869 that brought the port of Trieste, in effect, closer to the Middle East and Asia.

THOSE WHO WRITE ABOUT Trieste quote Chateaubriand's rough statement: "The last breath of civilization expires on this coast where barbarism begins."[11] To call the proximate Ottoman Empire—an eclectic civilization in its own right—barbarous, is of course entirely wrong, a reflection of one's own sense of cultural superiority. But Chateaubriand had a point in that Trieste signals a fault zone. It is a city that has hosted Romans from the West, Byzantines from the East, Goths, Venetians, Napoleon's empire, the sprawling and multiethnic Habsburg Empire, Italy, Nazi Germany, Yugoslavia, and Italy again since 1954. That last handover took years of diplomatic wrangling, as if to confirm that Trieste's very location—on a spit of territory that could have been placed in either Italy or Yugoslavia—constitutes proof of Trieste's unstable position on the map. The mid-twentieth-century American journalist John Gunther noted that between 1913 and 1948, Trieste lived under no fewer than five different occupations.[12] The race between Allied and Communist Yugoslav forces for control of Trieste in May 1945 was arguably the first major confrontation of the Cold War, perhaps providing a "reference point" for President Truman in the later crises of the Berlin blockade and the Korean War.[13]

Trieste marks the borderline not only between the Latin world and the Slavic one, but also between the Latin world and the German one. Indeed, this city of Italians, Germans, Austrians, Slovenes, Croats, Serbs, Greeks, Armenians, Jews, and so on registers Mitteleuropa, with its own unparalleled cosmopolitanism, broadening out into an international civilization. Though, if this neoclassical, utilitarian, and commercial city has one cultural identity or spirit above others, it might be that of the Austrian Habsburgs, who ruled here between 1392 and 1918, except for a short Napoleonic interlude.

Trieste does indeed put *empire* on your mind. I visit the castle of Miramare, just north of the city, built with round porthole-like windows by Maximilian, the younger brother of Franz Joseph, who believed that the Habsburgs had no choice but to control the Adriatic.[14] It is a monument to imperial delusion. Its gloomy, dark wood and red satin extravaganza is surrounded by sprawling Mediterranean seascapes on three sides, as if this entire overblown heap of boxy cold-weather furnishings has effectively appropriated the sunnier foreign environment, so far from the capital of Vienna. Maximilian, who believed deeply in liberal reform as a means of preserving and sustaining empire, was fated (of all things!) to go to far-off Mexico in 1864 as its new emperor—encouraged by his wife—only to be executed by indigenous revolutionaries three years later, completing his dark and tragic imperial fantasy.

Trieste reminded historian and travel writer Jan Morris "poignantly of the passing of all empires, those seductive illusions of permanence, those monuments of hubris which have sometimes been all evil, but have sometimes had much good to them." Because empires, by definition, are often multinational and multiethnic, it is when empires collapse that "racial zealotry," in Morris's words, can rear its head. When the Italians seized Trieste from the Habsburgs in 1919, they closed Slovene schools in the city and tolerated violence against the Slavs. When the Yugoslavs arrived in the city in 1945, they reopened the Slovene schools and forced many Italians to change their names. In 1946, when Morris first saw Trieste, the writer "pined" for a cohesive and "distilled" Europe, and imagined this city as "the ghost of that ideal." But the "false passion of the nation-state," Morris continues, "made my conceptual Europe no more than a chimera."

History isn't over, though. And as Morris says in old age, "One day the very idea of nationality will seem as impossibly primitive as dynastic warfare or the divine right of kings . . . a hobby for antiquarians or re-enactment societies."[15]

Indeed. In the present day, the port of Trieste will soon sign an agreement with Duisburg, the world's largest inland port, located at the confluence of the Rhine and Ruhr Rivers in western Germany, with the aim of increasing traffic on the new Silk Road that China is organizing. Trieste will acquire through Duisburg access to the northern—land—part of the Silk Road that terminates at the Pacific; while Duisburg will acquire by way of Trieste access to the southern, maritime Silk Road that runs through the Suez Canal and the Indian Ocean. A postmodern, multinational imperial system may re-emerge, this time supervised by the Chinese, and encompassing Trieste. A few months hence, I will get a message from a friend about "Chinese, Russian, American, and Mitteleuropean investors competing for bases in the port here—the second great opportunity after Maria Theresa," during whose reign the city became a vibrant, multiethnic hub. Yes, Trieste always did prosper under a big project—this time maybe with the Chinese, who will make Trieste another imperial reference point.

TRIESTE SERVES AS THE guiding spirit of the most erudite travel book I know, Claudio Magris's *Danube: A Journey Through the Landscape, History, and Culture of Central Europe*. Every spot along the Danube—every hillside baroque dome he sees—provides an opportunity for Magris, an academic from Trieste, to unleash a lifetime of learning on the page. After buying Magris's book in a bookstore in Geneva in 1998, I became infatuated with it. Magris's ruminations on Central Europe now constitute my entry into the spirit of this city. As with so many other authors I admire, I thought I would never want to meet him—for that would spoil the spell. I wanted to know him only through his precisely written words. And yet, as it would turn out, I would break my promise to myself, a full eighteen years since first encountering *Danube*, a riverine travelogue that commences in Central Europe and ends in Romania at the Black Sea.

Whereas the Rhine, he writes, "is Siegfried, symbol of Germanic *virtus* and purity, the loyalty of the Niebelungs, chivalric heroism," the Danube "is Pannonia, the kingdom of Attila, the eastern, Asiatic tide." More pointedly, the Rhine is about the "purity" of one race, while the Danube, with its link to the Austrian Habsburg Empire, evokes a "supranational culture" beyond ethnicity. In this way, he explains, the German language forever maintains the possibility to connote universal values. This Austrian mindset, both imperial and cosmopolitan, rooted as it is in a specific landscape, identifies the "stupid nonsense" that is postmodernism with its jagged juxtapositions, "while accepting it as inevitable." It doesn't take much for Magris to challenge the reader with abstractions, yet this is what encapsulates the beauty of his book, which is a bold experiment in taking the travel genre to another level of introspection that one can only envy.

The Danubian landscape leads Magris to reflect thus: "Life," paraphrasing Kierkegaard, "can be understood only by looking backward, even if it has to be lived looking forward." So begins Magris's journey into the darkest precincts of modern history.[16]

At Messkirch, in Germany, he spots a plaque announcing the boyhood home of Martin Heidegger, one of the twentieth century's great philosophers, who was also a committed Nazi. Magris connects Heidegger to Adolf Eichmann, the logistician of the Holocaust, both of whom, he explains, lacked the specific ability to imagine cold, abstract statistics as flesh-and-blood people. The contrast with Magris himself could not be more telling. This book seamlessly weaves the details of landscape and personalities into revealing abstractions, even as the abstractions themselves lead back to real events and people. "At Ulm," he tells us, "there bloomed a great flower of German inwardness. Hans and Sophie Scholl, the brother and sister arrested, condemned and executed in 1943," for their activities against the Nazi regime. Today a local university bears their names. "Their story is an example of the absolute resistance which Ethos opposes to Kratos," writes Magris. He quotes the historian Golo Mann about how the Scholls fought with nothing but "their bare hands" and a "cyclostyle" against everything and everybody around them. "They were young, they didn't want to die, and it was painful for them to forgo the enticements of such a glorious day," as Sophie said, before they were executed.[17]

Ulm is also "the heart of German Holy Roman Empire nationalism, that of the old Germany based on the law of custom, which sanctioned historical traditions and differences, opposing any central power, all forms of state interference," he notes with a tinge of nostalgia. The Danubian landscape evokes just so many associations with a traditional, almost romantic world, even as it is spoiled for him by the terrible ghosts of modernity, which started with Napoleon but progressed all the way to Hitler. And yet he revels in complications: observing Roman *limes* near Ingolstadt, he mentions that imperial pretensions to universalism have been "a mask for dominion" that predates modernity with all of its nightmares.[18]

The shadow of the Holocaust stains the baroque and Gothic splendor of Danubia, providing this travelogue with its moral power.

Magris writes about a Central Europe that is whole even though the fall of the Berlin Wall still lies in the future—*Danube* was published three years before that event, and had been in progress for many years. It is the lifework of an area expert on the verge of being an encyclopedist. Imagining the post Cold War between the lines of the text, the book nonetheless reflects the now-lost nuances of the Communist 1970s and early 1980s that I knew as a reporter: how the Slovaks suffered a lesser fate than the Czechs following the Soviet repression of the 1968 Prague Spring; how Hungary's internal political detente in the final decades of the Cold War allowed for a relatively freer climate there, in which even the regime wanted to forget politics; and how in Yugoslavia "Marshal Tito ended by resembling Francis Joseph more and more, and certainly not because he had fought beneath his banners in the First World War, but rather because of his awareness of inheriting a supra-national, Danubian legacy."[19]

The odyssey continues. As the Danube enters the region of Bulgaria and Romania, Magris explains the Thracian and Turkic origins of the Slavic-speaking Bulgarians and the way in which the Byzantine tradition filters into Romanian folk art. Near the Black Sea, the Danube splits up and spreads out "like wine from a broken *krater*, as the poem says when a wounded hero falls from his chariot."[20] Here then is the art of travel: contemplation in place of conversation, again, all because the most profound journeys are interior in nature. Magris's entire book, his sprawling exposition of Central Europe, has as its root the spirit of Trieste, his home, the maritime and southernmost outpost of Central Europe.

JAMES JOYCE LIVED IN Trieste between 1905 and 1915, scraping by as an English teacher and occupying a series of squalid apartments in the new section of town in its last years as an Austrian-controlled city. Here he wrote most of *Dubliners* and the whole of *A Portrait of the Artist as a Young Man,* and devised the outline for *Ulysses*. Trieste, in other words, was where Joyce became arguably the greatest writer in the English language in the twentieth century, though it would be decades before anyone became aware of this. This city with its polyglot and multiethnic population, which Joyce called "Europiccola," inspired the development of his own cosmopolitan literature.[21] Of course, inspiration does not equal happiness, and this was a decade of excruciating frustration for Joyce. There was the grinding poverty and dreariness mixed with the surging anger and self-doubt caused by his inability for years on end to find a publisher for *Dubliners*. It was an interminable period of near starvation and heavy drinking that led, in turn, to bouts of rheumatic fever. His wife, Nora Barnacle, though she loved him, did not understand him or his work. Once in a rage he threw the manuscript of *A Portrait of the Artist* into the fire, before it was quickly retrieved by his sister Eileen.

Only in 1913, after eight years of professional misery in Trieste, did he receive an unsolicited letter from Ezra Pound, who had heard about Joyce from the poet William Butler Yeats, and offered to help him in any way he could. The next year, indirectly through Pound's support, Joyce found a publisher for *Dubliners*—it had taken nearly a decade. Pound's moral and emotional support proved crucial in rousing Joyce to finish *A Portrait of the Artist* and begin *Ulysses*. Joyce seemed happy in Trieste more in retrospect, when he remarked that "the lax rule of the Austro-Hungarian emperor" was preferable to "democratic Utopias."[22]

While inspired by Trieste, Joyce never left Ireland in his mind. He held tight to his childhood memories as a form of sanity, almost. Yet he wrote about Ireland from an unimaginably objective distance, helped by Trieste's own cosmopolitan neutrality. Joyce's biographer Richard Ellmann notes, "Writing was itself a form of exile for him, a source of detachment."[23]

From the first page of *Dubliners*, describing the two candles that must be placed at the head of a corpse, Ireland, in its glowing, iron-dark madness and spectral intensity, as vivid as whiskey on the breath, enfolds you within a constricted and restrained narrative machine in which words have the musical precision of a Haydn or Monteverdi. The stories are at once exquisite and mathematical, complete with the names of streets and squares. Trieste, so radically foreign to the land of his birth, evidently helped Joyce see Ireland under a magnifying glass: the snuff-stained priestly garments and tawny gold sky at dusk; the dusty lace, the beef-tea, and the wiry note of a harp; and the lamps like "illumined pearls."[24] Meanwhile, there is the misery and pathos of common existence, in which the men drink and the women act bravely and suffer, all of them with their tragic flaws and narrow choices. Yet their absolution by the narrator, as cruel as some of these stories are, is as real and tactile as the tasteless taste of a wafer on the tongue in church.

Here is his biographer Ellmann:

> The initial and determining act of judgment in his work is the justification of the commonplace. Other writers had labored tediously to portray it, but no one knew what the commonplace really was until Joyce had written. There is nothing like Joyce's commonplace in Tolstoy, where the characters, however humble, live dramatically and instill wisdom or tragedy in each other. Joyce was the first to endow an urban man of no importance with heroic consequence.[25]

The fusing of real people with mythical ones, of the ordinary with the extraordinary, begins with *Dubliners* and its mournful stories.

Joyce's urge to see the individual within the group, and endow him with mythic qualities, was of a piece with his own journey from an Irishman to a European. To be European was to be cosmopolitan, and thus freed of the shackles of religion, ethnicity, and other forms of group identity. This process reaches an apotheosis in *Ulysses*, which owes as much to Dante as to Homer, to say nothing of the Old Testament, Aristotle, Milton, Shakespeare, and much else. The novel's hero, Leopold Bloom, is a total man: the totally average man, I mean, full of the commonplace. He is unreliable, middlebrow in his cultural judgments, "a pure amateur," filled with bawdy sexual urges, and thinks about sundry things such as Jews, women, the advertising industry, and on and on. Bloom is a complete interstellar cosmos inside one human being, through whose voice Joyce realizes his most profound and humanist statements on existence. For Bloom is gentle through and through, even to a fault. He nearly always sees two sides of any issue. He has difficulty making up his mind: a quality that makes him, for Joyce, immortal. Through him, Joyce laments anti-Semitism, the human condition, all that makes history "a nightmare," and to which the only answer is to assert one's power as a rational human being who does not give in to fate.[26] Trieste, with its intimacy and multiple identities, making it so hard to categorize, can reduce the mass to the quirky individual in the true Joycean spirit.

ONE STUDENT OF JOYCE in Trieste was the Swabian-born Ettore Schmitz, a successful middle-aged manager of a company that sold anti-corrosive paints for the hulls of ships. The Jewish Schmitz had a father who was Hungarian, just like Bloom in *Ulysses*. Schmitz, inspired by Joyce, became the path-breaking modernist of Trieste and the literary spirit of the city. Under the pen name of Italo Svevo (meaning "Italian Swabian"), his novel *Confessions of Zeno*, published in Italian in 1923, with its steely hard aesthetic and random refraction of memory, has almost attained the status of cult worship. *Zeno* reads not like a dream, but like the compulsive recounting of one, dominated as it is by racing thoughts with their comic, me-

chanical absurdity: "in the crowded Via Cavana," he writes, "I had
arrived more quickly at the truth than in the solitude of my study."[27]
It is a rare admission, and one not even fully developed, since the
Via Cavana is not really described at all.

Zeno is a completely interior book, nearly absent of both landscape and cityscape, and thus, inversely, it is a polished expression of
the disjointed, post-territorial sensibility that is, at the same time,
international, cosmopolitan, and European. Zeno Cosini, who enters psychoanalysis to cure a smoking habit, is a hypochondriac who
proposes marriage to three sisters, the third of whom accepts. He is
compelled to marry because he cannot cope with uncertainty. Yet
his marriage—alas, a drastic cure for his melancholy—leads only to
infidelity, as his mistress comes to dominate his conscious life. Zeno
also finds it impossible to communicate with his father, even as he
is later to be devastated by his father's death. This entire book
evinces the skeletal, chiseled nature of a patient's monologue. There
is the clinical flavor of the operating room about it, the odor of
Freud and Vienna throughout, in which the blinding preposterous-
ness of Zeno's circumstances forces you to break out laughing.

Whereas Henry James, a tireless precursor of modernism, probes
the surface of the inner life with his subtle rendering of consciousness, Svevo plunges vertically down into it, with all of its anxiety-
ridden, obsessive-compulsive aspects, as turbulent as, he says, the
life of Napoleon. James represents the Old World, whose natural
elegance manifests a finished culture, while Svevo is something
stark and alienating, like modern art or minimalist furniture. It is a
world where bodily pain itself stems ultimately from a guilty conscience. Here is the lonely mind standing athwart the stability of
bourgeois life: if not a prelude in the way that Stravinsky's *The Rite
of Spring* (choreographed in Paris in 1913) is to the civilizational
crack-up of World War I, then it is an early reflection upon it. Indeed, at the end of the book, Svevo says that because technology
makes men physically weaker, they must compensate with ever

more viciousness and cunning, leading always towards earthly destruction. This, of course, is sheer prophecy.

TO BORROW WORDS FROM Claudio Magris, the northeastern Adriatic is where "Venetian levity" is undermined by "*Mitteleuropa* gravity." In Trieste "no one has any illusions that the original sin was never committed and that life is virginal and innocent." There is a tragic, realistic mindset. Indeed, near Trieste at San Sabba, from 1943 to 1945, the Nazis ran the only extermination facility in Italy, where thousands of Jews and others were killed and more than 25,000 were deported to Buchenwald, Dachau, Auschwitz, and other death camps. And yet within such realism born partly of such atrocities, there exists a mediocrity and emptiness, for what, suggests Magris, is Mitteleuropa now without its Jews?[28]

Trieste has been a laboratory of ethnic politics, often not declared as such, which Robert Musil in his novel *The Man Without Qualities* dependably exposes in the manner of a surgeon. As he explains, this Hanseatic-like "Hamburg of the Mediterranean" was part of the Austrian Habsburg Empire and yet Italian in its heart. "Not a single flag" flies except on the administrative buildings and army barracks on the emperor's birthday, but on the birthday of the king of Italy, every clerk would have a flower in his buttonhole. And yet Vienna would do nothing about it, for fear of being "'accused of Germanizing.... After all, we're not Prussians!'" exclaims one of Musil's Austrian characters. On the other hand, the large Slavic lower middle class "passionately contested the favored Italian upper class's right to consider the city as its own property." Still, if the word got out "'that we're Germanizing, the Slovenes immediately side with the Italians,'" even as they hate doing so. For the real threat to peace within the Habsburg Empire was often the Austrians themselves.[29] Empire was a tense negotiation among ethnicities, which ultimately could not contain their struggle for greater political freedoms. But it is an irony that the monoethnic modern states that succeeded Austro-Hungary would, in quite a few cases, be less forgiving of minorities than the very empire that they undermined.

"I FEEL VERY MITTELEUROPEAN. I am Protestant. I have family roots in Hungary and the Hungarian part of Romania. My grandmother was half German, my maternal grandfather from Pula—to the south in Istria." Thin, smartly dressed, with white hair and glowing blue-gray eyes—and with a café manner that goes with a perennial demitasse in his hand—Riccardo Illy, the scion of a family of coffee producers and a former mayor of Trieste in the 1990s, meets me, too, in my hotel.

Again, I just listen.

"Remember that we flourished as an imperial melting pot, which allowed for local languages and reached from the Mediterranean to Galicia in Poland and western Ukraine. Turks, Romanians, Jews, what have you, came to Trieste from all over Eastern Europe. Even today, look at the phone book, or at the population breakdown. We are an urban population of 200,000, but with only a third from Friuli, another third from Istria and Dalmatia, and the rest Slovenes, Hungarians, Croats, and so on."

He continues:

"But that great Habsburg hinterland was lost after World War I. And after World War II, we found ourselves a small enclave backed up against the Iron Curtain," when Trieste became a Cold War spy center almost like Berlin and Vienna. After all, though Tito broke with Stalin in 1948, Yugoslavia was still part of the Communist bloc.* So in the 1990s, after the Berlin Wall had fallen, Illy, as the new centrist-independent mayor of Trieste, began to encourage

---

*   The split between Tito and Stalin led to bitter divisions within families of Trieste's Slovene minority.

Slovenia's integration with European institutions, as well as a reconciliation between Slovene-speakers and Italian-speakers in Trieste, in order to heal an ethnic conflict that particularly had its roots in the World War II atrocities committed by Yugoslav Communist partisans against the local Italian population. "You see," he explains, "Slovenia practically surrounds us. So I thought, if Slovenia could get into the EU and NATO, and also into the Schengen border-free zone, then we could get back our imperial hinterland," with the European Union functioning as a de facto replacement for the Habsburg Empire.

Of course, that is exactly what happened. But Illy now worries about the political state of European integration, upon which Trieste, with more autonomy than any region in mainland Italy, depends. "This is a part of Europe where borders and sovereignties have always shifted. And they must not change again, at least not officially." He explained that because Trieste's geographical identity, much more so than other Italian cities, is multiethnic and thus truly European, a so-called return to history and hard ethnic borders following the happy decades of the Cold War and post Cold War could be disastrous. For Trieste's whole raison d'être has been to operate in a cosmopolitan world without borders.

I AM NOW ON a street named for the prodigious nineteenth-century opera composer Gaetano Donizetti, where Trieste's neoclassical synagogue is located. It is perhaps the most beautiful synagogue in Europe, built in a style of restrained grandeur, its intricate motifs evocative of the late Roman period in the Middle East, before the ostentation of Byzantium set in, and when synagogue-building in the Holy Land first became commonplace in order to replace the function of the Temple in Jerusalem. Constructed between 1908 and 1912, the synagogue was fully restored after its use as a warehouse under the Nazis. Amidst such symbols of high culture, I also find the Caffè San Marco, the haunt of Clau-

dio Magris, the writer of my beloved *Danube*. The café, opened before World War I, is decorated in warm yellows and chocolate
browns, with wall-length mirrors reflecting globular lamplight, the-
atrical mask paintings hung inside gold medallions, and masses of
fleshy marble tables. It is spacious, yet intimate; busy with explo-
sions of conversation, yet quiet; the sounds disappearing into the
high ceiling. There is an element of both Austria-Hungary and
Manhattan: of a complex and completed civilization, ill at ease with
itself, that is. Time is savored here, a place where Italian intellectuals once plotted against the Habsburg Empire.[30] No one looks at
their watches.

Magris appears, unwinds his scarf, and sits down. His sweater
and sports jacket are in dark cozy shades. Born in 1939, he has a
worn, sculpted face that is sharp with intelligence. His eyes flare
with light as he talks, as if replacing the need for gestures. He can
just as easily discuss the Istro-Romanian Cici minority in the hinterlands near Trieste as he can the future of greater Europe.

Both he and his first wife, Marisa Madieri, now deceased, have
family roots in Italy and Croatia, in the Latin and Slavic worlds, he
tells me. This is common, for "there were medieval poets who wrote
in both Italian and Croatian." Moreover, his late Italian wife spoke
Croatian as a child, and the burial places for her relatives stretch
from Serbia to Friuli-Venezia Giulia. The Adriatic basin, in other
words, is actually more unified than one can ever imagine. "There
was always nationalism," he goes on, which could be liberal, like
in the nineteenth century, "but it was only after nationalism was
forced inside formal and bureaucratic *national* states" that it became
illiberal.

We talk about Central Europe, which he says was originally sustained by a "borderless fusion of German and Jewish culture." Thus,
Hitler's destruction of the Jews effectively finished off Mitteleuropa, because of how it undermined Germanism itself. Nevertheless, a notion and memory of Central Europe was preserved "under
the layers" of Communist-inflicted poverty and repression during

the Cold War. Although Central Europe as a concept returned briefly upon the weakening and collapse of Communism, "now globalization is destroying what's left of it.... Whether you're in Prague or Warsaw, it's Wall Street that's important."

Nevertheless, Magris finds optimism in the fact that he can drive to Slovenia—formerly on the other side of the Iron Curtain— and not pass through any border at all, and also use the same currency. What had existed cannot come back, that is true, he says. After all, the Jews are nearly gone, and German-Austrian culture will never be whole again, even as *Europe* as an idea may yet have other lives to live, if only the European Union can survive.

He fishes two books out of a battered briefcase, a novel by himself and a memoir by his late wife, inscribes them both, and gives them to me. Earlier in the day, a woman at a small museum surprised me with the gift of a book about Joyce's movements in Trieste. I carry these precious books home as totems of the encounters I had.

In the novel he gives me, Magris writes that "the realization of having failed is part of the ability to see the objectivity of History," for such knowledge "comes only from a lengthy familiarity with defeat."[31] Yes, only when you have been proven wrong, demonstrably wrong, can you appreciate that History is neither a game nor a pastime to read about at night beside a fire, but something real and horrible that can destroy not only the lives of others but your own life as well.

I AM NOW IN another café in Trieste, where another man, this one in sharp jeans and a sports jacket, who is bald with glasses and a clipped white beard—and a knife-like penetrating expression— hands me more books as gifts. They include his own travelogue, which covers the area from Finland to Ukraine. I will read it that night in my hotel and be stunned by its aromatic detail: to wit, crossing from a neat and tidy Protestant Estonia to a muddier and more disorderly Catholic Latvia is like crossing from one landscape-aesthetic to another kind. "To understand which way the world is heading, you have to go to train stations, not to airports," he writes. "But because diplomats prefer airports, their governments are no longer capable of foreseeing events."[32] This extraordinary man is Paolo Rumiz, a local Italian journalist, who, among so much else, covered the war in the former Yugoslavia from beginning to end. "It is all a long story," he begins in a low voice both haunting and distinguished.

"My grandmother thought of history as a carnival. After all, there had been six border changes in Trieste in the course of her lifetime. She was one of those who never experienced the horror of any of it, unlike the Jews, of course. I was born on December 20, 1947, the day that the free zone following the liberation from Fascist Italy and Nazi Germany was divided between an Anglo-American sector and a Yugoslav sector. My family came under the jurisdictions of the British and the Americans. Well," he goes on, "sixty years later, again on my birthday, in 2007, Slovenia became a member of the Schengen Area. So I went to the Slovenian border, a few miles from my home, and joined a party between Italians and Slovenians where everyone distributed little parts of the former border fence. Suddenly, for the first time since the fall of the Habsburg Empire, we in Trieste were in a region of no borders. But I got scared. If there were no more borders, then there would be no more reason to travel. For my wanderlust came from Trieste's claustrophobic confinement. So I decided to make a journey through a part of Europe where hard and difficult borders still existed. I wanted to become sick of borders altogether, to cure me of my psychological need for them.

"And what did I find?" he continues. "I found that the soul of Europe is not truly inside the European Union. As a European, I felt more at home in Lviv [in western Ukraine] than in Paris. In Lviv and such places, I could still feel deep inside me the spiritual presence of the Jews, Germans, Poles, and others: precisely because they were gone, I was forced to concentrate on them." There is a sterility in Western Europe that Eastern Europe lacks.

"On the former Eastern Front, I found that World War I," the war that gave the twentieth century in Europe its tragic trajectory, "is obscured and unstructured in memory. Yet, precisely because of that, and because of all the unfinished business with Communism, you feel strictly connected to 1914. But on the Western Front, they have made a tremendous effort to structure the past and put it all in a beautiful museum, so that you are not afraid of its power anymore, so that you don't feel any of it. In Western Europe you are never afraid and you should be afraid. This is why the eastern countries do not take NATO and the EU for granted. Since they are still afraid, they feel the need for these institutions more than people in Western Europe do.

"Trieste, too," like the rest of Western Europe, he explains, "is stricken with historical amnesia. Many people here fought for the Austrian Habsburg side against the western allies in World War I. And they returned from the war and forgot about it. Only in recent years have memories of that time been unleashed in this city. Now nostalgia for the Habsburgs grows while the problems of Italy mount. Our politicians here and in Brussels tell us, 'It's okay, there is no need to be afraid.' But I want our politicians to tell us to be afraid," he repeats, afraid of repeating the past in some way, given Europe's history, even the history before the twentieth century. "And they should have told us exactly that in 2014 on the centenary of World War I." How else is Europe to avoid tragedy? he suggests.

"Yet, the refugees [from the Middle East and Africa] have brought history back to us. The barbed wire erected by the Slovenians in order to prevent refugees crossing over from Croatia scares people. Suddenly there are hard borders again with Istria. These refugees are the messengers, telling us, in effect, that trouble is coming to Europe again, in some form." For ethnically based nations may not remain so ethnically based forever.

He goes silent for a moment. Then says, slowly, speaking at a more human scale:

"When refugees tell their stories they become individuals, not a wave, and each individual, no matter how destitute, can be hiding a god within himself. Wasn't Homer's Ulysses the first refugee, a war veteran, who had lost all his companions in a desperate journey across the eastern Mediterranean, who wandered for years, at the mercy of storms and hunger: passing through dangerous places, and then arriving nearly naked in a house filled with strangers?"

THE RISIERA DI SAN SABBA lies twenty minutes outside downtown: a memorial built on the site of a small hellish satellite of the larger Nazi death apparatus. It is a place notable for maintaining the only crematorium in Italy, where thousands of Italians, Slovenes, and Croats were murdered and burnt, while many more thousands of Jews were packed into tiny, filthy cells, before transport to the death camps in German-occupied Poland and elsewhere. The northeastern Adriatic and its Alpine shadow zone—Trieste, Gorizia, Ljubljana, Pula, and Rijeka—constituted, in and of itself, yet another geography of the Holocaust under direct German rule, as opposed to Italy proper, where the Nazis worked with Mussolini's Fascist government. The conversion of this former rice-husking factory and extermination camp to a national monument simply, powerfully *works:* you immediately feel oppressed by having to walk through a long and narrow passageway between towering slabs of concrete, which open out into a courtyard of more concrete slabs reaching, it seems, to infinity, where steel spikes and metal paving mark the footprint of the crematorium itself. There is no design element, no overt symbolism of any sort: just hard, blank, impossible-to-scale walls evoking annihilation.

I think of something Hannah Arendt observed in *The Origins of Totalitarianism* about Auschwitz and the other concentration camps. She intuited that the Nazis could only explain their ideology to themselves by creating such places. Auschwitz, and everything that went on there, was the very laboratory of National Socialism: it is what gave it reality; and from such deeds Central Europe will never recover.

Riding back in the taxi from San Sabba to the Grand Hotel, I see the other Trieste, more authentic in its way: miles of rusted factories; endless, pressed-together stacks of cheap apartment buildings; and the massive port with its merchant ships and gantry cranes. Here graffiti is more conspicuous. I remember what Monika Bulaj, a knowing Polish-Italian photographer who lives in Trieste and has worked in Iraq, Afghanistan, and the Coptic hinterlands of Ethiopia, among other places, said to me a few days before over a leisurely cup of tea: that this Grand Hotel where we were sitting, the great square with its lovely architecture, and adjacent streets with their fantasy-inducing boutiques, are "literally just a salon, an illusion," while the real Trieste and Europe were all around us; the ugly mass society, that is, which has obliterated the past and memory. And it will be further obliterated by China's local port project, as part of its Belt and Road imperial dream. Indeed, an antiseptic global dimension will be overlaid on the ugly mass society.

Rilke, Joyce, Svevo all lived in a smaller, more intimate world, a world that came before the creation of this vast ugliness, though the three of them imagined its arrival through their writing. They were modernists just as the modern world began to produce its nightmares. Their brilliant art had internalized the coming crisis of Europe and the West in the twentieth century.

EUROPE, THE WEST—WHAT IS it, exactly?

Beyond the Greeks, the definition of the West arguably builds with Rome's legacy of law and governance, the increased awareness of both Greek and Roman values during the High Middle Ages and the Renaissance, the Protestant Reformation with its work ethic that is an implicit rebuke to fatalism (a distant and indirect legacy of Judaism with its moral code), and the Enlightenment with its gift of rationalism and scientific exactitude: these are what we imperfectly and commonly define as the foundation of the Western tradition, even as we must be aware that other civilizations, Indic and Sinic, to name but two, have strong elements of the above as well. For it is quite true that, as the historian Norman Davies charges, "Western civilization is essentially an amalgam of intellectual constructs which were designed to further the interests of their authors."[33] The West and the East, according to Stanford historian and classicist Ian Morris, who goes even further than Davies, are at the end of the day mere "geographical labels, not value judgments."[34]

Indeed, geography may actually be the surest way to approach a definition of the West, one that minimizes cultural arrogance and self-deception. Europe—Rome, that is—right up through the time of Saint Augustine encompassed North Africa, which was Christian in the early centuries of the Common Era. Throughout antiquity, the cultural divide between the northern and southern shores of the Mediterranean was somewhat unclear: Rome had earlier destroyed Carthage less because it is was culturally different than because it was a rival. It was the swift advance of Islam across North Africa in the seventh and eighth centuries that, by virtually extinguishing Christianity there, to a significant extent severed the Mediterranean into two civilizational halves, making the "Middle Sea" a border more than a unifying force.*

The loss of North Africa to Islam would lead European history *as a process* to adopt a northward orientation, with the Germanic people now truly entering the story in a pivotal and defining sense for the first time. This development led the Spanish philosopher

---

* The survival of the Christian Copts in Egypt was the most obvious exception. The Nile Valley, after all, was a vertical artery of civilization that went south, away from the Mediterranean, rather than the cities and towns of Libya and the Maghreb, which were situated horizontally along it.

José Ortega y Gasset to observe that "all European history has been [*as a process*] a great emigration toward the North."[35] Of course, the Germanic peoples were themselves diverse: the Goths, Vandals, and Lombards being long exposed to Roman civilization, the Franks much less so, while the more northerly tribes would not adopt Christianity until much later.

More specifically, the West may have truly emerged in the tenth century when Frankish-German civilization forged the semblance of a structured society with a basic notion of the rule of law. Rome still remained an inspiration, if not a renewable fact at this historical juncture. And because of feudalism, power became "noncentralized, consensual, and consultative," encouraging a rather rudimentary form of individuality, even as "a new polity had emerged, the German *Reich*," explains the Harvard-trained Australian historian Paul Collins, echoing Francis Oakley.[36] Later, the continued rebirth of the Greco-Roman tradition in the arts, literature, and politics would bear full flower in the anti-clericalism of Machiavelli and the *raison d'état* of Richelieu. Thus did the West emerge in full force out of Christendom. Early modern multinational empires would further complicate political identity and values. Revolution and nationalism would then produce modern states and capitalism, further refining individualism. "Liberty grew because it served the interests of power," observes the Danish-American scholar David Gress.[37] The ultimate consequence was an art and literature that probed deeply into the psychology of personal life, providing it with both sanctity and moral responsibility: something that may have begun originally with ancient Greek sculpture. This all occurred within the claustrophobic confines of the western extremity of the Eurasian super-continent, blessed with many natural harbors, indented and protected coastlines, advantageously patterned river systems, and an invigorating cool climate. *The West*—namely the political and economic prominence of Europe throughout modern history—was, again echoing Oakley, as much a process as an inheritance: meaning its permanence cannot be taken for granted. The West may be quite transitory; the ground is always moving beneath our feet. Again, I think of the Chinese, who want to make Trieste part of the same maritime geography as the South China Sea, connecting Trieste more with the Indian Ocean than with many other parts of Europe.

Nobody probed this transitory aspect better than Oswald Spengler, the German philosopher who shocked the intellectual world with his *The Decline of the West*, published in two volumes in 1918 and 1922. Spengler found no special position for the West in world history, interacting and fusing as it does with other cultures and civilizations, and maturing and disintegrating as they do. The maturing, creative phase, he explains, emphasizes the role of the countryside, which culminates in the materialism and intellect of the city, that, in turn, produces imperial civilization, so that world empire announces the beginning of the end of the Western cycle in history, punctuated by cultural decadence. The "great Cultures," as Spengler puts it, "accomplish their majestic wave-cycles. They appear suddenly, swell in splendid lines, flatten again and vanish, and the face of the waters is once more a sleeping waste." The "money culture," the rise of global cities, and "the popular embrace of avant-garde . . . sensibilities, awash in cynicism and cosmopolitanism," have all been predicted, if not specifically then spiritually, by Spengler, writes the American historian and journalist Robert W. Merry. Spengler describes the process thus: "The higher a Culture rises— Middle Kingdom, Brahman period, Pre-Socratics, Pre-Confucians, Baroque—the narrower becomes the circle of those who possess the final truths of their time. . . . the human pyramid rises with increasing sharpness, till at the end of the Culture it is complete—thereafter, bit by bit, to crumble." In other words, the more sophisticated and erudite the elite become, the more that the masses slip away beneath them. The nineteenth-century Russian intellectual Alexander Herzen had this to say: "Modern Western thought will pass into history and be incorporated in it, will have its influence and its place, just as our body will pass into the composition of grass, of sheep, of cutlets, and of men."[38]

It may be that, just as the spread of Islam helped define the West and give some geographical structure to Europe, partially severing the Mediterranean as it did after millennia of unity in early and middle antiquity, Islam, by way of human migration, has, in recent decades, been helping to modify the very European construct it once helped establish. It was by separating from North Africa and the Near East that Europe was helped in defining itself, through the development of imperial and state structures central to the *idea* of the West. Now, saving the West can only mean advancing into a sturdy cosmopolitanism that can accept and absorb migrants, and not retreating into a coarse and reactionary nationalism: for the West grew gradually and inexorably, if not always directly, in the direction of liberalism. Europe, in other words, in order to save itself and the West, must become a system of states whose societies internally are international in scope and tradition. As Ortega suggested, just as nationalism led Europe out of the chaos of feudalism, Europe has no choice but to grow out of the confines of nationalism, so as to continue its inexorable evolution. The European Union, in some form, will have to adapt and be reinvigorated, or else become another feeble contrivance like the late Holy Roman Empire.

THE DRAMA BETWEEN ISLAM and the West makes me think of Sir Richard Francis Burton, for whom Trieste was home for eighteen years, until his death in 1890. Burton was the epitome of the Victorian-era romantic explorer. Born in 1821, he was described as "gypsy-eyed" and "darkly handsome," his face marked by a spear wound received in a fight with Somali bandits. He reputedly spoke twenty-nine languages as well as many dialects. Disguised as an Afghan, he made the pilgrimage to Mecca. He passed as a Romani laborer on the Indus River canals, and as a seller of trinkets and holy man while exploring Sind, Baluchistan, and Punjab. He was the first European to enter the sacred Muslim city of Harar in East Africa, and to lead an expedition to search for the sources of the Nile in Central Africa.

It was in Trieste in 1872 where Burton went into what he himself considered exile, to take up the job of British consul. He compared his plight to the Latin poet Ovid, exiled to the Black Sea port of Tomis in A.D. 8 by the Emperor Augustus. At first, he and his wife, Isabel, occupied a ten-room apartment on the top floor of a building close to the sea. Some years later, they moved into a palatial house outside the city with a view of the Adriatic, in which Burton chose a large room to both live and work. Like Joyce would be some decades later, Burton was often depressed and frustrated in Trieste, even as he got much of his most important life's work done here. For in these generically Central European surroundings he translated the *Arabian Nights,* the book with which he is principally identified.[39]

The Thousand Nights and a Night, of which Burton's translation in the mid-1880s remains the most well known, arguably offers, more than any other document, including the Koran, the most profound and panoramic interpretation of Eastern civilization between Europe and China, with stories that are Persian, Arab, and Indian. Burton explains: "The framework of the book is purely Persian, perfunctorily arabized." He compares what Persia achieved for Mesopotamian art and literature to what Greece did for Egyptian art and literature. "Hellas and Iran instinctively chose as their characteristic the idea of beauty, rejecting all that was exaggerated and grotesque."[40]

The so-called frame story is about the angry Persian king Shahriyar, who avenges his first wife's adultery by marrying virgins and beheading them the morning after their deflowering. Scheherazade saves her own life by telling the king a thousand and one interrelated stories that are always left unfinished at dawn, thereby continually delaying her execution, as the king is curious to hear more the following night. It is no accident that Scheherazade is able to do this: as we are told at the beginning of *The Thousand Nights and a Night,* she had amassed a great library, "had studied philosophy and the sciences, arts and accomplishments; and she was pleasant and polite, wise and witty, well read and well bred."[41]

Scheherazade weaves a maddening, multiplying maze of stories within stories, and about stories, each flowing into the next, confusing, Borges-like (of course, Borges himself was influenced by the *Nights*). It is a webwork of orality, of tales told by one person to another. A fisherman finds a jar containing a djinn who threatens him with death, which leads the fisherman to a great store of fishes that entrance a king, who is led to a palace by a lake where appears a young man with legs made of stone and a story to tell. . . . There are no resolutions, often no linearity, no goal or purpose, just as in the structure of Bloom's wanderings about Dublin in *Ulysses,* only wonder upon wonder. The ambience is chromatic, sensuous, wine-laden. Here is Baghdad with the tasteful opulence of Andalusia. To be sure, *The Thousand Nights and a Night* constitute a subversive document for a postmodern age of puritanical belief. The title itself, not comprising a neat "thousand," but a thousand and one, suggests infinity, a process of storytelling that never ends. After you read for a while you cannot remember where it all began. This is how we dream, and *live:* life begins in darkness in the middle of some drama, and ends in the middle of another, also in darkness. The *Nights* realistically captures human experience more than do the Western classics. Burton mentions "the popular superstition . . . that no one can read through them without dying."[42] For there is nothing beyond them.

Joyce wrote the modern version of the *Odyssey;* Burton translated multiple equivalents. For example, the seven voyages of Sindbad the Seaman, with their shipwrecks, monsters, and drugs, parallel Homer's story, and portray the Arabs as the seafaring race that they were. But in the *Nights* there is also a touch of Sophocles and the Old Testament, complete with Freudian tales that recall *Oedipus* and a city turned to stone. The Abbasid caliph Harun al-

Rashid walks abroad at night in disguise, in search of reality, by listening to stories of people he meets along the way. If only our presidents were so wise.

For even the most successful among us has lived through some tragedy or setback, and has awful, edifying stories to tell. What was it that Bernard Berenson wrote? "Human life, consciously lived, rests on tragic foundations."[43] Truly, only on the surface do *The Thousand Nights and a Night* have a fairy-tale quality, since their common motif is a journey gone astray. It is the root of many of life's mishaps: the most determined strivings take their place within a larger fate, which fades and erodes against other fates, until it all dissolves into oblivion. Again, it is Berenson that I place on my bookshelf alongside Burton's *Nights*. He writes: "There is no more ironical and yet more soothing comment on human fate than the sight of ruins . . . like Karnak and Palmyra . . . gnawed by the tooth of time and falling under their own weight; while gigantic statues and obelisks evaporate like ether, although in thousands of years instead of in so many seconds."[44]

Everything we do or build is forgotten, even as struggle is all we know. This is the silent elemental truth of the *Nights:* of every story putting the ones before it, and the ones before them, further back in memory, until only a trace remains. But as Berenson goes on to intimate, we require this process. It is natural. What is unnatural, and breaks us utterly, is when something is brutally smashed or suddenly obliterated out of the normal pattern. That is why the destruction of Palmyra in our own time is like the slaying of a person still young.

IT WAS THE WORK that Burton did at his desk in Trieste, as much as the travels he undertook in Africa, Arabia, and the Indian subcontinent, that made him the supreme orientalist. But merely by generalizing about the East from a Western point of view, he became an object of scorn to contemporary academics, notably the late Edward W. Said of Columbia University, who have accused Burton in so many words of essentialism and determinism. Burton's right to generalize about the East—what Said in his eponymous book calls "Orientalism"—was a privilege granted to Burton by the blunt fact of empire. British imperialism, in Said's view, allowed Burton and others to appropriate the East as their own private intellectual and aesthetic terrain, as though trinkets in their libraries. And because the Arab world was closer to Europe than Persia or India, it became the heart of Orientalism, the heart of Burton's world, where clichés about the "Arab mind" and "psyche" could be "bandied about" by Western specialists. Europe, in other words, further defined itself by announcing its cultural differences with the Islamic world, by way of those like Burton.⁴⁵

And yet, *not* to generalize immobilizes discussion and analysis. "When people think seriously, they think abstractly," writes the late Harvard professor Samuel P. Huntington; "they conjure up simplified pictures of reality called concepts, theories, models, paradigms," without which intellectual life simply cannot advance.⁴⁶

That's partly why I choose to see Burton differently, as a first step. In truth, Burton's translation of the *Nights* has helped bring the genius of Arab-Persian-Indian literature and civilization to Europe, a giant step in constructing the cultural bridge we call cosmopolitanism; in a way, he constitutes a much earlier phase of Said's own work. Before there can be understandings, there must be the misunderstandings that are the natural outgrowth of first contact.

Nor is Burton necessarily derogatory. As he himself writes: "Eastern despotisms have arrived nearer the idea of equality and fraternity than any [Western] republic yet invented."⁴⁷ Indeed, it has often been the imperialists themselves who have experienced foreign places firsthand, and consequently have a more nuanced appreciation of foreign systems than their untraveled compatriots at home. This is why imperialism, cosmopolitanism, and universalism are all connected. Conquest effects subtle changes upon the culture of the conqueror, whether it be the Romans in Egypt, the Mongols in China, or the British in the Near East. Burton helped lead the way. Said has severely and rightfully corrected his errors. One paradigm has replaced another, more or less as Huntington suggests. But it is all part of a process that may lead us to a common culture, or at least to something beyond East and West, so that the stories in *The Thousand Nights and a Night* have led in my case directly to those in Boccaccio's *Decameron*.

Trieste was a place of exile for Burton and Joyce—and an essential piece of Central Europe for Magris. It is a transition zone between the Mediterranean and a more wintry, northerly hinterland, and between Europe proper and the troubled Balkans. A geographical and cultural fault line is a great stimulus to the imagination.

PIRAN, KOPER, LJUBLJANA, AND RIJEKA

*The Early Modern World
Awaiting Us*

IN 1935, THE ANTI-NAZI WRITER AND AUSTRIAN-JEWISH intellectual Joseph Roth published a story, "The Bust of the Emperor," about an elderly count at the chaotic fringe of the former Habsburg Empire, who refused to think of himself as a Pole or an Italian, even though his ancestry encompassed both. In his mind, the only mark of "true nobility" was to be "a man above nationality," in the Habsburg tradition. "My old home, the Monarchy, alone," the count says, "was a great mansion with many doors and many chambers, for every condition of men." Such a patriotism is almost contemporary, even futuristic, in its character. Indeed, the horrors of twentieth-century Europe, Roth wrote presciently, had as their backdrop the collapse of empires and the rise of uniethnic states, with Fascist and Communist leaders replacing the power of traditional monarchs.[1]

Yet, this imperial collapse was probably inevitable. In his classic work, *The Radetzky March* (1932), Roth's chronicle of three generations of the Trotta family—his metaphor in the flesh for the decline and crack-up of the Habsburg Empire—he depicts a calcified imperial machine, rotting from within, unable to assuage the tumult of rising ethnic and national consciousness. Though worse would follow the Habsburg demise, the empire, because of its own forces of reaction, is unable to reform or adapt. Imperial collapse would only leave a vacuum, even as it was not born of simple fate. As Roth writes of one post-Habsburg outpost: "Things were going badly with these people. They prepared their own destiny and yet believed that it came from God."[2]

Fate is what we do to ourselves while blaming an outside force. And the self-destruction of the Habsburg Empire, that is, its inability—its unwillingness, really—to adapt to change through the middle and late nineteenth century proved to be supremely tragic: in significant measure it gave us World War I, from which emerged Hitler, for one thing. The Habsburg Empire, were it to have evolved more dynamically, with greater internal freedoms, would have been something well worth preserving in its own right, let alone for the enormous good it might have done the world: since relative to its own era on the continent, and to much that followed it in the 1920s through the 1940s, the Habsburg Empire represented stability, high culture, tolerance, and the protection of minorities. In fact, its various nationalities might have steadied their exuberance in return for more understanding from an impartial and enlightened imperial power, had only the Habsburgs offered them that. Empire in such a circumstance does not have to mean colonies, but rather can mean a vibrant multiethnic cosmopolitanism.

Because the Slovenes were part of the Habsburg domain for centuries, and tied to the Holy Roman Empire since the High

Middle Ages—even as they were Slavs who had migrated over the centuries into Europe from inner Asia—Slovenia signified Central Europe, Mitteleuropa on the Mediterranean. Here it might be said Europe begins its slow metamorphosis into the Near East and Eurasia, a process that according to my own travel experience does not reach finality until the Caspian Sea. Slovenia thus was the beginning of the bridge to the Balkans and beyond. Yet, because culture is dynamic, changeable, and not a fixed proposition, subject to the differing characteristics of empires and other influences, it is as if I am continuing my journey north and west towards Vienna and the European core, not south and east away from it.

AFTER A FEW MINUTES of driving along the Adriatic south of Trieste I am at the border of Italy and Slovenia, marked only by a sign, a casino, and a few gas stations, as gas is cheaper on the Slovenian side. But there is no border post; nowhere to stop and show a passport, as this former frontier between Communist and capitalist Europe, between Latinity and Slavdom, is now in the midst of NATO, the European Union, the Eurozone, and the Schengen Area. My taxi driver barely slows up. I marvel, simply because I knew Slovenia firsthand during the bad old Cold War days.

The road continues with its gleaming fresh asphalt and flashing signals, exactly as on the Italian side. Slovenia, despite the forty-four-year-long historical intermission of Titoist Communism, was always far more anchored in Central Europe than the rest of Yugoslavia, with much of its territory part of the Habsburg domain for half a millennium until the end of World War I. The seaboard towns of Koper, Izola, and Piran appear in succession, their old parts actually Venetian rather than Austrian, as the Adriatic shore here constituted the only part of Slovene-speaking territory where the late medieval and early modern centuries saw the rule of the Venetian doges for much longer than that of the Habsburg emperors. In this way, I am now closer to Venice than to Trieste, even as I have entered a country spiritually closer to Vienna. This is all natural, yet complicated. Little about civilization is pure, and almost nothing is one or the other. Through the satiny mist of early morning, amidst the oak trees, olive groves, and cypresses, I notice a long stretch of umbrella pine trees that remind me of Rome.

Thirty-five minutes after leaving the hotel in Trieste, I am at the hotel in Piran. Croatia is visible across the bay. The exact maritime frontier between the two states, both of which seceded from Yugoslavia in 1991, has been a subject of dispute.[3] All the borders are extremely close: Slovenia's Adriatic coastline is only twenty-nine miles long. Like the hotel in Trieste, this one in Piran is from before World War I, but the Old World elegance is now missing. A generic luxury lobby gives way to rooms with the plywood flavor of the dormitory and budget tour groups. I feel a tinge of nostalgia for the period of late Communism in the 1980s, when I was a young journalist and experienced the new provincial hotels of Yugoslavia.

I take a walk. A light wind etches lines in the sea, which owing to winter has a nocturnal quality though it is only late afternoon, and yet, by the harbor, it delights with its calm fishy breath. Piran is one of those places where you wish you owned a sailboat. This little town is just so perfect. Its human-scale squares and alleys are graced by scabrous pastel facades that mix neoclassical and Venetian Gothic, with a touch of the baroque. The pilasters and pediments barely protrude from the building surfaces, making for an understated and minimalist beauty. The starkly neoclassical Church of Saint Peter on the main square was designed in 1818 by Pietro Nobile, the same architect of the Habsburg Court—a man of Italian-Swiss lineage—who designed the neoclassical church at the head of the Grand Canal in Trieste. The early-seventeenth-century campanile at the top of the hill is a smaller version of the one next to Saint Mark's in Venice.

Away from the sea the stone squares and houses become more beaten down and weather-stained, the kind of beauty that, as Brodsky says, must emerge naturally as the work of time. I climb the tortuous alleys and steps to the parish church of Saint George, consecrated in 1637. Each late-Renaissance and baroque altar niche lining the white-walled nave is like an offering on a mountaintop, a magical clutter just short of being gaudy; this is apparently the most that humankind can do in order to demonstrate its appreciation to the Almighty. It is pathetic and magnificent at the same time. I stop before every altar: a feast of oil paintings framed by veiny columns with Corinthian capitals, each column somewhat different from the other. Blocks of tea-rose marble highlight the chalky stone, complete with medallions and vases in some cases, the whole clutter under a triangular pediment. *The genius of the baroque*, I think—whose reigning psychology is the "passions of the soul," in which mere reason is abandoned in place of deliberate exaggeration and abundance.[4] Though a bride of the East, the religion of Venice was Roman Catholicism, which is nowhere more powerful than in this church: as much a dynamic force of imperial expansion as were the pagan cultures of Greece and Rome.

I came to Piran because here Giuseppe Tartini was born in 1692, the Italian violin master and composer of the baroque music I so much adore. Whereas the sound of Bach is one of inexhaustible, almost cerebral complexity, Tartini, at least to my untrained ears, constitutes intense, lighter-than-air energy, complete with torrents of passionate longing, so that just a few string instruments sound like a dozen. Tartini's birthplace off the main square that bears his statue has a small and cheerful memorial room on the second floor, with the violin he played, his death mask, a few woodcuts of the period, Italian rococo furniture, and some of his philosophical manuscripts. There is a fine-mannered woman who maintains this exquisite place and is an expert on Tartini and his music. One other visitor besides myself is also here, a fellow American who is touring the birthplaces of baroque composers. He talks tenderly about how different musical modes connote different emotions: those in the "major" mode tend to be sunnier and optimistic; those in the "minor" mode darker and more introspective.

At dusk the main square and side streets by the harbor are crowded with people strolling. The spit and spray of Slavic consonants overshadow the operatic vowels of Italian. The women try hard to be elegant and nearly succeed; the men look shaggier and working class, walking in packs of four and five, slightly hunched over and often nursing cigarettes, wearing mismatched baggy jackets and running shoes. The scarves, fine leather shoes, designer jeans, tight-fitting sweaters, and other dash of the men in Trieste is a memory; so is the complex interior decorating of Trieste with its curtains, gold picture frames, and flower vases, all from which intimacy emerges: these are admittedly small things but ones that you cannot help but notice. How many cultures can match the stylish precision of the Italians? Truly, despite the collapse of borders, I have passed through a frontier: a frontier, mind you, that may mean less and less as the years go on, as the Italian and Slavic worlds find their way back to a semblance of cultural sympathy as in the days of Claudio Magris's ancestors, but a frontier, nevertheless. Here slivovitz is offered on the house by the waiter instead of limoncello like in Trieste.

Even within the Schengen Area, the European Union is a sprawling territory of starkly different cultures and national histories, governed to a significant extent by a remote and only partially democratic bureaucracy located in a faraway capital in the northwest of Europe, with many of its subject nationals now demanding more direct representation. Functionally speaking, isn't this a form of late and declining empire? Though, with its overwhelming emphasis on legality and small states, it might also be defined, in the observation of Yale historian Timothy Snyder, as an answer to the question of what comes *after empire.* For as he explains it, World War I saw the collapse of European land empires (Habsburg and Russian), while World War II began the process of demise of the maritime empires (British and French). What followed was the EU.[5] In any case, the EU is best historically situated within the discussion of empire and its different forms. The EU did not evolve out of nothing: it contains echoes of the past.

Having moved on from the busier cities of Ravenna, Venice, and Trieste, in Piran I retreat to seaside hotels in the off-season that are three-quarters empty, where the café tables on the flagstones are desolate except for a few people in overcoats defying the weather, facing the cut-glass beauty of the sea as if at the edge of the world. In winter, a harbor town truly becomes itself, with its singular isolation against the elements. There is only one restaurant open for dinner. The sailboats are stacked against each other, their brilliant aluminum masts and spreaders bobbing in the water like hieroglyphs of holiday seasons past and yet to come. Wealth, whatever your bank account, is to have sailed a clean and shattered coast when the autumn days are still warm and the nights cold and delicious under the deck blankets, and the crowds have already departed. The best place in the world to sleep is on a sailboat.

These are thoughts that come to me as I wander about. I need to linger in each place with nothing to do. Travel is the art of usefully wasting time. I read a good serious book for two hours over a double espresso in a café. I get more out of reading when away from home, where I am less burdened by worries and thus able to concentrate better. Later I walk every alley until I notice a new detail, or one that I thought I knew but which has to be corrected. I consciously thank the spirits for being alive, and enjoin myself to henceforth complain less. For nothing lifts my mood in the Mediterranean like the pale winter sun, which delivers just enough warmth to constitute a miracle. Only after I get a little bored do I know it is time to move on.

I HAVE JUST LEARNED that Boris Pahor, the great Slovenian writer and Holocaust survivor, is ill and cannot see me. He lives outside Trieste and I was prepared to retrace my route in order to visit him. He is 103 now, born in 1913, and for me a part of the attraction was simply to meet someone that old, with just so much life experience to relate.

Pahor's *Necropolis* is a document from hell, composed of memories of the Holocaust that shift inside him "like algae when stagnant water is stirred." This is a world of slow starvation "in which all the precepts of civilization collapse under the tyranny of the stomach lining." His experience, moving as a medic and prisoner from one concentration camp to another, reduces the epic evil of the Holocaust to one death and one cruelty at a time: to one guard beating a half-naked and starving prisoner, before dousing him with ice water in the midst of the winter. Riding in a death train close to the engine car, Pahor "could feel the warmth of the steel like the belly of an animal. The end of humankind," he thought, is here, "because all that's left is the compassion of hot metal." Only by renouncing all memories of his past and not thinking about the future could he manage to stay sane. And after so much bad blood between the Italians and the Slovenes, in which the former tried to erase the identity of the latter, it was the "shared fear of the ovens" that brought the two groups together in the camps.[6]

Such a man is a realist who has never lost his humanity. Observing tourists at one of the concentration camps in the 1960s, Pahor recognizes that Europe "emerged from the immediate post-war years as an invalid, fitted with glass eyes so it wouldn't frighten good citizens with its empty sockets." Europeans, in Pahor's view, became "standardized" men full of complacency and cowardice, lobotomized by their past, rather than sensitized to it. But never, through it all, did he become cynical. He writes that once the sight of a newspaper in the barracks "released a wave of warmth and light," for the headlines contained the names of Italian cities "which suddenly presented themselves to me in all their splendor, medieval vaults and Gothic arches, the romanesque portals, the frescoes by Giotto, the mosaics of Ravenna."[7]

Because comparison is the basis for all serious scholarship, those who have direct experience with previous eras also have the deepest insights on our own. Since my early thirties, I have found old people endlessly fascinating and have wanted to be around them. Young people look the same the world over, always swarming together, their heads in their smartphones, while old people often sit alone or in quiet, lonely pairs and look distinctive; and their expressions contain all the tribulations of life. Whatever their regrets, they are more original. The beauty of youth obscures one's true character, which emerges more clearly with the battered visage of age. I'll never forget these lines from Solzhenitsyn:

"Idolized children despise their parents, and when they get a bit older they bully their countrymen. Tribes with an ancestor cult have endured for centuries. No tribe would survive long with a youth cult."[8]

KOPER, TEN MILES AWAY along the coast, was known to the Romans as Capris (for "goat," thus the Slovenian name, Koper), to the Byzantines as Justinopolis, and to the Venetians and other Italians as Capodistria, meaning "head of Istria." Following its fall to Venice in 1278–79, Koper had its own governor and agricultural hinterland, much like other cities of the Adriatic's eastern seaboard under Venetian control. Istria, in particular, the large peninsula at the head of the Adriatic, was for Venice a strategic defense line against the Habsburg and Ottoman Empires, as well as a base for a class of traders, administrators, and other go-betweens to facilitate the complex relationship between the Venetian and Ottoman Empires. With the fall of Venice toward the end of the eighteenth century, Koper, like other towns in the region, came under Habsburg control. Between the world wars it was governed by Fascist Italy, and later became part of Yugoslavia. In 1991, after a war with Belgrade that lasted just a few days, Slovenia seceded from the Yugoslav federation.

Koper is not a pretty, toy-town stunner like Piran. Even its old part is crowded with cars, with tacky and nondescript buildings mixed in. The first thing you notice upon entering is the massive port with its gantry cranes and some luxury car dealerships. There is blasting pop music even in the quaint alleys. The restaurants and cafés have decor that is post-Communist without being quite post-modern. Again, this is not Italy, where the fabric of art and material culture as it evolved over the centuries is so much richer; nor is there the velvety Habsburg warmth and elegance of Trieste. As for the legacy of Venice, despite the powerful sculptures and dim oil paintings of early modern Venetian podestas in the regional museum, Venice's rule ended here more than two hundred years ago, and Koper was only an imperial outpost.

Of course, peeling back layers of history and culture is an uncertain and dangerous business. To wit, Koper has a large ethnic-Italian community and though it fell under the rule of Communist Yugoslavia for decades, nevertheless, it constituted one of the most prosperous and cosmopolitan parts of the federation.

In Koper's very defiant religious intensity, the world of late Communism ironically flickers on here. This being Sunday, the immense fifteenth-century Cathedral of the Assumption is jammed with worshippers singing "Hallelujah." In the baroque interior I feel among the Slovenes the same poignant emotion that I know from Polish and Croatian Catholicism: fighting religions close to the frontier with Orthodoxy, born of decades of struggle against Marxist atheism, which erased so much of tradition and thus left behind a moral vacuum. The chants inside the cathedral, a veritable stone fortress with its blind Gothic arcades, are a sturdy refuge.

Outside the cathedral, you have to block out all the distractions in order to appreciate the Renaissance, Gothic, and baroque masterpieces nearby. The chipped stone facades with their heraldic decorations and coats of arms, rubbed and blackened by time, inspire analysis and introspection in a way that the cheerful pastels of Piran, which emphasize surface over volume, do not. It is always the detail that holds you. At the end of an alley marred by dangling electric wires and metal gutters and downspouts, I find a seventeenth-

century mansard roof topped by a triangular point and lateral vo-
lutes like cake swirls, the worn-away stone still a triumph. The
Praetor's Palace, with its origins in the late fourteenth century, built
after a war between Venice and Genoa that consolidated Venetian
rule here, sums up the Venetian Gothic power of Koper, with its
crenellations and lancet arches, amid busts of podestas that, while
not exactly lifelike, force you to concentrate on history as the work
of individuals as well as of larger forces.

Behind the palace and cathedral, I admire the municipal library
with its baroque and slightly classical limestone facade; stirring relief images of biblical scenes just beneath the architraves. This used
to be the eighteenth-century palazzo of the Bruti family. I know
this from a book I have recently read that has unleashed urgent
thoughts within me.

THOUGH HISTORIANS KNOW ABOUT the vast difference between
the early modern world and the modern world, journalists and pol-
icymakers are often confused about the distinction. The distinction
is crucial, and grants an insight into where human society might be
headed next. The early modern period is often popularly defined as
beginning with the Renaissance and ending with the Industrial
Revolution, or, similarly, from the end of the Middle Ages to the
defeat of Napoleon.[9] The modern period begins after that. A key to
early modernism is how it generated identities far more multiple
and elastic and, therefore, benign compared to those wrought by
the ethnic straitjackets demanded by modern nationalists. In many
a place in the early modern world, someone could be a Muslim or a
Jew or a Christian and yet a citizen of the same city and multinational empire; in the modern world someone's religion could re-
strict his or her identity to a specific monoethnic state.

Indeed, the main point of the late Harvard professor Samuel P.
Huntington's *The Clash of Civilizations and the Remaking of World
Order*—a book that everyone in the 1990s owned an opinion about

but which far fewer had actually read—is that political identities based on ethnicity, culture, and civilization are not primordial, but integral to the very process of modernization.[10] Yet, if modernism is itself just a stage of history, are identities—despite the headlines about reactionary populism, sectarian war, and the conflict between Islam and the West—moving imperceptibly in the direction of something more flexible? Might the early modern era offer a relevant and actually more hopeful guide to the future?

Arguably the most sophisticated view into Europe's early modern past was published in the last few years: Noel Malcolm's *Agents of Empire: Knights, Corsairs, Jesuits and Spies in the Sixteenth-Century Mediterranean World*. Malcolm is the definitive academic historian: a research professor at All Souls College, Oxford, intimidatingly multilingual, a trained archival detective, a fiercely engaging writer, a biographer who knows that the art of biography is to illuminate the entire period in question, and one who can write a rich portrait of a country encompassed within a smartly drawn geopolitical panorama. *Agents of Empire*, which is roughly about the contest for supremacy in the Adriatic and the eastern Mediterranean between Venice and the Ottoman Empire in the late sixteenth century, is a "microhistory" of a family within an encyclopedic, almost Proustian vision of early modern Europe.[11] Because Malcolm is writing academic history and not popular history, relatively little here is assumed. Emotions don't bleed off these pages: you are told only what the archives themselves and other records reveal. The result is a certain dryness, combined with extreme erudition. Thus, the reader is led backward in time, even as he or she has to work hard to follow it all.

And I myself had to work particularly hard reading this book. Almost thirty years ago, Malcolm wrote a devastatingly harsh review of my own book *Balkan Ghosts: A Journey Through History* (1993). My ground-level reporting of Yugoslavia and elsewhere in the 1980s, on which the book was based, warning as it did of a coming conflict and serialized in *The Atlantic* some years before war erupted and even before the Berlin Wall fell, did not come remotely close to meeting Malcolm's standards of objectivity and research. Though my instincts about the region were correct and my writing vivid, my initial rage over the review gave way over time to a deliberate resolve to learn from such criticism, seeing it as an opportunity for self-improvement, rather than for resentment. And thus I dived into Malcolm's magnum opus, struggling against my bad memory of his review. Life is about grasping every opportunity to learn, however uncomfortable it may be.*

Malcolm's narrative begins in Ulcinj, located on the Adriatic Sea in the extreme south of Montenegro, close to Albania: a place similar in some respects to Koper. Originally Illyrian, then Roman, absorbed into Byzantium and afterwards into Slavdom, Ulcinj came under Venetian rule in 1405 and under Ottoman rule in 1571. Of course, Ulcinj still mattered greatly to Venice in the sixteenth century because it stood on a vital frontier. For here was the messy Venetian-Ottoman borderland of periodic atrocities, where clan conflicts mattered more than religious ones. Nevertheless, the Ottoman conquest fashioned subtle changes, not an upheaval. As Malcolm writes:

> . . . it may seem that an alien element took over at every level. . . . This impression is false. With a few exceptions (soldiers, and some others), the Muslims were not immigrants brought in from distant Islamic territories; they were local Albanians who happened to convert to Islam. Reasons for conversion were various, and in many cases probably had more to do with advancing one's social and economic position than with any religious concerns.[12]

---

* I wrote about the circumstances surrounding *Balkan Ghosts*'s publication in a sequel-of-sorts, *In Europe's Shadow: Two Cold Wars and a Thirty-Year Journey Through Romania and Beyond* (New York: Random House, 2016).

In other words, yes, there was in fact a clash of different empires with different religions, but it was not as stark as meets the eye. The Ottoman Empire was still an important source of grain for Venice. For there were long periods of peace between the two empires, when Venice used the Muslim Ottomans as a source of pressure upon rival Catholic city-states in Italy. "Venice," Malcolm says, "was the only [European] power whose naval policy was primarily concerned with the protection of trade routes; and since the trade in question was with the Ottoman Empire, the usual policy involved cooperation, not conflict." There is an even larger point here: that geopolitics, because it is somewhat refreshingly amoral, stood above bloody religious clashes with all of their moral absolutes. For example, Catholic Poland could live with the Ottoman-ruled Romanian principalities, "but it could not accept the idea of their becoming clients and creatures of the [fellow Catholic] Habsburgs," who were too close by for comfort. Moreover, there was the "overriding determinant" of Ottoman policy in Europe in this period, the struggle against fellow Muslim Persia in Asia, which further encouraged—along with the Ottoman hold over Syria and Egypt—the sultans' desire to dominate the eastern Mediterranean and Cyprus in particular; this, only in turn, helped bring them into rivalry with Catholic Venice.[13]

Because this is as complete an account of a period and a particular geography as one can reasonably imagine, the author also recounts the nastiest sides to this Venetian-Ottoman rivalry: such as the dispatch of irregular forces from the Balkan interior to burn villages and seize livestock, in order to make life utterly wretched for the Venetians, whose slither of a coastal empire on the eastern Adriatic was particularly tenuous, and subject to Ottoman whims. On the other hand, owing to the rugged terrain of Albania, Ottoman attempts at administration in that part of the Balkan interior encountered stiff martial resistance, so that while the Ottomans could destroy an existing power structure in Albania and its environs, they failed at constructing a new and pliant one. (Sometimes the anarchy originated on the coast itself, as when the Uskoks, based in the port of Senj in Habsburg-ruled Croatia, launched raids into Ottoman territory.)

And it is the *Ottoman* Empire that Malcolm is talking about—not the Turkish one, even as Ottoman and Turkish are in many cases synonymous. But they are certainly not synonymous in many other cases—given that the Ottoman sultanate was a rich and cosmopolitan confection of different cultures and even religions, with many different kinds of self-governing polities and non-Turkish cliques (Bosnian, Albanian, and so on) within it. As Malcolm tells us in one of his asides, the "upper reaches" of the Ottoman administration included "many 'renegades' (converts to Islam) from Italy, Croatia, Hungary, Austria and elsewhere, whose native language and mental formation were Western." This whole system "of government, taxation and military organization" made the Ottoman Empire in the fifteenth and sixteenth centuries "the envy of Western Europe."[14]

Malcolm's efforts, particularly in searching out archives, are not centered on the larger social, military, and geopolitical canvas, but on the Bruni and Bruti families of Venetian-Albanians, who inhabited a world of connections and status at the borderland of Venetian and Ottoman power around Ulcinj, where the Italian and Slavic languages were used almost interchangeably. "The Brunis and the Brutis," the author writes, "were genuine linguistic and cultural amphibians. And that . . . was essential to their success in the wider Mediterranean world."[15]

This extended family included, for instance, a Catholic archbishop in the Balkans; the captain of the papal flagship at the Battle of Lepanto in 1571; an interpreter who worked for both the Venetians and the Ottomans; and a member of the Spanish spy network in Istanbul, who later became chief minister of Moldavia. (Gasparo Bruni himself owed loyalties to Venice, the pope in Rome, and the king of Spain.) While Venice and Istanbul were the Adriatic basin's "two important early modern centers of cultural production," in the words of scholar E. Natalie Rothman, the Brunis and Brutis were part of a "trans-imperial" world that "clearly violated the mythic representation" of each side as the feared and hated *Other*.*

Here is where Dubrovnik (also known as Ragusa) comes into the picture. A storied, semi-independent city-state north of Ulcinj on the Adriatic's Dalmatian coast, it functioned as an intelligence hub and communications center between East and West during the second half of the sixteenth century. Dubrovnik's wealth came originally from being the export center for lead, silver, and other commodities originating in Bosnia, Kosovo, and elsewhere in the Balkan interior. Because it was virtually enclosed by Ottoman territory, Dubrovnik could not resist the sultans militarily, even as the city-state depended on the Ottoman Empire for food. But, partly because it was such a reliable supplier of intelligence to Istanbul, Dubrovnik was not required to supply soldiers to the sultanate, or assist the Ottoman soldiery in any substantial way. Dubrovnik represented the ultimate ambiguity, in other words: "a Christian state nestling on the edge of Ottoman territory, practically autonomous but regarded by the Sultan as part of his empire."[16]

This was a world in which vast Muslim armies operated deep inside the Hungarian heartland of Central Europe; and yet it was also a continent engaged in the most complex of geopolitics that triumphed over civilizational clash. And thus it forces reflection on our own world. The knowledge and policy elite among us inhabit a very cosmopolitan milieu that should make the Brunis and Brutis quite familiar. Anyone who has experienced the upper social reaches

---

* Noel Malcolm, *Agents of Empire: Knights, Corsairs, Jesuits and Spies in the Sixteenth-Century Mediterranean World* (New York: Oxford University Press, 2015), p. 34 and 99. E. Natalie Rothman, *Brokering Empire: Trans-Imperial Subjects Between Venice and Istanbul* (Ithaca, NY: Cornell University Press, 2012), pp. 30 and 251. This eclectic interweaving of identities has my mind wandering to many things, such as the *convivencia* (coexistence) in medieval Spain, with its Mozarabs (Christians under Islamic administration), Mudejars (Muslims under Christian administration), muwallads (non-Arabs who converted to Islam), and Moriscos and conversos (Muslims and Jews who had been baptized). Medieval Spain and the eastern shore of the Adriatic in early modern times were both to some extent cultures of negotiation and compromise on both the personal and the political level.

of London, Washington, New York, Berlin, Shanghai, and innumerable other cities, as well as the fancy and influential international conference circuit, as I have, is aware of so many people with extraordinary multilingual gifts and eclectic loyalties. This is a world of, for instance, someone born in Singapore, whose parents come from France and the Punjab, who may speak English, French, Chinese, and Hindi, and owns at least two passports, with relatives serving in multiple governments and non-governmental organizations (NGOs) at reasonably high levels. This is a world of a former narrow and aristocratic elite morphing into a larger global upper class, one full of opportunities and risks: somewhat akin to that of the Brunis and Brutis.

It is also a world of Dubrovniks: that is, of transactional city-states—think of Singapore and Dubai—whose loyalty, deep down, is to business and trade rather than to any larger power or political philosophy per se. And, of course, it is a world of secular geopolitics that increasingly transcends religious divides: Israel and Saudi Arabia in a very real, albeit unspoken, alliance against Iran; former enemies America and Vietnam lining up together against China; largely Eastern Orthodox Romania tilting away from Orthodox Russia while Orthodox Bulgaria and Serbia tilt increasingly toward Moscow. Divisions of religion and sect, obviously, cannot be denied, just as they could not be in the early modern world, but, as in that world, the closer you look, the more the cross-cutting complexities and contradictions abound.

At a more profound and perhaps less obvious level, there is, as the French philosopher Pierre Manent intimates, a growing emphasis on city-states and the half-hidden traditions of empire, even while the problems of modern states increase.[17] I mean that powers such as the United States, China, Iran, and the European Union, while not officially empires, have many of the frustrations and challenges of former imperiums. Meanwhile, on almost all continents, cities grow into both megacities and region-states of their own.

Isn't this all, then, to a much more amplified and enlarged, high-tech extent, a version of early modernism? Just as the young Henry Kissinger saw an answer to the possibility of nuclear armageddon in the 1950s in concentrating on the post-Napoleonic court diplomacy of Metternich and Castlereagh, Noel Malcolm's answer to where so-called postmodernism is heading is to concentrate on the early modern exploits of an extended, multinational family amid a world more multicultural and purely geopolitical than we realize. In this way, early modernism and postmodernism merge.

I consider all this as I stand before the former Bruti palazzo in Koper, a town that was a crossroads of empires and civilizations during the late medieval and early modern eras—just as it may be still.

TO FURTHER UNDERSTAND THE influences bearing upon Koper, I must now journey to Ljubljana, Slovenia's capital, ninety minutes away by bus to the northeast, tucked into the gloomily beautiful, conifer-clad Slovenian interior close to a corner of the Alps: a place where I can just listen to people talk about the culture and geopolitics of Central and Eastern Europe.

I have always felt that the twin crises of the European Union and the Eurozone will ultimately have their sharpest effects not in Western Europe, but farther to the east. With all of their problems, Western European countries have stronger states and bureaucracies than their counterparts in the east, where nearly a half century of Communism has left a lingering legacy of institutional decrepitude. In such a circumstance, the declining power of Brussels leaves countries in the eastern half of the continent more vulnerable to Moscow. So rather than listen to the platitudes and clichés of big shots at conferences in Munich and Davos, where everyone is performing for an audience, I would rather have one-on-one conversations at café tables in Ljubljana, closer to the borders of the Near East and Orthodox worlds, where geopolitical risk is more immediate, less abstract.

Ljubljana: known in German as Laibach, a place more historically associated with the Habsburg Empire than with any particular
nation-state. Here in 1821, one of the crucial congresses was held to
stabilize Europe after the Napoleonic Wars. Thus, in the very sound
of its name Laibach recalls such personages as Metternich and
Castlereagh. I was last in Ljubljana in October 1989, just a few
weeks before the Berlin Wall fell, on a concluding trip through
Yugoslavia, from where I had reported often during the 1980s. This
was still twenty months before the start of the war there. But I
would ultimately leave Slovenia out of the final version of *Balkan
Ghosts,* even though it had been a member of the Yugoslav federation, while I would include Greece in the manuscript though it was
a long-standing member of NATO. Greece, I had argued to my
editors, was Near Eastern despite its ties to the Western alliance,
while Slovenia was Central European despite being for so long a
part of the largest Balkan country.

Ljubljana in 1989 has left a deep imprint on my memory. A section of my diary from the period, published as a travel essay in *The
New York Times,* records: "Mornings are a blank canvas. Not until
9:30 or so does the autumn fog begin to dissolve. Then the outlines
of steep roofs, spires, leaden domes, statues, and willows and poplars emerge like an artist's first quick strokes. At first it is a pen-
and-ink with charcoal. By mid- or late morning come the richer
colors of the palette: facades of orange and yellow ochers, pinks,
sandy reds, and dazzling greens. As for the architecture itself," I
went on, "it is not only baroque and Renaissance but also Art Nouveau, Art Deco, and so forth. This was partly because, with the exception of five years of Napoleonic rule, Ljubljana between 1135 and
1918 was inside the Habsburg Empire, and thus artistic influences
from the far-flung domain filtered in." Truly, I was infatuated with
the city.[18]

But there is even more from my notebooks about Ljubljana that
I did not publish at the time: Men smoking in the damp and cold
hotel restaurant while waiters talked and ignored customers amid

loud rock music (Blood, Sweat & Tears singing "Spinning Wheel"). People had ravaged eyes under matted hair, without the blow dryers and designer glasses that were already ever-present in nearby Austria at the time, and everyone with bad-quality shoes. It was a place where people began to drink early in the day.*

And yet one after another of the persons I interviewed back in 1989 complicated those initial impressions. For Yugoslavia was already starting to fall apart, even if it wasn't yet in the news. "The Serbs look backward while we look forward: away from the archaic system" of Tito's Yugoslavia. "In Slovenia, Tito [a half-Slovene] has been completely forgotten." "Slovenes are like conscientious objectors in the Yugoslav federation." "We watch Austrian television, not Serbian television." "We are a small country that looks out, Serbia is a great country that looks in." All in all, in October 1989, Slovenia was a poor and downtrodden place by Western standards that, nevertheless, evinced a distinct bitterness about having to prop up the even poorer and yet more powerful states within the Yugoslav federation, notably Serbia. Yugoslavia had, in a political and cultural sense, dragged Slovenia southward into the Balkans, and away from its rightful place in Central Europe, to which Slovenia's own Habsburg legacy entitled it. Indeed, it was Slovenia's very resentment over that fact which caused it, like Poland and Hungary, to fiercely aspire towards membership in the West, and thus towards liberalism and free markets.

THAT WAS ALL THREE decades ago. Revisiting Ljubljana is like returning to the same house but one with new fixtures and furniture, as if the city has been brought into finer focus by the same artist, now employing the thinnest paintbrush. There are the new

---

* As I wrote back then: "Here in Ljubljana Haider might be in his element," referring to Jörg Haider, the late leader of the populist and vaguely neo-Nazi Austrian Freedom Party, who hailed from the province of Carinthia just over the border, and whose support was ultimately circumscribed by Austria's own middle-class prosperity.

cars, the portable speed bumps, the new signage, pedestrian streets, artistically designed recycling bins, and a hotel with a stage-lit, digital quality. The service is over the top, with waiters gesturing like ballet dancers. People look thin and sharp with fashionable scarves and umbrellas. In Ljubljana, I feel much closer to Italy than in either Piran or Koper, despite their Venetian historical influence and the Habsburg one here. Global brand names are plastered all over the streets, and there are many Asian tourists on shopping sprees.

Žiga Turk, a two-time former government official now at the local university, has, like many people I will meet here, a cool, neutral clarity of expression and thought, without that burdensome intensity of the late–Cold War Balkans that I used to know. Talking to him at a smart café, I feel as if we are in Brussels, not in the former Yugoslavia. "We are only just out of the woods," he tells me, "and seeing good growth for the first time since 2008, when the financial crisis exposed how weakly institutionalized we were. Take Koper, once a stronghold for the Yugoslav military. It has in fact become a better managed, less strike-prone port than Trieste. In the future there will be a rail link from Koper into Central Europe. Not constrained by nearby hills like Trieste and Rijeka, Koper's geography is allowing the port there to expand. On the other hand, look around the region," he goes on, never raising his voice. "It is as if the fourth successive empire is breaking up around us. First it was the Habsburg Empire that collapsed after World War I, then the [Yugoslav] Kingdom of the Serbs, Croats, and Slovenes that broke apart in World War II, then the breakup of socialist Yugoslavia after the Cold War, and now the European Union is in deep crisis. Do you know why there is no pan-European populism? Because Europe as a whole has no emotional identity."

He favors a stronger European Union because it would re-create the relative peace of the Habsburg and Ottoman Empires in the Balkans, a situation that would allow historic sub-regions to flourish. "But for now, given the crisis, we Slovenes agree that we must

stick with Germany—not with Italy, not with Visegrád [a grouping
of north-central European states], and not with Croatia." Europe
still means Germany to him. And Germany is safe as long as its
chancellors maintain an Adenauer-like sense of obligation to the
memory of World War II and the Cold War.

"Of course, we are not anti-Russian. Russia never really threatened Slovenia. Russia must increasingly become geopolitically integrated with Europe, since Russia's alliances with China and Turkey
ultimately cannot hold." He means that Russia will always be a junior partner in any alliance with China, something Russia would
never tolerate, even as a Russia competing with the United States
in Europe would raise Russia's stature. As for Turkey, it competes
too much with Russia in the Balkans, the Caucasus, and the Middle
East. Slovenia, which ironically had little to do with the Soviet
Union during the Cold War, even though it was inside the Communist world, now has some Russian investment in banks, steel
plants, and a proposed natural gas pipeline.

"It is like the European power politics of previous centuries are
returning," he sighs. "Russia is back in, and the U.S. is a step removed." As for the former Yugoslavia, "we are lucky to have the
Croats to the south—because they are so anti-Yugoslav and anti-
Serb, they have the effect of pushing us further north into Central
Europe." The borders of the border-free Schengen Area, I am told
over and over again during my stay here, approximate the borders
of Germanic Europe: of the Holy Roman Empire. Thus, Slovenia
finally has a historically natural border. And yet there is a certain
insecurity in his message: the fear that somehow Slovenia can still
be cast away from a weakening European Union, even as Slovenia
is no longer (and never really was) part of the Balkans.

Matej Avbelj, a young professor of European Union law who
arrives at a café on a little scooter, explains to me that "Slovenia is
still obtaining a middle class. The political parties have no funds,
they are institutionally weak, the parliamentarians are too often no-
bodies. We don't really have party structures in the liberal demo-

cratic sense, like, for example, you have next door in Italy. It is still too much a matter of us and them, of Slovenia and the European Union, of Ljubljana and Brussels." As I would find farther south along the Adriatic coast, in Croatia, Montenegro, and Albania, the problems of Communism still lingered, long after Communism has dissolved.

Peter Grk, former chief foreign policy advisor to the prime minister, and Alenka Košir, a foreign ministry official dealing with the western Balkans, are certainly not willing to give up on the European Union. They take me out to lunch at a designer restaurant that could be located literally anywhere in the West, and tell me that the European Union means nothing less than a constructive, problem-solving mentality, a belief in legal states over ethnic nations, the sanctity of the individual over that of the group, and the rule of law over arbitrary fiat. Such a system must eventually succeed in one form or another since there is, ultimately, no other alternative— whatever the result of this election or that. "Only the European Union offers a form of unity within a greater diversity," they say. And it is only the European Union that can save the failing parts of the former Yugoslavia that lie to the south beyond Slovenia and Croatia. "The Russians will use Serbia as a beachhead only if the European Union lacks the *will* to compete there."

And even if there is to be a multi-speed Europe, then Slovenia, they say, is perfectly positioned to be in the fastest economic and political group, since it is small—thus easily manageable—and is well situated geographically, bordering Italy and Austria.

Though Grk and Košir are both unwilling to give up on the European Union in some form, they also admit that the current state of the former Yugoslavia mirrors the old divide between the Habsburg and Ottoman Empires, with Slovenia and Croatia (the success stories) falling within the Habsburg realm, and the much weaker states to the south being legacies of the Ottoman.

Indeed, Grk and Košir are young and idealistic, but they are not unknowing. They simply believe in agency. And they know that the danger in Serbia, Bosnia, Kosovo, and Macedonia is not necessarily *now,* when memories are still relatively fresh concerning the bloody cataclysm of the 1990s, but *later,* years from now, when memory of the last war fades and passes into distorted myth, like much of Balkan history.

I HAD TO REMIND myself that Ljubljana is only one hour or so by car from Trieste, a place that might have been an independent city-state with open borders—rather than part of Italy—had the post–World War II border settlement worked out differently. Dimitrij Rupel's father was from Trieste, and his grandfather was a Habsburg customs officer there. Rupel, born in 1946, was Slovenia's first foreign minister after independence from Yugoslavia, and afterward became ambassador to the United States and mayor of Ljubljana. He is a natural diplomat and politician: tall and imposing, with white hair and a short white beard, a real presence, that is; avuncular in the way of indicating good judgment, without necessarily being an intellectual. I fall easily under his spell.

"Napoleon wanted to close the nearby sea door to German-speaking Central Europe," he begins. "There is actually a statue to Napoleon here. After Napoleon was defeated, the czar of Russia, Alexander I, and the Habsburg emperor, Francis I, walked the streets of Ljubljana together during the 1821 Laibach Congress. What I mean to say is that Slovenia and Ljubljana used to be much more important than they are now. The problem is that our identity was too long submerged within multiethnic empires, and we were minorities living in different regions such as Styria and Carinthia," now in Austria. "The cry in 1848 [Europe's year of failed liberal revolutions] was for a united Slovenia, but that didn't happen. When we finally did get our own state in 1991, it occurred so fast that people here didn't see it as a great accomplishment. After all, the war with Yugoslavia—it was with Serbia really—lasted only a few days and cost sixty lives, though it began the greater Yugoslavian disaster."

The escape from Yugoslavia was ironic, he explains, because "Slovenia, feeling oppressed by Austro-Hungarian rule, enthusiastically joined the Kingdom of the Serbs, Croats, and Slovenes following World War I, in a fit of pan–South Slavic feeling. Slovenia had been an outlier in the Habsburg Empire, and accounted for one of its less developed parts. So we were not at that time thankful for its benefits." This anti–Central Europe feeling, he goes on, "was strengthened by the fact that Serb soldiers helped stop Italian aggression against the Slovenes in the early years of the Yugoslav kingdom. Only much later," as the Yugoslav kingdom became unstable and its successor state—socialist Yugoslavia—became a prison, "did we finally realize that we had been better off under the Austrian Habsburgs all along." But by then Slovenia was functionally trapped inside the Balkans, he laments.

"Our best time in history," Rupel exhales, "has just passed, when we were inside an EU that still had Britain as a member, keeping Germany from dominating Europe." He worries that whereas Germany has exercised a benevolent influence in recent decades, a return of German nationalism in some form in a post-Brexit EU would only be natural and therefore cannot be ruled out.

DAMIR ČRNČEC IS A COLUMNIST, law professor, and former head of military intelligence in Slovenia. He takes me to a folkloric restaurant and over a lunch of grilled meat with mustard explains that because Slovenia is at a geographical crossroads—pressed during various periods of its history by Italians, Germans, and Hungarians—it is also a perfect listening post for evaluating developments in both Central Europe and the Balkans, which Slovenia is crammed in between. "Both the Serbs and the Croats continue to try to seduce us into joining their side against the other, and of course we stay neutral." He then talks of old "Turkish" lines and sieges, of the relevance of ethnic and historical grudges despite the age of digital communications. Damir is tough and intense, and harbors the pessimism and realism that is more natural to a military background than to a civilian one. But the vision he suggests for Europe is almost completely in line with the one that I had just heard that morning from two suave former ambassadors at the Slovenian foreign ministry.

According to this vision, the Schengen borders are natural in just so many ways. They hark back to the old *Antemurale Christianitatis*, the "Bulwark of Christianity," proclaimed in 1519 by Pope Leo X, in a reference to the Roman Catholic Slavs as the front line against the Ottoman Empire, Croatia being the first line of defense against the Muslim sultanate and Slovenia the second. "When Communism collapsed," said one of these former ambassadors, "we thought none of this earlier history was important. We assumed the existence of socialist Yugoslavia and before that the Kingdom of the Serbs, Croats, and Slovenes had erased such differences among us. But three decades after the collapse of Tito's Yugoslavia we find that we are back to late medieval and early modern history [in which the territory of Yugoslavia was once divided among three empires—Habsburg, Venetian, and Ottoman].[19] Look," the diplomat continued, and then proceeded to rattle off the following statistics from his head:

The Slovenes toward the end of the second decade of the twenty-first century had a per capita income of $32,000. They were in "first-speed" Europe. The Croats' per capita income was $22,400. They were in "second-speed" Europe. Croatia, after all, offered a mixed history. Istria, Zagreb, and some other areas of the country were heirs to the Austro-Hungarian Habsburg tradition, the Dalmatian coast to the Venetian one, and the rest of the country to the Ottoman one. (There were, in truth, multiple Croatias.) But then came the rest of the former Yugoslavia, which fell almost completely within the Ottoman imperial system. Here we had Montenegro with a per capita income of $17,000, Serbia with $14,000, and Macedonia, Kosovo, and the former Ottoman part of Bosnia with similarly low numbers, if not lower still. Indeed, despite the existence of a South Slav federation clean across the western Balkans for most of the twentieth century, all that is left are the economic and social distinctions from older, imperial divisions. This, mind you, is not ethnic or racial determinism, since as it turns out the Slavs of southeastern Europe have been shaped politically and economically more by the actions of these foreign imperial systems than by their own blood and language. In sum, the former Byzantine and Ottoman part of Europe, the part closest to the Near East, is still the poorest—and the least stable.

A word of explanation is due here. For centuries, the Habsburg and Ottoman Empires ran rich, sprawling, multiethnic, and bureaucratically vibrant empires that, among much else, protected minorities like the Jews better than the uniethnic democracies that would follow them after World War I. Yet, there were differences. The Habsburgs had their roots in Alpine Europe whereas the Ottomans harked back to Central Asia and the Caucasus. The Habsburg domain was comparatively more developed, wealthier, and less chaotic than the Ottoman one. As a journalist in Yugoslavia during the Cold War, I can attest that this unwieldy federation got progressively poorer and less organized as I traveled south from Habsburg-influenced Slovenia to Ottoman-influenced Macedonia.

The view from Ljubljana—the city where Tito died in 1980—is that the Yugoslav war of the 1990s continues without the shooting. That is, historical divisions are still raw. Croatia and Serbia still compete for control in Bosnia. Bosnia itself is divided into ethnic and religious cantons. The Serbs and the Albanians remain psychologically at odds. And the unification between Albania and ethnic-Albanian Kosovo, however unwieldy it may be and however bloody it may become—and however implausible it all may seem now—could eventually happen unless both places, along with Serbia, get into the European Union.

So we are back to the issue of the European Union, which, with all of its pathetic inadequacies, offers the best possible way forward for southeastern Europe. Without the European Union— amplifying as much as containing German power as it does—there is mainly the economic and political influence of neo-authoritarian Turkey and Russia in the Balkans. In other words, a new Iron Curtain of sorts now meets a new early modern imperial division of Europe. Just consider: the civil society programs of the Hungarian-American billionaire George Soros have been under attack for quite some years now in the former East Bloc—programs that did so much to bring Western values to the old Communist East in those heady first decades of the post Cold War. Meanwhile, as my Slovenian acquaintances remind me, the day after the April 2017 referendum in Turkey that approved authoritarian powers for President Recep Tayyip Erdoğan, Erdoğan went not to the tomb of Mustafa Kemal Ataturk, the founder of modern Turkey, to pay homage, but to the tomb of Mehmed II "the Conqueror," the fifteenth-century Ottoman sultan whose armies marched westward from Constantinople as far as Bosnia. For Slovenia, the future looked troubled, unless Brussels could match Ankara and Moscow in its strength of vision.*

I DRIVE SOUTH, BACK in the direction of Koper, through a shaved Alpine landscape with the pruned and tidy exactitude of Switzer-

---

* In the years following my visit, a far-right prime minister rose to power in Slovenia, Janez Janša, a devotee of the former American president Donald Trump and the right-wing populist leader in neighboring Hungary, Viktor Orbán. Janša traded in disinformation and with Orbán's help built a propaganda network that garnered many followers. It was an example that we are truly at the end of the modern world and into the postmodern one, in which absurdity combines with globalization to produce unimaginable outcomes. It was humbling to see a country whose experts had impressed me with such probity now drift for a time into illogic. Again, all a traveler or journalist can do is catch a moment in time. The future will always remain a mystery. See Domen Savic's "Slovenia's Prime Minister Is a Far-Right Conspiracy Theorist and Twitter Addict Who Won't Admit Trump Lost," *Foreign Policy*, November 11, 2020.

land or Austria. Then I veer slightly eastward, still heading south, in the direction of the Croatian border. My passport is stamped as I leave Slovenia and stamped again a few yards away as I enter Croatia. I exchange my euros for Croatian kuna. I have never left the European Union nor the former Yugoslavia, but I am now leaving both the Schengen Area and the Eurozone. This is a real border.

Soon I am descending through tunnels in the mountains until the infinite sprawl of the Adriatic appears again with the peninsula of Istria and great offshore islands rising like the backs of dinosaurs. The port city of Rijeka emerges suddenly as a blight: stout lines of graceless apartment blocks, their verticality a violent interruption of the landscape. The car's descent continues into the gritty center of the city: stolid peeling buildings, blackened and pebbly, eaten away by time, punctuated by the occasional, brooding cedar and cypress. This is the baroque and neoclassical legacy of Austria-Hungary, interspersed with the oppressive modernism of late Communism and the West, too. One row of apartment blocks alone, with its smears of cement and potted flowers on the cruddy balconies, bears traces of several different eras of post–World War II history. The skyline is crowded with gantry cranes. For in addition to the ferries and Tito's famous yacht on the piers, this is a vital container port.

My hotel, with its prefabricated wooden furniture and brown wall-to-wall carpeting, is quite comfortable but not *evolved* like the hotel in Ljubljana—not plush like the ones in Rimini and Trieste—here I am still stuck in the twentieth century. Whereas the lobby and café in Ljubljana was like an advertisement from a glossy fashion magazine, now, less than two hours later, I am in one of those elegant black-and-white movies. I have come from the capital of a much richer country to a less-touristed, industrialized port of a poorer one. Rijeka is more Balkan than Ljubljana, but that is only a question of relativities, as I am still in the former Habsburg Empire. In this part of the world, too many people think that every place to the south and east of where they stand is where the Orient begins.

Rijeka constitutes another gradation en route eastward: a place with raw depth and intimacy and character. Whereas Trieste is immaculate old money, Rijeka is the detritus of Communism. Global tourism has yet to sanitize Rijeka. And so this dirty old town remains beautiful and distinctive in its way.

The Croatian Rijeka of today, with 129,000 people, was once the cosmopolitan city of Fiume, featuring its Piazza Dante and other Italianate place-names, inhabited up to 1947 by Italians, Croats, Hungarians, and Slovenes, before it fell under the sterile and repressive rule of Tito's Yugoslavia. When I think of Fiume, I think of Claudio Magris's late wife, Marisa Madieri, and the diary of her childhood, *Aqua Green*, named for the color of a skirt her mother had given her, with money earned from a pawnshop at great sacrifice. A critic said the diary makes one yearn "for an existence that is outside of history and of time." For it is a book that celebrates the indestructible quality of inspired memories associated with love. Whenever the author passes below the Church of Villa del Nevoso, now called Ilirska Bistrica, "it seems to me that the edges of time touch and that the mantle which shrouds it has become transparent," for in her mind her parents "are still getting married up there," with her mother "walking in a flowing white veil" in the August warmth.[20]

The poignancy of these thoughts arises from the travails of refugee life that were to follow. In 1947, as Yugoslav Communist forces swept into the area, Marisa Madieri's family chose to leave for Italy, thereafter suffering a year of persecution before the actual departure. Her father lost his job and was briefly imprisoned, and the family was evicted from their apartment and reduced to a one-room existence with all their possessions piled to the ceiling. Once her family came to Trieste, they lived in a grim refugee camp and were viewed with suspicion by the local Italians outside.

Rijeka—Fiume—was a place of conflicting sovereignties long before the 1940s. Beginning in the late fifteenth century, Rijeka was an important seaport of the Austrian Habsburg Empire, and after the establishment of the Austro-Hungarian Dual Monarchy in 1867 much of it came under the rule of Budapest, with new rail links connecting it deep into Central Europe. If Trieste is a fault zone, then Rijeka is the very border of that fault zone. In fact, following the First World War, ethnic conflicts among the urban population and the decision of foreign diplomats to hand over the city to the new Kingdom of the Serbs, Croats, and Slovenes led 9,000 ethnic-Italian legionnaires to establish the vaguely anarchist and Fascist "Regency of Carnaro" here.* That lasted a year, until 1920, when the Treaty of Rapallo declared Fiume a free state under Italian rule. In 1924, it became part of Fascist Italy. Through it all, the drama between Slavs and Italians nearby on the Istrian peninsula became a microcosm of the drama between East and West; between the free West and the Communist East. Though, given the cruelty and general insensitivity of the Italians towards the Slavs, something not restricted to Mussolini's Fascists, one side was not always and not necessarily morally superior to the other.

For example, I look up at the balconies in Rijeka and think immediately of the leader of the Italian Regency of Carnaro, Gabriele D'Annunzio (1863–1938), a name that emerges from time to time in conversations here as a vague and occasional background noise: mentioned quickly in passing, but rarely explained. D'Annunzio was a charismatic intellectual with a lust for power and adulation, who consequently loved balcony appearances. For him, the purpose of politics was to supply an arena for glory and the erection of the perfect state. In Fiume, in 1919, with the collapse of the Habsburg Empire and the city the object of rival claims and protracted negotiations by Italy and the new Yugoslav kingdom, D'Annunzio seized power at the head of the far-right legionnaire movement, itself supported by flaky youthful idealists. Though he didn't last long, this romantic thinker stylistically paved the way for Mussolini: he was a warning against hazy ideas and intellectual conceit. For lofty

---

* The name refers to the Gulf of Kvarner, where the city is located.

themes, if not grounded in moderation and practicality, can be the enemy of healthy politics.[21]

GIACOMO SCOTTI IS EIGHTY-EIGHT at the time I meet him, spry and diminutive, with combed-back white hair, and nattily dressed in a tie and sweater underneath a sports coat. I meet him for lunch at the University of Rijeka. Since 1948, when he was twenty, he has been furiously writing essays and novels on the whole problem of the Italian-Yugoslav borderland, where he has lived during most of his life. A prolific writer and fervent anti-Fascist in his youth, Scotti tells me, bristling with passion, that no chief of state in Italy has ever really asked forgiveness for the crimes of World War II, as the leaders of Germany have repeatedly done. Italy is a bit like Austria in this manner: a pro-Axis country for much of the war that afterward thought of itself as a victim. That is why extreme right-wing movements can take root in Italy (and Austria, too), and hint of a return of Istria and Dalmatia to the Italian fold; whereas such nationalism and irredentism has, at least until the present, been much harder to imagine in Germany. "Thousands of Slovenes, Croatians, and Montenegrins died in concentration camps in Italy and Italian-controlled territory. These figures are not taught in Italian schools. Italians cannot feel the pain of others," he says. Scotti disputes the notion that without the alliance with Hitler, Mussolini might now be remembered as no worse than Franco and Salazar. "Remember, Mussolini invaded Ethiopia in 1935, four years before the formal alliance with Hitler. Mussolini wanted to dominate the whole central Mediterranean," and indeed occupied practically the whole eastern Adriatic seaboard unto Albania and Greece during World War II.*

---

*   As early as 1934, Mussolini spoke of conquering North Africa. Davide Rodogno, *Fascism's European Empire: Italian Occupation During the Second World War*, trans. Adrian Belton (New York: Cambridge University Press, [2003] 2006), p. 47.

Scotti, an old man, living in one of those anonymous, high-rise apartment blocks in the former Yugoslav section of Rijeka that had not been part of old Fiume, is a living example of the power of memory to pass on vital facts and objective truths. In his own way, he is a *Fiumani:* that is, an ethnic-Italian who believes in a cosmopolitan sovereignty looser than that associated with the Italian state. He mentions to me the two-headed eagle that had just been put back atop the bell tower in downtown Rijeka. "It is a Habsburg emblem, not a Croat, Hungarian, or Italian one. It was taken down by the Fascists, and symbolizes the local freedom and autonomy that this city enjoyed under the Habsburgs." Rijeka in its heart, he suggests, has always been independent.

ONE NIGHT I HAVE dinner in the seaside village of Kantrida, a few minutes' drive to the west of Rijeka. With me are three local academics: Sanja Bojanić, who teaches philosophy; Vanni D'Alessio, a historian; and Vanni's wife, Sanja, an anthropologist. The restaurant is one of those simple, unpretentious affairs, reminding me of the Greek islands in the 1970s, less and less common these days, where under wooden beams we enjoy a glimpse of the grandeur of the Istrian coastline. We polish off grape brandy, *malvazija* (a local white wine here served in jars), and brill fish.

The discussion is about borders, and all agree that the twentieth century was a catastrophe. As Vanni explains, the coast just half a mile farther to the west came under the rule of Trieste, and here, where we sit, as well as part of Rijeka, was oriented towards Budapest. Rijeka itself was actually divided, and the other part of it was politically oriented to Zagreb. But despite all of these complex, cross-cutting tensions, the imperial system worked, since everyone was ultimately loyal to the Habsburg sovereign. Underneath the fraying tent of empire lay a host of subtle identities that the post–World War I peace arrangements obliterated with the creation of modern, more uniethnic, and sometimes nasty states. Yes, Rijeka (Fiume), like Trieste, should have been an independent urban republic, I will be told over and over again.

It is dark now and the Istrian coastline has disappeared except for the sprinkle of lights on the shore. This is the extremity of the Julian March, that narrow belt between the Alps in the north and the Istrian peninsula where up to 350,000 Italians, following World War II, were displaced from the Italy-Yugoslavia borderland as Tito reconsolidated the South Slav state. The University of Michigan academic Pamela Ballinger writes of the "nostalgia for a lost 'Italian' world" of Istria among both those Italians who left and those who remained here.[22] Again, I think of Marisa Madieri's *Aqua Green*. For the wounds between the Slovenes and Italians over the Slavs' ethnic cleansing of the latter in the Trieste-Istria region have reopened with the end of the Cold War. Debates over guilt and victimhood are no longer suppressed.[23] Everywhere in this historically contested, northeastern corner of the Adriatic there is this tension between the need for the *nation* and the need for *pluralism* at the same time: something that might actually be achieved with the help of the sea itself, "a promiscuous, middle, neutral territory, an open field to the commerce of all the Nations of this gulf," in the words of one of those cautious nationalists quoted by Dominique Reill.[24]

The dinner conversation quickly drifts to the problems of Bosnia, Kosovo, and Macedonia. Yugoslavia may be dead, but people talk as if it still existed, and as if Rijeka were still a part of it. Indeed, the next morning Natasha Sardzoska, a young visiting academic and translator who lives in the Macedonian capital of Skopje, tells me about her concept of "phantom borders," old frontiers that "still exercise a reality in people's minds," and which, by the way, have in some places come back with a vengeance, owing to the different reactions of local governments to the Arab refugee and migration crisis. I ask Natasha about the situation in Macedonia and she tells me about how Skopje was transformed into a pageant of expensive sculptures of Alexander the Great and related personages from

Macedonian antiquity. "The government wanted to combat the historic claims of Greece and Bulgaria on its territory, but the result is just kitschy, Disneyesque." Macedonia, she goes on, is very poor. People there hate *Europe* because "the Greeks keep Europe from recognizing us. Meanwhile the Turks are trying to take over the local economy." (In fact, a compromise was reached, with Macedonia changing its name to North Macedonia in order to satisfy the Greeks.)

My time in Rijeka constitutes a whirlwind of discussions about a panorama of topics related to local history, the former Yugoslavia, and existence itself. Here as in Slovenia are people who have experienced firsthand the collapse of Communism: they or their parents know what disintegration is about, and not only from textbooks.[25] The city is steeply hilled and hard to walk therefore, connected as it is by a series of serpentine staircases. The morning air is sharp and tangy, as if lignite were still being burned to heat the houses. The great Austro-Hungarian buildings are in every shade of yellow, bone, and gray. They form an amphitheater that opens out to the stage set of the harbor with its skyscraper-scale gantry cranes. It is a cityscape that deduces memories from the great and calamitous events of the past.

I cross the river from the former Italian Fiume—Rijeka's city center—to the part of the city that lies within the old Yugoslav kingdom, which existed between the two world wars. Despite the passage of a hundred years, there is still a difference in the two sides of town: the part of the city that used to be Fiume evokes a poorer Trieste, while the Yugoslav part evokes a vague, socialist sterility with its masses of apartment blocks.

Along with Sanja Bojanić, my host, I meet the vice rector of the local university, Snježana Prijić-Samaržija, in the rector's office over an espresso and pastries. As a traveler, you never quite know what you will end up discussing. I usually break the ice and then let the conversation go wherever it wants. It turns out that the two academics are deeply worried about the loss of truth and objectivity in the digital age. Since the Renaissance, there has been a search for facts and disciplined analytical thought that arrives at the correct answers to problems. Truth is a value in and of itself, obviously. Without it there is no science, and no resolution to things. But Sanja and Snježana define postmodernity, with its moral equivalencies and different, subjective narratives, as leading to the destruction of all that. Sanja calls it an "entropic" process. The academy, with its deconstructionism that dismantles ideas, experience, and memory itself, is not altogether innocent in this regard. This is certainly not a new idea, but it is one that ties intellectual elites in Europe together with their counterparts in the United States. We see each other as taking part in the same moral struggle, directed against the subversion of reasoned argument by populist emotion on both sides of the Atlantic. Thus, the fact that Sanja, Snježana, and I agree on so much is itself an indication of the divide that exists between us and many of our compatriots in our own countries.

I am now with young people and the better for it. The students I meet at the University of Rijeka are also worried about the same things as American analysts: for one thing, they are concerned about a weakening European Union, combined with a future possibly more nationalistic and politically unreliable Germany. One student, from Romania, who was in Britain at the time of the Brexit vote, says that the European Union is more than just an impersonal, bureaucratic organism. "Many of my friends cried after the results of the vote became known. It was truly a tragic experience for us." (A little bit like the collapse of the Habsburg Empire, I think.) That is a common elite viewpoint, to be sure, but yet another indication of how Central Europe and the Balkans were not distinct *others*. These regions were not really separated from each other and from America: rather, their elites were going in the same direction as elites everywhere.

The conversation with these students and academics continues the next day in Opatija and Volosko, old Habsburg resort towns to the west of Rijeka. Here is the generic Mediterranean of the travel

supplements, dead ringers for the Côte d'Azur, with fast cars, elec-
trifying blue water, a *lungomare* along which Franz-Josef once
walked, wedding-cake houses that dazzle with their light, cafés
adorned with wrought iron, and luxurious gardens in the early
spring of palms, pines, evergreen oaks, magnolias, and wisteria,
punctuated by dark cypresses that, just maybe, because they express
the beauty of a math theorem, brighten your state of mind. With
their boutiques and men in silk ties and expensive sports jackets,
Opatija and Volosko are places that scream good taste and whisper
money.

I think for a moment of Vladimir Nabokov, who stayed with
relatives here as a boy of five in 1904, when "Abbazia," as Opatija
was then known, evoked the fin-de-siècle, aristocratic world of the
Austrian Riviera soon to be extinguished by war. By far the most
refined and lapidary of the Russian literary giants, Nabokov fits
perfectly with Opatija. Nobody remembers his or her own childhood with the passionate exactitude of Nabokov. His was a height-
ened state of consciousness that embodies *memory* itself. There was
just so much joy and life force contained in his slightly withering
sneer.

The bora is blowing—the wind that they say is born in Senj to
the south of here, marries in Rijeka, and dies in Trieste. The students and I drift from a café to a restaurant, between long walks.
Eyeing the pageant of wealth by the sea, we talk about how Marx
was wrong about the primacy of economics. It is not all about economic self-interest. After all, says one of the graduate students, "the
rich vote for the Left in Europe, and the poor and lower-middle
class vote for the Right. Why? Because each section of society identifies culturally with these tendencies." Another student adds: "The
pseudo-communist Left is hip and radical chic, with its NGOs and
fashionable causes. That draws the wealthy and attractive people.
The poor, meanwhile, are attracted to the ethnic nationalism of the
Right." This is partly why, as someone else says, "Soros is now being
condemned by the populist Right in the former Communist coun-

tries. The NGO culture that Soros helped create unawares is seen, fairly or unfairly, as an elitist transplant." This leads to a discussion about the "snobbery" of academia, with its own class system of tenured professors and poor graduate school teachers, and the vicious, egotistical fights over the accuracy of footnotes and much else. The names of obscure academic texts fly back and forth, with arguments about their worth. I copy down the names of some to read and to judge for myself.

As we are discussing books, I bring up the name of Milovan Djilas, the great World War II partisan fighter who was once Tito's heir apparent, and later the original East European dissident, a man who wrote such classics of World War II and Cold War literature as *Wartime, Conversations with Stalin,* and *The New Class.* I interviewed Djilas every year in the 1980s in his Belgrade apartment behind the Parliament building. Through a clinical interpretation of history Djilas saw the vague outlines of the future, and specifically foresaw the war of the 1990s.

"Who is Djilas?" the students at the table exclaim, practically in unison. Though all are former Yugoslavs, these students and teachers have simply never heard of him. It turns out that the combination of censorship lasting into the 1990s, when they were young and in school—Djilas, after all, was a longtime dissident after he broke with Tito—and the constricting, often abstract, and theoretical reading lists of their university and graduate courses left no room for this great chronicler of an entire era in the second half of the twentieth century: an era that gave birth to the 1990s' wars of the Yugoslav succession. Books and manuscripts vastly proliferate nowadays, even as less is really read, and so much of what is vital does not get passed down from generation to generation.

There is an air of depression and consternation at the restaurant table. And it isn't just about the state of academia. Europe and especially the Balkans do not look hopeful. I am now told about how, among other things, Montenegro has become a colony of the Russian mafia and Albania the colony of the southern Italian mafia, accounting for the eruption of designer restaurants, bars, expensive hotels, and jewelry stores in Podgorica and Tirana. And there is, by now, the familiar litany about the poor and nasty ethnic climate in Bosnia, Serbia, Kosovo, and Macedonia. In this part of Europe at least, it seems that NATO is only a superficial layer of reality, and the European Union is simply out of gas and credibility.

I return to my hotel room, amid my books and notes, and consider that all cannot be so depressing. Linear thinking often leads down dark holes, but has a flaw in its logic. I don't believe there will be another war in the Balkans, because the war in the 1990s was structurally caused by the very messy process of Yugoslavia's dissolution and the consequent breakup of the Yugoslav army, with all of its weaponry. Yugoslavia has already broken up and, therefore, something else will happen: perhaps a redivision of Europe—not in cinematic and ideological terms with a new Berlin Wall, but something far more subtle and, yes, early modern. And considering what that future might be leads me to consider other writers and what they have to say.

"MODERNITY IS IN THE first place a project, a collective project formulated in Europe, implemented at first in Europe, but intended from the beginning for all of humanity," explains the French philosopher Pierre Manent. This helps explain the thinking of the French intellectual Julien Benda in the 1930s, who believed in a rational and abstract, de-nationalized Europe, which as the contemporary Dutch-American intellectual Ian Buruma points out, has proven unsatisfactory to the masses who want something more culturally tangible.

Europe, in other words, especially in the immediate aftermath of the Cold War, replaced its own cultural and civilizational ideal for that of humanity as a whole. And that has been a problem. Indeed, while European elites talk about universal rights, the citizens of European countries themselves want governments closer to their own ground-level emotions and concerns. And because the European Union super-state has proved inadequate to many, we may be back to what Manent, once again, calls the age-old political formulations of city, empire, and tribe or *ethnos*. To be sure, European cities continue to grow and become ever more vibrant forms of identity, expressing the triumph of civilization today just as they did for Borges's imaginary eighth-century Lombard warrior in Ravenna. Meanwhile, old European empires exist unofficially in the differing economic and social patterns they have bequeathed to the various parts of Europe, from the Carolingian Empire in core-Europe to the Habsburg Empire in Central Europe, to the Byzantine and Ottoman Empires in the less-developed Balkans. As for the tribe, it is represented by populist nationalism, perhaps the swan song of the modern state, given that hundreds of millions of people now live outside their own country of origin and more than a billion cross borders every year.[26]

To wit, Hegel calls the *nation* that which appropriates, in Manent's words, the "mediating function" of religion. For it was religious divisions, Manent writes, that "provided the most powerful and the most specific reason for the erection of the modern State."[27] But the same nationalism that replaced religion, and which once gave European states their lofty ambitions as well as liberal values (witness the 1848 uprisings), can be a fossilizing and even reactionary force: a reason for the momentary decline of centrist political parties in parts of Europe, which often seem spent of ideas. Of course, at the other extreme is cosmopolitanism, which runs the danger of putting too much emphasis on rationality and the "self-centered," egotistical individual.[28] This is why, according to Manent, the less institutionally secure nations of Central Europe are so viscerally opposed to such cosmopolitanism and postnational liberalism. Countries such as Poland, Hungary, and Slovenia simply could not have faced the same multicultural pressures as France with its millions of Muslims, for example, and yet still maintained social peace.

Oxford professor Jan Zielonka, however, says all is not gloomy, since a vibrant "neo-medievalism" may come to the rescue: a dynamic overlapping of identities and sovereignties—supranational, national, and local—as cities and regions vie with the European Union for a claim on people's loyalties. But unmistakably the Westphalian world of "concentration of power" and "clear-cut identity" is in decline.[29]

The European Union was built on the shoulder of this modern world of strong states willing to cede some of their sovereignty in order to end, once and for all, the bloody power politics that had given birth to two world wars. And because the United States represented the world of power and the awful choices that come with it, Europe, sheltered under an American security umbrella, for a long time believed itself morally superior to America while protected by it at the same time. Alas, the European Union has not worked out quite as expected, and this vision of paradise has been undermined by competing national interests inside the continent and new threats from outside it, often emanating from Russia and the Middle East.

Yet, hope and opportunity, as well as danger, may lie ahead. Europe may actually be in a situation akin to that of Adam and Eve in Milton's *Paradise Lost,* cast out of the Garden of Eden, yet as Milton writes, "The World was all before them."[30]

For by accepting struggle and the battle against fate, Adam and Eve become fully human. The Tree of Knowledge, from which they have tasted the forbidden fruit, allows them for the first time to know both good and evil; "if they had not eaten, they would have continued to know good alone" and thus be unable to value it, notes the twentieth-century Oxford don Maurice Bowra in an essay on Milton. Moreover, because of their disaster, Adam and Eve now learn "true modesty." Bowra explains that "Milton's solution to the Fall of Man is that out of it a new kind of goodness is born and that man can show heroic qualities by doing his duty in the face of great obstacles."[31] And because man was now subject to disease and death, labor and progress become for the first time possible.[32] Likewise, a Europe cast out of paradise—its elites and citizens both having discovered a new modesty—now has the opportunity to forge good out of a world beset with difficulties and outright evil. Insecurity builds character.

This new modesty or insecurity means falling back, to some extent, on the nation, that "deep, horizontal comradeship," in the words of the late Cornell scholar Benedict Anderson, something for which people have been willing to give their lives. Indeed, there are no tombs of unknown soldiers for Marxists or liberals, or for members of non-governmental organizations, as Anderson slyly notes, only for patriots, whose nations are forged out of primordial elements like language, religion, ethnicity, and culture.[33] Nationalism saves us from "personal oblivion," writes the late Anthony D. Smith of the London School of Economics, by giving individuals a destiny beyond themselves.[34] Therefore, going forward, neo-medievalism and early-modern-style cosmopolitanism will always require as their foundation the kind of building blocks of identity that non-elites in particular can feel instinctively in their bones, without the requirement of explaining or intellectualizing about it. Because the European Union has not as yet provided such a psychic, emotional bond, its power must therefore remain limited, and it will constitute only one layer of Europe's emerging political map.

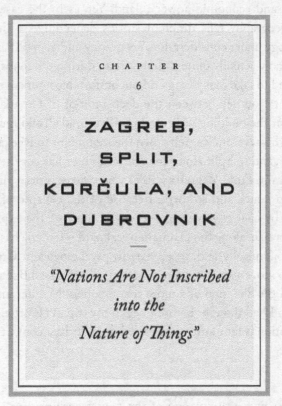

CHAPTER

6

ZAGREB,
SPLIT,
KORČULA, AND
DUBROVNIK

—

*"Nations Are Not Inscribed
into the
Nature of Things"*

The LATE CROATIAN HISTORIAN AND EMERITUS PROFESSOR at Yale Ivo Banac writes that the "nucleus" of medieval Croatia was the Adriatic seaboard, but the Venetian expansion south along the Adriatic, coupled with the Ottoman conquest of adjacent Bosnia, "occasioned the slow migration of Croat nobility toward the north and effected a lasting change in the political map of Croatia," distancing it from its Adriatic roots. With this, Zagreb, the nexus of old Slavonia, deep in the interior, emerged as the Croat capital.[1] The Federal Republic of Yugoslavia also had the effect of further pulling political and economic power inland. Yet, as in the case of Italy, where geography tells different stories depending on the age of technology under consideration, geography and geopolitics in Croatia are now actually quite different than during the 1990s war.

It used to take many long and uncomfortable hours in a bus, car, or train to journey between the deep interior of Croatia and the coast. But the building of several massive, graded, and multi-laned superhighways from Zagreb down the mountains to Rijeka, to Senj, to Zadar, and to Split along the Adriatic coast has cut the distance dramatically. From Zagreb to Rijeka now takes ninety minutes, to Senj two hours, and so forth. Because of the collapse of distance effected by civil engineering—to say nothing of the explosion of global tourism along the Dalmatian seaboard—Croatia has changed both economically and, to an extent, psychologically. Croatia has begun to move away from a more ethnically obsessed Balkan orientation in the direction of a more cosmopolitan Mediterranean one.

Or so I had thought before I began my trip. As is often the case, the situation is far more complicated upon further contact with the evidence.

FROM RIJEKA I TAKE one of the new superhighways inland, to Zagreb. It is nearly three decades since I was last at the Esplanade Hotel with its aura of fin-de-siècle Vienna. I vaguely recall from the 1980s, before the hotel was remodeled, a lobby of gold-framed mirrors, velvet curtains, and purplish carpets, with a dining hall resembling a cluttered art gallery: the universe of Freud, Klimt, and Kokoschka. The intent of the remodeling is to make the Esplanade more generically international. But the effect is mixed: the heavy browns, the dim brass and gold leaf, the white marble dripping in black veins all make for an intimate gloom: the signature of Central Europe not yet conquered by the edgy globalism of Austria and Germany.

Later on, after a rainfall, I leave the hotel and go for a walk. Zagreb means "behind the hill," the hill being the site of the upper town, which dominates the lower one. In the lower town are the Esplanade and the turn-of-the-twentieth-century neo-Renaissance, art nouveau, and Secession-style buildings and pavilions, separated by leafy expanses. High on the hill, staring down at the lower town, is the fortified Gothic Cathedral of Zagreb, a veritable Catholic mini-Kremlin, consecrated in the thirteenth century and restored at the end of the nineteenth. Just outside the cathedral, sometime in the mid-1980s, Monsignor Duro Kokša and Slavko Goldstein, both now deceased—and both of whom I knew back in those days— spent hours in a car late one night arguing about just how many thousands and tens of thousands and perhaps even hundreds of thousands of Serbs, Jews, and Romani were killed at the concentration camp of Jasenovac by the Croatian fascist Ustashe during World War II: the Catholic church official claimed much lower numbers than the Jewish community leader.[2]

The issue, as I would learn, has not gone away.

The first people I meet here are Nebojša Taraba and Ivana Ljubičić, a television producer and a philosophy student, who quickly inform me that "behind it all," the public conversation in Croatia is still psychologically dominated by the local Roman Catholic Church, trapped as it is in the 1980s within a debilitating reactionary worldview, as if it were still fighting the old Communist regime by an appeal to tribe and little else. It is an old story: a frontier church hard up against the borders of Eastern Orthodoxy and Islam, feeling too insecure to shed its prejudices against—as it now happens—Jews and Muslims.* I want to write about a new, global cosmopolitan and Mediterranean Croatia, to serve as a contrast to what I wrote about the country in *Balkan Ghosts*. But the people I meet in Zagreb will not wholly cooperate.

Like Ljubljana, Zagreb constitutes an exhausting feast of con-

---

* Croatia is actually the last Western Christian, Catholic country going east until one reaches the Philippines.

versation against a backdrop of global consumerism. In 1989, during
my last visit, the horrors of the 1940s still seemed close, as the Cold
War was a postscript to World War II; now, my initial hope is that
even the war of the 1990s will appear remote. For history, I tell myself, is less of a burden as wealth and technology obscure the past.
But that, it turns out, is exactly the problem: among the most populist and reactionary elements of the population are not the old people with long memories but the young ones, with little sense of the
past. And many of the young people who are, in fact, progressive
have been emigrating en masse for jobs and new lives abroad, leaving the reactionary ones behind. Alas, Croatia is, to some degree, an
extension of the conservative populist rejoinder to liberal politics
that is occurring in Hungary, Poland, and elsewhere: fueled by economic anxiety and the failure of the European Union to establish a
meaningful sense of identity and belonging.

Ivo Goldstein, the late Slavko Goldstein's son, is a historian, like
his father, as well as the former Croatian ambassador to France and
UNESCO. His father died only two months before we meet.
"When my father passed away," he tells me, "a priest on the island
of Hvar wrote on the Internet that he was so happy that an enemy
of the nation of Croatia was dead. As is often the case with the
Internet, the message spread." The government, so as not to offend
the Church and the populist right wing, sent only a single, very
low-level official to the funeral, even though the elder Goldstein
was a locally famous historian, a journalist and publisher, the president of the first non-Communist political party in Croatia, and a
pillar of the Jewish community.

I ask simply, "What is the problem with this place?"

The decades dissipate, and in Goldstein's careful, complex, and
hesitant answers—the mark of an academic who knows just how
complicated the truth can often be—I am suddenly reminded of his
father. "I am fifty-nine," he tells me, "but only in the last two or
three years have I become a pessimist. In 2009 [upon the worldwide
Great Recession], the economy contracted by nine percent or some-

thing like that. It will take us some time to return to where we were then. But that is a side issue," he says with a frustrated shrug that indicates more factors than he is able to articulate at the moment. "When we were admitted to the European Union in 2013, they [the EU officials] told us in so many ways, without actually spelling it out, that we had homework to do: that because we were a big and sprawling country, because we were war-ravaged, and therefore a regional fulcrum, our success was key to the entire future of Central-Eastern Europe. So what was that homework which went unspoken? At the heart of it all was that we had to be more inclusive, like all successful Western democracies, especially those with relatively small populations like ours: like Holland, for instance." The degree to which minorities felt welcomed would in the end define Croatia, a country of four million, he explains.

"But what is happening instead?" he continues. "Revisionism is flourishing, helped by the same revisionism on the Serb side, with reactionaries in both countries feeding off each other, usually arguing over the Internet," which provides an inter-communal ecosystem in basically the same language. The Internet, in the worst sort of way, is the last remnant of Yugoslavia, I am told. Thus, the debate his father had with Monsignor Kokša in the car that night over three decades ago "still goes on."

"I had once thought that with the death of the perpetrators and the victims of the Ustashe crimes at Jasenovac this issue would be settled by dispassionate research. I was naive. I now know we in Croatia find it hard to normalize."

"The long process of joining the EU was better than membership itself," Vesna Pusić, a former Croatian foreign minister, tells me. "The process forced us to aspire to liberal democratic values. But once we were admitted to the EU we put membership in our pocket, so to speak, and reverted to our old ways." It didn't help that by the time Croatia got accepted into the EU in 2013 "the EU itself was tired and troubled, with idealists like [Vaclav] Havel and [Adam] Michnik no longer the brand names of an emerging unified continent. Political development requires ideals, not just realism," she emphasizes.

At the local level, "the problem is that Croatia is the only country in the former Yugoslav Federation that was both a victim and victor in the 1990s war," explains Dejan Jović, a colleague of Goldstein's at the University of Zagreb and the head of the International Relations Department there. "Yes, I know, Slovenia was also a victim of Serbian aggression, but Slovenia was only at war for a short time and had few casualties. We in Croatia, on the other hand, had many casualties and much destruction, but we also won in the end. So if you believe that you are both victim and victor the result is that you become full of yourself—you become nasty. The world," Jović continues, "is supposed to feel sorry for you while at the same time you feel dominant. We have had no truth and reconciliation commission. We are still anti-Serb."

Ethnic cleansing has helped this sad development, with only 7.5 percent of the Croatian population listed as minorities, as opposed to 22 percent before the war. "Communism," Jović says, "is now seen as equally reprehensible as fascism. But how can you compare the genocidal Ustashe regime with Tito's relatively restrained version of Communism?" Jović, because of his mild face and commonsensical demeanor, is all the more devastating in his analysis. "Because national identity in Croatia is still built around the 1990s war, the populist right wing has the advantage. War itself has not been delegitimized here the way it was in Western Europe after World War II."

It ultimately has to do, he explains, with the failure of Tito's Yugoslavia to ever develop a *demos*, which Jović translates as a "meaningful sense of citizenship." Yugoslavia, "like the EU in a way, for decades meant little except an impersonal bureacracy."

Could it all have been different?

Ivo Goldstein suggests that rather than a great ideal or a great horror, originally the very idea of Yugoslavia merely offered a practical solution to the Slavic western Balkans at the time of the collapse of the Habsburg and Ottoman Empires following World War I. But interwar Yugoslavia with its Serbian kingship—and prime ministers who were generally Serb—proved unfair to the Croats and others. Of course, after World War II, Tito diminished the role of the Serbs, but because he did so in an authoritarian manner, as Jović says, no real *demos* ever emerged.

Ivana, the young philosophy student who is my guide, interjects with passion: "It is in fashion at my university nowadays to be pro-Tito, since the very word 'Yugoslav,' after so much war and ethnic cleansing, means simply to be a global cosmopolitan."

"TITO WAS AS BAD as Stalin," says Željko Tanjić, rector of the Catholic University here. "The problem of Western elites—the very same people who as university students manned the leftist barricades in 1968—is that they see the Fascists in World War II as absolutely evil, without contextualization. But they have all these contextualizations, rationalizations, justifications, and explanations for Tito. To Western elites, Communism was a good idea that just happened to go wrong. Meanwhile, Tito to them appears especially liberal compared to the other Communist leaders because he was independent of the Soviet Union," Father Tanjić says, full of animation and excitement. "But Communism under Tito was still Communism. It still eliminated elites. Tito killed hundreds of priests and nuns. And Tito killed historical memory with his decades of repression, so that all these questions and all the problems of Communism continue unresolved in the former Yugoslavia—here in Croatia."

Father Tanjić is exceedingly warm, with a friendly expression, sitting in a well-lit office with modern decor, his iPhone at the ready. Yet his positions on the concentration camp of Jasenovac, and on the controversial role of wartime Croatian Cardinal Alojzije Stepinac—a fascist collaborator in the view of the Serbs; a cleric who may have done too little, too late to help the victims of fascism, in the view of objective observers; and yet a martyr to the Croats—

are the same positions as I heard three decades before in the last days of Yugoslavia from the austere and forbidding Monsignor Kokša in his office near the Cathedral. Like Kokša, Tanjić defends Stepinac and questions the statistics regarding the concentration camp of Jasenovac. Jasenovac was a tragedy, but was Tito much better? he seems to suggest.

In crucial ways, Croatia remains unchanged: trapped in the issues surrounding national identity and war guilt that drain political energy and thus impede social and economic development.

THE HANDSOME, VAGUELY CHARISMATIC former center-left Croatian prime minister Zoran Milanović overflows with random knowledge about all the books he has read. Milanović, who would be elected Croatia's president in 2020, tries hard to communicate complexity. He is intense and pedantic, a bit unusual for a politician. "It is important to realize," he begins, "that we have not gone as far to the right as Poland and Hungary. Those governments convey the sheer desire to overwhelm institutions—the media, the courts—with a winner-take-all mentality. That has not happened here. We have only been flirting with the basest feelings of the electorate." Croatia, he continues, does have certain advantages, at least historically and geographically. "Remember, Croatia is the only Slavic polity in the world that is decisively maritime." Poland and Bulgaria may have coastlines, but the sea does not define what they are. "Whereas Venice, without really colonizing us, opened us up to the world much more than any imperial power elsewhere in Europe." Croatia's potential is therefore still untapped, he implies.

More accurately, Croatia, the academic historian Tvrtko Jakovina tells me, "is a country of distinct regions, that never functioned as a united entity under the Austro-Hungarian monarchy." The sea is only one, albeit a major, element in the Croatian historical experience. Because of this problematic identity—because of this very geographical unwieldiness—"there is a degree of insecurity here which expresses itself in right-wing, populist politics," Jakovina explains.

I console myself with the hope that these conversations are period pieces only. The situation is bound to evolve, perhaps by the time the reader encounters these words on the page.

I DRIVE BACK DOWN the highway from Zagreb to the coast. The great, mustard-colored Habsburg piles of the capital quickly recede and I pass down through long tunnels cut into the mountains, and then into forests mantled with fresh snow where the last leaves of autumn bear the dull gold hue of Byzantine icons. Dizzying switchbacks bring me out of the snow and into another Croatia. The Adriatic at Senj, where the northern wind originates, is a cruel steely blue. The wind is so strong that the sea, solid with foam from a distance, looks like frost on a darkened window. On the other side is the island of Krk, looking as bleak as Mongolia. This wind is simply extraordinary, rising and crashing wave-like against bare trees and banging shutters. The bora devastates the landscape. Bad weather here means wind, not rain, a local who rents me a room says. All the hotels are closed. Nobody is in the street and most of the houses are empty for the season.

I find an open bar by the sea with loud pop music and cigarette fumes that offers grilled meat and a bottle of cheap local wine. From my table I see the ocean spray lifting above the few parked cars. There is a small grocery open where I buy bread and cheese for breakfast. I carry with me a collection of poems by Lawrence Durrell. I have all I need for the moment to be happy. Emails are blessedly few.

Eyeing the water through the window in the bar, I reflect on the conversation I had the other day with the former foreign minister Vesna Pusić about Croatia's Adriatic future. She was a candidate for the job of United Nations secretary-general and has a very sophisticated global perspective.

There is the challenge of Africa, she told me. With Africa's population set to climb over the course of the century from 1.1 billion to perhaps 3 or 4 billion, migration will be a permanent issue for a country like Croatia with a Mediterranean coastline and a negative birthrate: yet Croatia is a country that has no experience as a multiracial society.

"Then there is the era of natural gas awaiting us," she went on. For there is much talk about building facilities for liquefied natural gas on the island of Krk near Senj and Rijeka, in order to import gas from—who knows—the Persian Gulf, Israel, or even the United States. It looks like natural gas might also be found in significant quantities in the seabed off Istria itself, which then could be exported by new pipelines north to Hungary, Poland, and Ukraine even, making all these countries less dependent on Russia for energy. Also, there is the Trans-Adriatic Pipeline to consider, which could transport hydrocarbons from energy-rich Azerbaijan through Turkey, Greece, and Albania, and under the sea to Italy, with a spur line going north from Albania through Montenegro to Croatia. Russia fears that such pipelines would lessen dependence on its own energy reserves, and thus is quietly helping friendly, far-right political parties in Croatia and elsewhere, she explained.

"Finally, there are the war refugees principally from Syria." Though they only passed through Croatia without staying, the very influx of several hundred thousand people in 2015 and 2016 "made us suddenly aware how much geography is shrinking. The Middle East is closer than we ever thought, and because of gas and pipeline politics, so is Ukraine." Croatia, thus, is a gateway to Eurasia, even as, Pusić hopes, it will also be more of an Adriatic country—connected to Central Europe via pipelines with their seaboard gas terminals, allowing Croatia in at least one respect "to escape the Balkans."

The sight of the Adriatic, with its openness to the world—however grim it appears on this day—communicates all of this. In Senj I feel for the first time that I have left the Italianate region of greater Trieste, encompassing Istria and the Gulf of Kvarner by Fiume-Rijeka, even as the Venetian Empire now really enters the picture again.

The wind groans on and on. I think about the barrenness of the coast just south of here: partially attributed to the Venetians who, during their long occupation, cut down oaks, pines, and beeches for their shipyards.[3] I look at the hills and think of the Spanish philosopher José Ortega y Gasset, who once said: "The past is the only arsenal where we can find the means of making our future real."[4] There is nothing but the past, especially when it is relitigated. But because the past demonstrates never-ending metamorphosis, I know that the future must be open to many possibilities. So much has happened along this dramatically shattered shore, as I will now try to explain.

Dalmatia, "land of mountains," is the name used for the Adriatic coast of what is now Croatia. It is also the name of a group of tribes, the Delmatae, which declared independence from the rest of Illyria (perhaps the ancestor of modern-day Albania) and organized itself here. In the late fourth century B.C., the establishment of Greek colonies in the vicinity led to Roman incursions. But it was only after its conquest of Syracuse in 212 B.C. that Rome turned its attention in earnest to the Adriatic's eastern shore, this time to counter pirates and Macedonian kings who had aligned themselves with Carthage. Two centuries of warfare followed, as Rome tried to subjugate the Delmatae and other Illyrians along this shoreline. Finally, in A.D. 9, after another Illyrian revolt, a fed-up Emperor Tiberius abruptly concluded an armistice in Bohemia, and along with his nephew Germanicus he traveled south to crush this uprising. "From that year," writes the historian Giuseppe Praga, "Dalmatia settled down submissively in the shadow of the Roman eagles."[5]

Following the downfall of Rome in the West in A.D. 476 and rule by the Ostrogoths, Justinian annexed Dalmatia to the Byzantine Empire in the early sixth century, so that Dalmatia was now governed from Constantinople. But Constantinople was far away and

Dalmatia continued to be influenced by the Latin language and its close ties to Italian cities such as Ravenna. The Slavs arrived here en masse from points farther east in the seventh century. With the help of the Byzantine emperor Heraclius (A.D. 610–641), the Slavs managed to drive the Huns and Avars out, and in exchange for Heraclius's help, thereafter adopted Christianity.

The Venetian Empire, unknown yet even to itself, was born in these waters with an anti-pirate expedition down the coast in A.D. 1000, even as the medieval kingdom of Slavic Croatia in the interior was extending its rule to this seaboard. In the twelfth century, the kings of Hungary assumed the Croatian crown, and began a protracted fight with Venice for domination here, a contest Venice would win by the early fifteenth century, inaugurating hundreds of years of rule by *La Serenissima* ("The Most Serene" Republic). Whereas the Hungarians had seen the conquest of Dalmatia as an end in itself, completing the extension of their state to the warm waters of the Mediterranean, the Venetians needed some of these Dalmatian outposts to secure sea lanes for their possessions in Crete and Cyprus. Undermining the Hungarian effort in Dalmatia was the Ottoman advance toward the Danube and Bosnia, so that Hungary perforce could no longer focus as intently on Dalmatia as it once did.

Until 1635, Venice, too, struggled against the Ottoman Empire, with Ottoman agents and outposts literally hovering in the mountains close by. Of course, it was under Napoleon that Venice ceased its existence, and after a brief French interlude, which constituted a period of hope and expectation, Dalmatia was ruled indifferently at best by the Habsburgs from Vienna until World War I. At Versailles, Dalmatia was divided between Italy and the new Yugoslav kingdom of the Serbs, Croats, and Slovenes. During World War II, Mussolini took much of Dalmatia, which after the war passed back to Tito's federation under the guise of the Yugoslav Republic of Croatia. With the 1990s wars of the Yugoslav succession, Dalmatia became part of an independent Croatia.

So many transformations!

I glance up again at the mountains and think of the Mongols who had come through them, all the way down to this coast in 1241–1242. It was only the death of Ogodei, the Great Khan, and the power struggle that would ensue to choose his successor, that caused the Mongols to head home to Central Asia, so that in Oxford historian Peter Frankopan's words, they "took their foot off the throat of Christian Europe."[6]

It was as though this squiggly and picture-perfect seaboard represented literally the end of Europe, with Asia beginning right there in the mountainous Balkan interior, just within eyesight: mountains of which the French historian Fernand Braudel, considering their history, writes: "One could hardly imagine a region more primitive, more patriarchal and, whatever the charms of its civilization, in fact more backward."[7] Allowing for Braudel's overstatement, allowing for the immense possibilities and mutations throughout history, and allowing for my own experience of travel over the past few decades, one of subtle gradations rather than of stark contrasts— nevertheless, the coast of Dalmatia, like the city of Trieste itself, does in fact represent a fault line of sorts. Along it you are in the warm and cosmopolitan embrace of the Mediterranean; leaving it to journey upward into the mountains, you enter a somewhat colder, more insular environment, one far more influenced historically by the Austrians, and farther south by the Ottomans and the Near East.

Indeed, Venice in the eighteenth century saw Dalmatia as "balanced between civilization and barbarism," and hence in need of a "civilizing" mission. Thus was born a Venetian version of Edward Said's Orientalism, undertaken in order to clarify Venice's own standing in the West, given how *La Serenissima* itself was imbued by its association with eastern Byzantium. Venice would henceforth define itself in opposition to Dalmatia, and attempt half-heartedly to save it at the same time, writes Larry Wolff, a professor of history at New York University, in *Venice and the Slavs: The Discovery of Dal-*

matia in the Age of Enlightenment.[8] Eighteenth-century Venetian Orientalism is the focus of Wolff's densely detailed academic study, a subject that might seem obscure from afar, but which acquires striking immediacy once you are here. As I get older, travel increasingly awakens in me a fascination with such academic books: books that reward complexity rather than simple answers.

The human summation of the *otherness* of this coastal hinterland, the people who were the very "exemplary" of "primitive Slavdom" in Venetian eyes, were the Morlacchi, a people who, as Wolff explains, "were not truly Slavs at all, but Slavicized Vlachs, the herdsmen of the Balkans, of Latin or Illyrian or even Asiatic Turanian descent." The Venetians considered these mainly Eastern Orthodox herdsmen "ferocious" and "barbarous." They were compared to the Laestrygones, the tribe of giant cannibals who nearly ate Odysseus. The Venetians had, in fact, artificially constructed an entire identity, however vague, for a group of people "whose name," as Wolff reminds us, "has now been completely forgotten." The Morlacchi survive as an Italian family name and as H. G. Wells's apelike Morlocks in his 1895 work, *The Time Machine.**

Ernest Gellner, the great twentieth-century British-Czech philosopher, observes that "nations are not inscribed into the nature of things," so that modern nationalism comes from the "crystallization of new units" derived from previously "overlapping, intertwined" cultures.[9] Thus, the loosely defined early modern categories that allowed for the invention of the Morlacchi in the first place would later give way to stricter modern groupings in which, along with others, the Morlacchi became Serbs and Croats. Yet, simply because identities are so often artificially constructed does not mean that they do not have a psychological reality all their own in which people believe deeply in them and consequently are capable of going to

---

* It was the late-eighteenth-century Venetian traveler the abbé Alberto Fortis, Paduan by birth, who first wrote in detail about the Morlacchi. Larry Wolff, *Venice and the Slavs: The Discovery of Dalmatia in the Age of Enlightenment* (Stanford, CA: Stanford University Press, 2001), pp. 2, 13, 128, 129, 134, 267, and 348.

war over them. We might assume that in coming decades and centuries there will be further reinventions of how people communally define themselves, not only here but elsewhere. For the populist nationalism that we see now in the West may be but a swan song for the ultimate decline of nations themselves.

The best argument for this approach that I have found is in John V. A. Fine Jr.'s *When Ethnicity Did Not Matter in the Balkans: A Study of Identity in Pre-Nationalist Croatia, Dalmatia, and Slavonia in the Medieval and Early-Modern Periods.* Fine, a lifelong expert on Byzantium and the Balkans, and a professor at the University of Michigan, demonstrates that until modern times in the western Balkans, "the labels denoting peoples change[d] frequently": that "identity" was "a matter of choice," and people were "not inherently ethnically anything." In the Middle Ages, to be a Croat was a geographical designation only, he notes. As for Dalmatians, "they habitually referred to themselves by their city's name, thus basing identity upon citizenship."[10] Given that this mutability of identity occurred during ages of comparatively little technological change, long before the onslaught of postmodern globalization, just imagine the possibilities for the reinvention of identities at a time of technological tumult like now!

Indeed, a mistake I made as a younger writer in the Balkans was to accept as fixed and permanent such ultimately ephemeral identities. I was a reporter and travel writer who recorded what people told me. That gave me an insight—one which proved to be vaguely correct—as to where the region was headed at the time in terms of war and peace. But I lacked a deeper awareness about how identity was more about ideology than blood. Only in recent decades could I properly appreciate an observation like this one from Ivo Banac:

> It is characteristic of the South Slavs that the civilizations that separated them were not always territorially constituted. Folk costumes could incorporate elements of Levantine and Occidental urban dress; a Glagolitic mass could be heard in

one church and the Orthodox liturgy of a slightly different Church Slavonic recension in another. Still farther to the east, oddly, one could attend a Latin mass in a rural church and hear the muezzin's call from a nearby minaret.[11]

In that same spirit, consider that while Yugoslavia was seen in the 1990s as a straitjacket from which its various nationalities wanted to escape—so that each group could literally get away from the other one—a hundred years earlier, the very concept of Yugoslavia was synonymous with freedom and idealism themselves, a mechanism for the South Slavs to move beyond the imperial prisons of the Habsburgs and Ottomans. And this brings me to an urgent World War I–era book, *Dalmatia and the Jugoslav Movement* by Count Louis Voinovitch.* Count Voinovitch, from an old Ragusan family, sees the dream of a united Yugoslavia emerging from the singular civilizational mix of his own Dubrovnik and Dalmatia at large. His starting point for this dream is the historic need for the South Slavs to escape from Venetian imperialism. As he writes:

> It is quite true that the Venetian Government did not inflict upon Dalmatia the scourge of feudalism. It is quite true that it did not allow the Turks to install themselves on that Slavonic coast, lit up by the Latin smile. It is quite true that the memory of common struggles for the defense of civilization and of *Te Deums* at St. Mark's kindled feelings of pride among the Dalmatian families. But this foreign Government did nothing for Dalmatia: it brought neither schools nor hospitals nor roads. . . . The fairy beauty of Venice, her military glory and the fame of her art . . . could not console the Dalmatian people for their ruined life; and hence they remained fiercely Slav.[12]

---

*   The preface is by Sir Arthur Evans, the great archaeologist who at the turn of the twentieth century excavated the palace of Knossos on Crete.

The book proceeds in this rousing manner, combining the grace of an aristocrat with the argumentation of an intellectual. Venetian imperialism, at least in Voinovitch's telling, was not at all of the civilizing variety. There was no higher purpose, or question of imposing Venetian language and culture. Venice's Orientalism, in his view, was limited to defining itself in opposition to an imagined *other* (the Morlacchi, for example). The Serene Republic in five centuries never demanded anything unconnected to urgent military necessity. Venice "never considered Dalmatia as her own territory, as a continuation of her soul, but always as a military colony. . . . She was superbly indifferent," writes Voinovitch, since it wasn't so much Dalmatia that Venice required but the "waterway of the Adriatic itself" to the Levant.[13]

Yet the Italian nationalist historian Praga counters that whatever the limitations of Venetian rule, the very presence of Italy led to "the dissemination of liberal ideas," while some degree of Venetian-Slavic solidarity existed as a counter to Islam and later to the absolutism of the Habsburg Empire.[14]

Of course, what united the South Slavs at the end of the early modern era was not only the desire to escape from the Venetian hold on the Adriatic coast, but the combined legacies of Habsburg and Ottoman imperialism in the interior. While the spirit of the 1848 revolutions across Europe brought Bosnians, Serbs, and Croats together, they also felt themselves a Slavic civilization apart from everyone else in Europe: they were a people that, for example, had little sympathy for the struggle (in their eyes, at least) of a so-called liberal Hungary against a despotic House of Austria, since Hungary had also oppressed them in the past. This made the continent-wide awakening of 1848 problematic in the Balkans. Voinovitch chronicles the formal reconciliation of Serbs and Croats in 1903, a process hailed with particular passion in Dalmatia. To Voinovitch, writing from the vantage point of 1917, the Serbs and the Croats remain essentially united by "the cult of the common language." The fact that the Serbs are Eastern Orthodox and the Croats

Roman Catholic is explainable by their geographical circumstance: at the meeting place of the Greek East and the Latin West, which goes back to the division of Rome and Byzantium and runs through the heart of Yugoslavia. But Voinovitch does not see this as an impediment to unity at all, as he celebrates the liberal nationalist spirit of the age, embodied in the long process toward a South Slav union. (Indeed, the heroes of the nineteenth century's enlightened liberalism brought together both sides of the Adriatic: Cavour, the giant of the Italian Risorgimento, and Josip Strossmayer, the great Croat bishop who championed South Slav reconciliation.)[15]

Alas, the World War I disintegration of the Habsburg and Ottoman Empires gave the Serbs and Croats no great power to unite against any longer. And as the modern age took hold, with its subtle and not-so-subtle reformulations of communal identities, Serb and Croat tensions grew, to culminate in the fascist Ustashe regime in Croatia committing mass murder against Serbs and others during World War II. Yugoslavia was reborn only under Tito's Communist dictatorship, and in the aftermath of the fall of the Berlin Wall it disintegrated into civil war between Serbs and Croats in the 1990s. Yet, as postmodernism with its eclectic identities—similar in some respects to those of the early modern age—takes hold, might the South Slavs find some way towards reconciliation, all living under the umbrella of a NATO and European Union that might still—however much they struggle—manage to exist? It is precisely the march of such unpredictable change that still gives me hope for Count Voinovitch's proposition of ethnic healing.

NOW I MUST RETURN to the question of Croatia itself, a state that literally rose from the ashes of a war-torn Yugoslavia in the mid-1990s—its landscape then an interminable wasteland of burnt-out houses and ruined churches—to achieve real independence for the first time in roughly a millennium. Such violence has been the wages of Croatia being a borderland between Central Europe and the Balkans, between the Mediterranean and an inward-looking interior, and between the Latin West and the Byzantine Orthodox East. "The very shape of the country reinforces the impression of a frontier," writes British journalist and historian Marcus Tanner. "Nothing compact, square or secure. Instead the country curves round Bosnia in a narrow arc, in the shape of a crescent moon, or a boomerang." And "because," as he goes on, Croatians "inhabit the rim, or the ramparts, never the middle"—historically sandwiched between Hungary, the Habsburgs, the Ottomans, and Venice— they have never been relaxed about their identity: Croatians are historically a fighting Catholic people in front of a Muslim and Orthodox host.

Now comes another incarnation. Rather than a country politically and psychologically entrenched in its interior that also had a coast, the "center of gravity," as Tanner reports, has been shifting in recent years from the interior to the Adriatic seaboard, thanks to mass tourism. This country of just over 4 million draws 15 million tourists mainly to Dalmatia each summer. New trains, in addition to the highways I've already mentioned, have cut the distance from the capital of Zagreb in the interior to the Adriatic in half. And because the country's geography has symbolically shifted toward the coast, so, too, has its identity, at least somewhat.* Croatia, born in a sense on the Adriatic, may finally begin to return here, despite the depressing politics in Zagreb.

WHAT ABOUT SENJ, WHERE I am now? Senj, once part of the sprawling medieval Orthodox Patriarchate of Peć, headquartered far away to the southeast in Kosovo,[16] actually recalls the sixteenth-

---

* Marcus Tanner, *Croatia: A Nation Forged in War* (New Haven, CT: Yale University Press, [1997] 2010), pp. x–xi, 8, 36, 300–301, and 318–19. Nor is there anything artificial in Croatia's renewed seaborne identity. For example, there is Nin, farther down the coast near Zadar, lapped by the waters of the Mediterranean, which was a center of Slav resistance to Rome and an ecclesiastical capital of the nascent Croatian state in the tenth century.

century Uskoks, Christian refugees from the eastern side of the mountains, deep in the interior, who had fought and escaped from the Turks and made Senj a base.* "The Uskoks were indisputably ghastly," writes the British traveler Jan Morris. "They were epic villains." She describes their leader, one Ivo, who "was supposed to have routed 30,000 Turks with a handful of comrades and to have come home from another battle holding his own severed left hand in his right."[17] Wearing long hair and mustaches, with iron rings in their ears, the Uskoks were said to nail the turbans of Turkish prisoners to their heads. The Uskoks were part of a piratical and semi-criminal underclass that must have made Senj a robbers' den of a place.

The Uskoks were "not animals invented by Edward Lear. They were refugees . . . like the Jews and Roman Catholics and liberals driven out by Hitler," argues Rebecca West in a distinctly more sympathetic and understanding voice, writing during World War II. The Uskoks "found, as these have done, that when one door closed on them others that should have been opened suddenly were not." These poor Slavs were driven out of their villages, "out of the fellowship of Christendom," sold out by a pact between Venice and the Ottoman Empire, and consequently had no choice but to take up a life of iniquity. Pirates they may have been, but their ability to reconstitute themselves as a naval power—having arrived on the coast from the mountains completely destitute—"showed signs of genius," West maintains. But the situation was complicated, for the Uskoks also acted as raiders in the interior, which they did not completely desert, and their actions against the Ottoman Empire benefited the Habsburgs, even as the Habsburgs worked with Venice to suppress Uskok piracy along the coast, in order to prevent a permanent Ottoman naval deployment in the area.[18]

The Uskoks were brutal partly by reasons of circumstance. And the overriding circumstance was the realpolitik of Venice that allowed *La Serenissima* to appease the Ottoman sultanate as often as

---

* The name may come from the Serbo-Croat *uskociti*, meaning "to jump."

it countered it. This realpolitik, in which relative European order and the safety of trade routes constituted the highest ideal, was a good thing in general, as it allowed amoral geopolitics to assuage a clash of religions and civilizations. But it sold out the minority Christians of the Balkan interior adjacent to the Adriatic. It was a typical case of one good triumphing over another good that causes suffering (the essence of ancient Greek tragedy, according to Hegel),[19] with violence and some disorder in its wake. Because of the world's infernal complexity, international relations are never clean. That, at least, is one lesson of the Uskoks, whose actions were the upshot of imperial politics played between the Venetians, Ottomans, and Habsburgs. There is a vague echo of the Uskoks in the situations of the Kurds, Afghans, and Vietnamese in the second half of the twentieth century, victims of imperial-style superpower politics, who were alternately supported and sold out.

NEAR SENJ, I ALSO cannot forget, is the island of Goli Otok, where Tito established a gulag that for decades served as a prison and torture facility for political opponents. These included Stalinists (after the break with the Soviet Union in 1948), and Italian communists who had moved to Yugoslavia in order to build socialism following World War II and ended up as suspects of the regime. Goli Otok symbolizes how keeping the communal peace in Yugoslavia prior to 1991 went hand in hand with a chilling and unnecessary brutality: a theme of Father Tanjić's remarks to me in Zagreb. Since the collapse of empires in 1918, no political solution for the South Slavs of the western Balkans has ever really worked.

ALONE IN SENJ, WITH the bus service canceled because of the bora and freezing rain, I pass the hours writing in my diary. Deafened by the unrelenting and isolating sound of the wind, my thoughts cannot help but turn inward.

Knowing the future is easy, I tell myself, if only we are willing to see the present. Sometimes the most dangerous thing a writer can do is to describe what he sees in front of his face, since the very ideals and assumptions that many of us live by are dependent upon maintaining a comfortable distance from the evidence. For example, the world is simple in a place like Washington, where big abstract ideas about democracy obscure complex facts on the ground thousands of miles away. Thus, I have always believed that journalism is invigorated by a return to *terrain,* to the kind of firsthand, solitary discovery of a place best associated with old-fashioned travel writing. Travel writing has always meant much more to me than what appears in the Sunday supplements: rather, it can be a deft vehicle for rescuing geography and geopolitics from the jargon and obscurantism of academia at its worst. I recall Winston Churchill's *The River War* (1899) and T. E. Lawrence's *Seven Pillars of Wisdom* (1926), which employ the experience of travel to explore geography, warfare, and statecraft in late-nineteenth-century Sudan and early-twentieth-century Arabia. Owen Lattimore's *The Desert Road to Turkestan* (1929), another book that comes to mind, is about both the organization of camel caravans and Russian and Chinese imperial ambitions. Freya Stark's *The Southern Gates of Arabia* (1936) is as good a depiction of Osama bin Laden's tribal homeland of eastern Yemen as any you'll find today. Freya Stark, as I have written elsewhere, describes still-surviving caravan routes that obliterate borders, and Yemeni merchants who, "after a life of money-making, retire to an old age of guerrilla warfare in their valley." She is skeptical about whether the human race yearns for peace as much as it claims to do. She knows this uncomfortable truth in the way that good reporters know things. These reporters slip away from the pack in order to cultivate loneliness; they demand of themselves not to write a word about a place or a subject until they know it firsthand. And they will do this out of curiosity, for as the illusion of knowledge grows daily in this digital age, the reality of places themselves becomes more of a mystery.[20]

I cherish my early life as a traveler and reporter, when I went to places that are much harder to get to today: Syria, Yemen, Afghanistan, Pakistan's Northwest Frontier, and so on. These places were not as yet war zones when I was there. You could travel around nearly every part of these countries by bus, as I did, without a gun or bodyguard. Because of the danger now associated with these places, my experiences are encased in a special chamber of memory, as if they had happened not just decades but ages ago. And yet there are moments so vivid I can touch them almost.

I was following a wayward path, with little or nothing to show for it for long stretches—little that you could put on a résumé. Because I was young and the future seemed endless, I preferred not to arrive anywhere, except for brief stops. I had no plans except to travel for months and even years on end, accumulating nothing except what I could carry. It was an altogether linear existence, and therefore superficial. Yet, the things I saw proved useful, even if it took years of sedentary reading and reflection for me to properly interpret them.

You could say that my early life was defined by three one-way plane tickets. Bored with a job on a small newspaper in Vermont and unable to land a job on a bigger newspaper anywhere, in 1975 I bought a one-way ticket to Europe with a few thousand dollars saved up. From Europe, I went south by ferryboat to Tunisia with a companion, and from there drifted to Sicily, Egypt, Syria, and Jordan, before ending up in Israel almost a year later. I tried life in Israel for a few years, served a year in the military, and, approaching thirty, realized that I had no professional prospects, even as I had the screaming urge to travel again. I just felt there was more to life—much more—than my own ethnicity as a Jew.

In Israel I began to feel that I couldn't breathe, it was emphatically that claustrophobic: not just in a geographical sense, with enemies all around its borders, but in an intellectual sense, too, with Jewish security the issue around which every other issue revolved. So in 1981, I bought a second one-way plane ticket, this time from

Israel to Romania, a jumping-off point from where I spent many weeks traveling throughout the Balkans and Central Europe writing newspaper articles.[21] I then returned to the United States and proceeded to get all those articles published, but still could not land a good job in journalism anywhere. I was a thirty-year-old with little work experience and a degree from a middle-of-the-pack college: nobody wanted me.

So I bought a third one-way ticket. This time to Greece: a country that was in 1982 both lovely and cheap to live in, and which was close to both the Balkans and to the hot spots of the Arab world and beyond. In Greece I got married, became a father, began making a respectable living as a freelance foreign correspondent, and wrote my first two books: on the Horn of Africa and Afghanistan. From Greece my young family drifted to Portugal, where I wrote a third book, *Balkan Ghosts*, excerpted in *The Atlantic* four months before the Berlin Wall fell. The excerpt ended with this conclusion: "In the 1970s and 1980s the world witnessed the limits of superpower influence in places like Vietnam and Afghanistan. In the 1990s those limits may well become visible in a Third World region within Europe itself. The Balkans could shape the end of the century, just as they did the beginning."[22] Then, on November 30, 1989, less than three weeks after the Berlin Wall fell, I wrote in *The Wall Street Journal:* "Two concepts are emerging out of the ruins of Communist Europe. One, 'Central Europe,' the media is now beating to death. The other, 'the Balkans,' the media has yet to discover." Thus, I devoted the article to consider the ethnic fissuring of Yugoslavia.*

* Robert D. Kaplan, "Balkans' Fault Line: Yugoslavia Starts to Feel the Tremors," *Wall Street Journal/Europe,* November 30, 1989. Though my reporting depressed an American president regarding the possibilities of military action—something that will always cause me deep remorse—I supported military action from the beginning. In the March 1993 issue of *Reader's Digest,* the same month that *Balkan Ghosts* was published, I wrote: "Unless we can break the cycle of hatred and revenge—by standing forcefully for self-determination and minority rights—the gains from the end of the Cold War will be lost. All aid, all diplomatic efforts, all force if force is used, must be linked to the simple idea that all the people of Yugoslavia deserve freedom from violence." Soon after, I appeared on television (CNN, C-SPAN) to urge intervention. I unambiguously urged military intervention on

War broke out there nineteen months later. What had been a desperate freelance existence gradually began to stabilize.

But what followed was not only triumph but criticism. While books like *Balkan Ghosts* and, after that, *The Ends of the Earth* were commercial successes—and essentially launched my career—the reactions of some reviewers, people trained in history and political science at the world's finest universities, taught me how my own experiences as a young traveler, as valuable as they were, and as unique as they were, nevertheless robbed me of the intellectual discipline that could have made those early books much better than they were. So, rather than read only history and literature as I had been doing, I silently determined to henceforth explore also the best works of academia, in both history and political science, all the while writing and reporting to support a family. Travel writing, I began to realize, was by its very nature insubstantial.

The more reading I did, the more insecure I felt, as I realized how ignorant I had been all along, and how little I had accomplished compared to the authors I now read. I took solace in the fact that whatever one's education, by middle age we are all either learned or unlearned (at least to some degree), depending upon how deeply and seriously we have read on our own in the course of the intervening decades. And serious reading, like serious traveling, means getting away from the crowd, cultivating loneliness, and finding books in the silent mazes offered by bibliographies. With books as with people, obscurity is not necessarily a virtue, but neither necessarily are the recommendations of the crowd.

For example, there is the late Predrag Matvejević's *Mediterranean: A Cultural Landscape,* an encyclopedic survey of winds, soils, coastlines, weather, currents, maps, trade, history, cultures, dialects, and what-have-you. His prose is precise, mathematical, academic, and on account of its very comprehensiveness achieves a hard-to-come-by

---

the front page of *The Washington Post* Outlook section more than a year before we intervened ("Into the Bloody New World: A Moral Pragmatism for America in an Age of Mini-Holocausts," April 17, 1994).

beauty. Matvejević, a Bosnian-Croat scholar, understood that even inland Bosnia and Herzegovina were shadow zones of the Adriatic, and thus had certain Mediterranean traits, even as Europe itself, through the interplay of trade routes, religions, and empires, "was conceived on the Mediterranean." Because he knows this sea as both a local and as an expert, he has no use for the raptures of foreign travel writers.[23] I have to watch my step, in other words, since writers like him are everything that I am not. I am but a foreign interloper and generalist. I realize that this can be an imperialist enterprise simply by appropriating terrain that is not my own.

And as I grow older and continue to read and question, my early path actually becomes more and more of a mystery to me, even as I continue to realize its value and to hold tight on to its memories. Whenever I try to explain or to justify my early path, I think of Saint Augustine's consciously depraved early life as a quasi-pagan, which surely gave him greater perspective on people and on himself in the course of his later life as a solemn Catholic. Wisdom can be facilitated by moving through different layers of existence, economic and social, that have nothing to do with growing old. Life to Saint Augustine was not an abstraction, *he had lived it in all its aspects,* and thus he knew that many were saints or sinners according to their circumstances, and the two categories were at some level interchangeable. Many of us evolve in unusual ways, and I am certainly not the first person by any means to be inspired by—or to gain some justification from—the life of Saint Augustine.

BUS SERVICE HAS RESUMED, but because of the wind along the coast where large vehicles are in danger of tipping over, the bus south from Senj to Zadar takes an inland route. Very soon we ascend into the mountains, where the snowy landscape seems to belong to a more northern latitude. The trees on the lofty hillsides are a palette of dying yellows, punctuated by the sight of bare limestone escarpments: the Dinaric Alps. Pines and firs squirm in the wind.

After three hours we descend back to the coast. In Zadar I have a nice hotel, luxurious compared to the room in Senj. Travel is about the enjoyment of radical change, positive or negative, within short periods of time. In Zadar the bora of the last few days is suddenly but a memory. The weather here is mild. People sit outside on café chairs with their coats on. Children glide by on bikes over the glassy stone street, past dazzling shop displays of Italian lingerie and handbags. Littered around the old town with all its boutiques are Roman, Byzantine, Romanesque, and late medieval ruins and churches—as well as the occasional Communist-era architectural monstrosity. Nearby are yachts and catamarans. The travel industry has anointed Dalmatia "the Mediterranean the way it used to be." True enough in winter, I suppose. But when I think of Dalmatia, something more substantial affects me: something thrillingly eclectic (that is, not something generically and insipidly global). Take the Glagolitic chant that has not yet died out in the churches here: Roman Catholic yet Old Slavonic and Old Croatian at the same time, fusing Latinity and the Greek Byzantine East. Haunting and somber, layering different civilizational traditions, you listen and give in to the soaring undertow. You don't quite know where you are, and that is the beauty of it.

Dalmatia is a thick deposit of charms and climates. In the meditative silence of early morning, with the inviting smells of a pastry shop, I walk down a narrow street of Zadar that ends at a pane of blue water: bordered, in turn, by a line of pitch-dark evergreens and a single palm tree. I venerate the bright, chalk-colored walls of multiple Romanesque bell towers crowned by narrow pyramidal roofs, and a ninth-century circular Byzantine church—which, with its strength and purity, instantly reminds me of Istanbul's Hagia Sophia—that nevertheless has Carolingian design touches of northwestern Europe. A town's architecture, no matter how many centuries old, can affect the very style of its inhabitants, I believe. Indeed, I walk around and think that the local aesthetic of Mediterranean Slavdom is Italian joie de vivre mixed with the deadening legacy of scientific socialism, expressed through a strain of nasty

religious and ethnic politics. The municipal defense walls recall Venetian and Ottoman wars: inside is a medieval clutter, as well as
some lonely empty spaces that are a remnant of World War II
bombing. Allied air forces attacked Zadar after the Germans took
it, following a long Italian occupation that lasted practically from
World War I to World War II. Much later came the Yugoslav army
attack on the city in 1991 as the federation broke apart. The history
of the area is overwhelming: Hitler, Mussolini, Tito, and Milošević,
for example. Yet, at the café tables in the morning, young mothers
with designer sunglasses rock their babies in strollers with one hand
and and sip morning coffee with the other. Normality is the most
beautiful of all things, especially considering such a past.

BUS TRAVEL IS EASY in Dalmatia. It is a decidedly middle-class
affair over good roads and with dependable schedules. Towering
limestone karst formations follow me south, where olive and fruit
trees soon join the thick pageant of juniper and other shrubs. With
one change of buses I am in Split in under two and a half hours, and
head for the old city.

In Split, the moldy northern wall of the Roman emperor Diocletian's palace stretches before me, seven feet thick and fifty feet
high, scarred by the scrub growing from its crevices and punctuated
every so often by arched windows that were bricked up long ago.
The stones came from the nearby island of Brač, which would fur-
nish the stones for the White House in Washington some fifteen
centuries later. They get smaller and more anarchic in their arrangement as my eyes creep upward. It is history in progress: the Roman
period topped by Byzantine and later ones. Diocletian was not its
only inhabitant—it also housed Julius Nepos, the next-to-last
Roman emperor in the West, who fled here from Ravenna following a coup. He stayed for five years before being slain by his own
soldiers. I walk through a grandiose gate into canyon-like alleyways,
their stones blackened with age.[24]

I finally come upon the Peristyle, the ceremonial gateway to the imperial quarters. The alleyway ends abruptly and there is a submerged flagstone expanse. On three sides there are columned Roman buildings over which medieval Venetian ones were built. The effect is the same as on previous visits, except that in recent years awnings, table umbrellas, and a café have unfortunately cluttered this and an adjacent space. Nevertheless, I still feel as though I have entered a brilliant salon of, well, *History*—the only word I could think of whenever coming here. On my left is a line of six dull pink granite columns from Egypt, supporting a frieze and acanthus the color of bleached bone, charred in many places. Resting on a pedestal between two of the columns is a cracked black granite sphinx that Diocletian brought back, along with the columns themselves, from Egypt. Also to my left is Diocletian's mausoleum and temple complex. In the seventh century A.D., the mausoleum was converted into a cathedral by a bishop from Ravenna, and a Romanesque belfry was added in the late Middle Ages.[25]

To my right as I enter the ceremonial gateway are Romanesque and early Gothic palaces whose lintels and balconies were blackened and eaten away by the salt winds. And straight ahead of me as I enter is the Protiron, the monumental entrance to Diocletian's private apartments, where the emperor stood to receive homage from his subjects. Broken slabs litter the vast area. Byzantine crosses are etched everywhere.[26]

I remember my emotions coming upon this historical pageant so suddenly my first morning in Split in 1971—after taking the ferry across the Adriatic from Pescara, and sleeping fitfully that night on a park bench. My head felt light, my legs a bit wobbly. I stood there dumb, not knowing really where I was, convinced I had wasted my nineteen years of life up to that point.[27]

Gaius Aurelius Valerius Diocletianus was an Illyrian born in Salona, a few miles away. The first Roman emperor from the Balkans, he reorganized the empire after a sustained period of incipient anarchy. Realizing that Rome had become too vast for one man to rule anymore, upon becoming emperor in A.D. 284, Diocletian eventually divided the throne four ways. While he himself settled in Nicomedia, in western Asia Minor, to watch the East, he made Maximian, another Illyrian, responsible for the West, and established a new capital at Milan. Some years later he subdivided the two halves of the empire, giving Galerius control over the Balkans and Constantius I Chlorus control over Spain, Gaul, and Britain. The empire added new categories of administration, buttressed by additional pomp and ceremony—exorbitant in cost even as the tetrarchy restored domestic order. The secrecy and mystery that were hallmarks of Byzantium had their origins in Diocletian's court in Nicomedia. Diocletian's restitution, while impressive, was a balancing feat that merely prolonged, rather than arrested, Rome's decline. As Rebecca West writes:

> Diocletian had been born too late to profit by the discussion of first principles which Roman culture had practiced in its securer days; he had spent his whole life in struggles against violence which led him to a preoccupation with compulsion.[28]

The end of Diocletian's reign was clouded by the last great persecutions of the Christians. The persecutions were, in fact, carried out by Galerius, the ruler in the Balkans—Diocletian's vow not to spill blood went unheeded. The result was a resurgence of martyrs' cults, such as Donatism in North Africa, followed by Christianity's own conquest of the empire soon after. In A.D. 305, following twenty-one years in office, Diocletian voluntarily abdicated the throne, with Galerius and Constantius, two of the tetrarchs, succeeding him. He spent the last nine years of his life at this vast palace he had built for himself in Split (originally conceived as a military camp and filled in with houses and alleyways throughout the Middle Ages). It was an example that no previous emperor, and few subsequent emperors or Catholic popes, would follow.

Though illness may have had something to do with his abdication, it showed nevertheless the wisdom and humility of a lifelong soldier, whose sense of duty more than compensated for his lack of learning.[29]

I leave the flagstone expanse—where a tour guide is talking loudly about all the NBA players who come from Split—and walk up the steps to the reception hall of the imperial apartments: a large, barrel-vaulted chamber of thin bricks, stripped bare of its mosaics and with its dome open to the sky. I next enter the cathedral, once the emperor's mausoleum, which exudes a similar feeling of martial strength. The dome of the cathedral, a poignant yellow-gray hue, is wonderfully bare and smudged with the smoke of ages. Adjacent to the cathedral dome are the tombs of two bishops: composites of classical and medieval styles, they are visual demonstrations of a historical continuum that makes antiquity feel less far away.[30]

Split, between my visits in 1971, 2002, and 2017, is as good a place as any to chart the social and economic upheaval that constitutes globalization, in both its good and bad aspects. From a bare and beautiful town in summer with a lonely railway station and an old city plagued by drugs and prostitution, existing within the shadow of Tito's Communism where crime and pornography flourished, Split in the course of almost half a century has become a jam-packed morass of cheap kiosks, food stands, cafés, and boutiques that stay crowded with tourists deep into the autumn. Many an alley corner in the old city is marked by a new historical plaque that is marred by graffiti. The streets of the old city have become a veritable high-end shopping mall patrolled by tourist armies, wearing baseball caps backward and carrying selfie sticks. Because of the creation of a global middle class in the intervening decades, everyone the world over looks and acts increasingly similar. In this sense at least, travel has lost its magic; or, rather, I should say the traveler must now work harder to understand the mystery of places given that travel relies on the differences between us. And alas, we inhabit a world where we all are being ground down by the same sheet of sandpaper. Again, as in Venice, the only escape is into the past through art, literature, and the best works of academia.

I HAVE A COFFEE one morning in Split in an elegant café with dark wooden decor and an air of Vienna about it. There is an arresting view of the black granite sphinx and columns that Diocletian brought here from Egypt. My companion is Jurica Pavičić, a local columnist and film critic who is a veteran of the 1990s war. He has a smiling face and is someone with great enthusiasm for the world of ideas and how they apply to the political journey of the western Balkans. He enjoys talking about these things and I enjoy listening to him.

When I mention to Jurica that my conversations in Zagreb were in important respects basically the same ones I had thirty years ago, he answers: "Of course, nothing has been resolved, because this is a part of the world where a civil war occurred within World War II, with not only Croats fighting Serbs but partisan Croats fighting fascist Croats. So the feud continues. On one side," he goes on, "are the children and grandchildren of the partisans, and on the other side are the children and grandchildren of the fascist Ustashe."

I ask, "And so there is no final resolution concerning the status of Tito in the region's history?"

"No, no resolution. Everything bad that is said about Tito is true. But everything good said about him is also true. Tito remains ambiguous. He was a Communist who also created a sort of leftist middle class—or a class of reform Communists, whatever you want to call them—that is, people who could actually run things, institutions. But," he continues, raising his voice, delighted in the irony, "the Yugoslav leftists were never as left-wing as the Greek leftists, because the Greek leftists have existed within a real capitalist society which they hate.

"Look," he says, returning to the original question, "if Tito's system had been allowed to continue without the violent breakup of the 1990s, Yugoslavia today might be like China, prospering under a form of capitalism organized by a liberal Communist Party."

"And instead?"

"Instead, the debate that started in the 1940s continues, with the Catholic Church now the effective politburo of the populist right wing. Look"—his wonderfully expressive face lights up further—"what the Church really deep-down wanted all along in World War II was to be governed by a Franco or Salazar, not a Pavelić:* a Spanish or Portuguese traditional, pro-clerical rightist; not a Nazi right wing. It wanted the Ustashe but without the killing of the Jews."

"But that was impossible," I interject. "Spain and Portugal constitute Iberia, benignly enclosed by water on three sides. And Portugal has been vaguely sympathetic to the Jews in modern times because a significant part of its population are descendants of Jews themselves who converted to Christianity during the Inquisition; while in this part of the world Hitler would have tolerated only a Nazi puppet state."

"Of course."

His point was only that the Church in Croatia is really about conservative tradition, which, because of the legacy of World War II, happens to burden it with the baggage of fascist crimes. The inhabitants of Dalmatia, for example, are generally pro-Church and traditional mainly in the way of Iberians and southern Italians (and also because of migration from the conservative Balkan interior), not because of a particular ideological or historical leaning.

"Does the idea of *Europe* or being *European* mean anything here?" I ask, changing the subject, though not really.

"No," Jurica says thoughtfully. "Europe meant something here in the 1980s" when there was the expectation of positive change. "But it is too general a concept" to have real traction. He agreed with those I met in Zagreb that applying for European Union member-

* Ante Pavelić was the World War II leader of the Croatian fascist state.

ship forced Croatians to think about being Europeans, but once inside the EU, "there is the feeling that *we can do what we want now, just like the Poles and Hungarians,*" who have drifted into reactionary nationalism. "But Croatians have not taken the final step and wandered into an open argument with Brussels like the Poles and Hungarians. You see"—he pauses—"we are less secure about our Central European identity than our neighbors to the north, so we don't want to risk losing it. We are a people who deny publicly that we are even partially in the Balkans, but we admit our Balkan identity privately, among ourselves."

IN THE EVENING I locate a restaurant with fine food despite a drafty and freezing interior, and it goes well with the view from my table of palm trees lining the corniche. Palm trees in the Mediterranean are something that I have always associated with being cold. There is the myth of year-round summery weather in the Mediterranean and this accounts for the poor quality or even absence of central heating. I have never shivered in winter as I have in the Mediterranean. The Mediterranean can be inhospitable, barren. It is not only about the beautiful churches and alluring beaches of Europe. North Africa is as much a part of the Mediterranean as southern Europe. Winter, cold, the Muslim East, and refugees are all aspects of the Mediterranean experience in the early twenty-first century. The European coast of the Mediterranean is old and rich; the North African coast is young and poor. The age of migration has only begun.

SEEN FROM THE WATER, Split looks as handsome as ever, its centuries-old buildings and reconstructed Romanesque belfry in the foreground against a towering wall of karst: I am standing on the deck of a car ferry that will take me southeast past the islands of Brač, Hvar, and Vis, to Vela Luka on the western tip of Korčula. The passengers are few this weekday morning in late November: mainly grizzled truck drivers smoking cigarettes with tabloids rolled under their arms. I have the upper deck more or less to myself. I sprawl out with my books and notebook on a table. The engine begins its vibrating racket, a whiff of oil enters my nostrils, and the ship retreats from the pier and approaches the breakwater. Then this shattered coastline begins to emerge in all its sculptural magnificence. The water is a great sliding panel of sunlight as the first green islands, like sleeping crocodiles, sharpen into focus. There is nothing like a sea voyage to restore one's sense of optimism, a sense of being cleansed of your own past. This may be the real reason people buy sailboats.

I spot a small Catholic church alone on a rocky isle in the dark blue water. There is such nobility to it, I think. It calls to mind the Orthodox churches on the remotest Greek islands. Before the elements there is nothing but faith, and wars and struggle are mainly substitutes for the elements. What is reason—and abstract, bureaucratic reason at that, generally what the EU has to offer—compared to such faith: a faith, moreover, which is the very source of communal identity?

After three hours we approach land. I climb down to the dark hold of the ferry and remain sandwiched between two trucks whose drivers are preparing to move. The giant steel door lowers and sunlight blazes in, revealing an assemblage of one-story houses by a harbor. I arranged for a car and driver in advance, since there are no taxis this time of year. We make the forty-minute journey across the length of the island from Vela Luka eastward to Korčula town. The silence and mystery of island existence immediately descend on me like a benediction.

The road now threads through a dense quilt of olive trees, vineyards, and white pines, occasionally punctuated by young cypresses, with glimpses of sea scrolling up to the horizon. Korčula's old town is a fortified medieval masterpiece, as if carved by a great artist from the same piece of rock and humming loud with silence. "I write of

stone. I write of Italy," declared Adrian Stokes about the temple in
Rimini, where I began my journey. The words could almost apply to
this white limestone settlement that casts a spell like minimalistic
poetry. I pass through a Venetian baroque entranceway atop a Renaissance gate beside a Gothic chapel, all on one little square. The
shops and cafés are boarded up in the off-season, intensifying the
effect of the architecture. Only cats patrol inside the city walls.
Without too much imagination, the spare Gothic lines of triple and
double archways along one alley recall the Doge's Palace in Venice.
I walk inside the gem of a sixteenth-century Gothic cathedral that
is really only a modest-sized church, but what a sense of strength
and volume! There is a Tintoretto of three saints behind the altar
that is so mysteriously lifelike it seems almost to move. Like a perfect thumb, the old town juts far out into the water, making for
stunning seascapes. A bare ocean is like a desert, full of alienation.
But a sea such as this, studded with islands and with mainland
mountains close by, is a sight of endless fascination.

Directly before me is the Pelješac canal, separating Korčula from
the mainland. It once marked the dividing line between Rome and
Byzantium, and also indicated a seaborne approach to imperial
Venice. Korčula is yet another Adriatic fault zone, changing hands
during the Napoleonic Wars between the French, the British, and
lastly the Austrians, who ruled it for a century until the birth of the
Kingdom of Serbs, Croats, and Slovenes following World War I.
The Korčulan dialect is peppered with Italian and Venetian words,
and the local family names—Arneri, Boschi, Depolo—go back to
the *Serenissima*, when this tiny, double espresso version of Dubrovnik was the "arsenal of Venice," writes author and journalist
Michael Dobbs, who lives part-time in Korčula. The different
winds, too, Dobbs goes on, suggest a geopolitical frontier: the warm
and dry maestral on the western side of the city walls open to the
sea, the humid and wet jugo from the south, and of course the frigid
and destructive bora, more familiar to the eastern side of the island
and the Balkan interior to the northeast.[31]

I check into my hotel as darkness falls. The palm trees, oleanders, and stunted oaks that line the water have disappeared into shadows. I sip a glass of Pošip, the local dry white wine, which is light but richly distinctive. I think of the Dalmatian expression *fjaka*, which may translate as "indolence" or "relaxation," connoting an attitude toward life almost. I go back to the old town for a walk. The silence is so severe it is as though I am inside a seashell. Pools of blackness, making it difficult to see your feet, open out to miniature squares each lit by a single lamp. The alleys at night intimate chambers of just-remembered dreams and childhood. Five minutes' walking in any direction brings me back to the sea. Is there a better evocation of time, of centuries passing, than the sound of water lapping against medieval walls at night?

Before a late dinner with some locals (people I have met through friends of other friends elsewhere), I pass into the new section of Korčula where from inside the local library I hear music. Schoolchildren are singing a haunting and traditional Croatian melody as parents and friends listen in rapture. A few days later I will see a performance of the Moreška sword dance, which migrated to Korčula in the fifteenth century: mundane reminders of communal and regional pride, making me think of the church on the remote isle I saw from the ferry.

But at dinner my new friends lament (just like the people I met in Zagreb) about how Croatia is losing population, with the young moving to Ireland for higher-paying tech jobs, with the agricultural heartland of Slavonia emptying out, and with women having fewer children. Croatia's democratic politics has alienated the young, dominated as this politics is by the same old divisions between those who are nationalist and those who are not. "You have to constantly feed the nationalist beast with meat—with economic development—otherwise it will bite you as in the past," I am told. This leads to a discussion about the crisis of democracy in the West, and how, as one person at the table suggests, "maybe monarchy, after all, is the most historically natural form of government: a leader perceived as legitimate by everyone who can consequently make the difficult but necessary decisions." My friends are liberal cosmopolitans, which in the local context means that they are "Yugoslavs," like Count Voinovitch in a way, leading me to wonder if his century-old idea of South Slavic unity might yet be reborn. In Korčula the very intensity of its beauty keeps people prideful and rooted in place, giving them hope for the future. I had to escape the place where I grew up in order to find beauty. Here people don't have to leave.

And here of all places in Croatia the breath of the Mediterranean is strongest. For Italy is everywhere in Korčula, thanks to imperial Venice. It is where Italian influence on Slavdom is most tactile: in the Church, in the architecture, in the coffee and the cuisine, in the dialect even, Stanka Kraljević, a teacher of Latin, tells me. In fact, it is the Italian influence that accounts for the exquisite Greek Byzantine icons in a church and museum here: for Byzantium, as we know, left a deep impress on Venice.

PERHAPS THE MOST IMPORTANT event in Korčula's history was the sea battle fought here in September 1298, just off the old town's eastern wall, between the Genoese and the Venetians, which saw the Venetian fleet commander, Andrea Dandolo, and Marco Polo, who commanded one of Dandolo's galleys, both taken prisoner among thousands of others. Dandolo, unable to bear the disgrace, committed suicide; Marco Polo was imprisoned in Genoa.* It was during his confinement, finally freed from the burdens of his commercial and military responsibilities, that he was able to carefully dictate the story of his travels in Asia.

Marco Polo, who began his twenty-four-year-long trek to Asia by sailing down the eastern shore of the Adriatic in A.D. 1271, would

---

* Admiral Andrea Dandolo should not be confused with the Venetian doge of the same name.

spend considerable periods of time in Palestine, Turkey, northern Iraq, Iran in its entirety from the Azeri and Kurdish north to the Persian Gulf, northern and eastern Afghanistan, and China's ethnic-Turkic Xinjiang Province, before arriving at the court of the Mongol emperor Kublai Khan, in Cambulac (modern-day Beijing). From Cambulac he would make forays across the whole of China and down into Vietnam and Myanmar. His return route to Venice would take him across the Indian Ocean: through the Strait of Malacca to Sri Lanka, up India's western coast to Gujarat, and on side trips to Oman, Yemen, and East Africa.

If the early-twenty-first-century world has a geopolitical center, this would be it: the Greater Indian Ocean from the Persian Gulf to the South China Sea, and including the Middle East, Central Asia, and China. The current Chinese regime's proposed land and maritime Silk Road, called in newspaper parlance "the Belt and Road Initiative," duplicates exactly the routes Marco Polo traveled. This is no coincidence. The Mongols, whose Yuan Dynasty ruled China in the thirteenth and fourteenth centuries, were "early practitioners of globalization," seeking to connect the whole of habitable Eurasia in a truly multicultural empire. And Yuan China's most compelling weapon was (despite the Mongols' bloody reputation) not the sword but trade: gems, fabrics, spices, metals, and so on. It was trade routes, not the projection of military power, that emblemized the "Pax Mongolica."[32] Mongol grand strategy was built on commerce much more than on war. If you want to understand China's grand strategy today, I would think, look no further than Kublai Khan's empire, of which the Venetian Marco Polo leaves such a unique record.

Yet for Kublai Khan it didn't altogether work. Persia and Russia became autonomous, and the Indian subcontinent, separated from China by the high wall of the Himalayas, with seas on both sides, remained its own geopolitical island. Though, all the while, the Great Khan strengthened his base in what has always been Chinese civilization's arable cradle, in central and eastern China, away from the Muslim minority areas of the western desert. Here, too, the geopolitical characteristics of Marco Polo's world roughly approximate our own.

Marco Polo equated the future with China itself, even as traveling in Tibet he had seen the dark side of Yuan Chinese rule, with its wanton destruction and forced incorporation of a distant province. Coal, paper money, eyeglasses, and gunpowder were Chinese marvels unknown in Europe at the time, while the city of Hangzhou, with a moat and hundreds of bridges over its canals, was as beautiful in Marco Polo's eyes as Venice itself.

Aside from the geopolitical island of India, two especially consequential territories that Marco Polo describes in his *Travels* are Russia and Persia. Russia he observes from afar as a profitable wasteland rich in furs, whereas Persia dominates much of his itinerary. Persia is second only to China in Marco Polo's eyes—in a similar way that the Persian Empire dominated the routes of Alexander the Great and Herodotus, when it was history's first superpower in antiquity.[33] For, as so often in history, it was all about Persia. Or Iran, as it is now called. Thus, a map of thirteenth-century Eurasia during Marco Polo's lifetime—whose organizing principles were the "Empire of the Great Khan" and the "Khans of Persia"—is actually the proper point of entry into our own geopolitical world, and where it is going: a world in which Europe, especially the Adriatic—encompassing both Western and Eastern Christianity as well as Islam—is more and more integral and organic to a larger Eurasian whole.[34]

Picture-perfect, winter-haunted Korčula, a veritable city-state of its own along the Silk Road, concentrates one's thoughts on all these matters like no other place I know. There is even a local claim, questionable really, that Marco Polo was born here.

I AM ON A balcony in Lumbarda, south of Korčula town, overlooking a silent bay close to where the sea battle involving Marco Polo was fought over seven hundred years ago. There are potted plants:

hortensia and hibiscus; and nearby pomegranate, olive, and bougainvillea trees growing. This is the home of Toni Lozica: guide and opera baritone, from a family going back many generations in Korčula. He is a tall and massive man, whose iron-gray hair, tied in a ponytail, and clipped white beard give him the air of a monk on Mount Athos.

His balcony, under a pergola, opens into a vast and delightful room where pasta is cooking and books and paintings line the walls. The books are in several languages and deal mostly with the history of the Balkans and the greater Adriatic. They are in just enough disorder, without being chaotic, to give his library the sense of actually being used. There are brocaded pillows and half-burnt candles and old trunks from an earlier age of travel; two of the trunks were once owned by the British war hero Fitzroy Maclean himself. On a long wooden table Toni pours me an ice-cold glass of slivovitz followed by Grk, a local white wine with a clean metallic taste. This is a classic Mediterranean existence at the very edge of the Slavic world. I am in the home of someone warm and soulful and highly cultured, who cooks and reads and thus can enjoy his own company, a home suffused with the ecstatic odor of the sea.

As two fat and fluffy cats walk in from the balcony, Toni announces that the pasta is ready and we begin to eat and talk, or rather I begin to listen. Toni seems to have read all the books by authors that matter most to me: Fernand Braudel, Predrag Matvejević, Lord Norwich, and so forth, writers who observe the essential unity of the Mediterranean as a civilization, while also being a theater of rivalry and conflict, but with a common destiny nevertheless. Toni nods to himself as he tells me how different and less tragic the twentieth century might have been had this assassination not taken place or that election gone differently. The older he gets, in spite of Braudel and Braudel's brilliant determinism, the more Toni believes that history is a matter of odd contingencies and individual passionate encounters.

Finally, as usual, the subject turns to the former Yugoslavia.

"Will Yugoslavia return?" I ask.

"Yes, Yugoslavia must return. It is the potential EU of the western Balkans. We all speak more or less the same Slavic language, and we all must trade with each other, so there is no alternative to a new and informal Yugoslavia. As long as there is an EU," Toni continues, "there will have to be a process to re-create Yugoslavia in some form or other," however diluted and immersed it is in a common civilization of the Mediterranean basin. "Yugoslavia was an empire. The EU is an empire. And what is the EU really about? Is it about trade and economics? Ultimately, no. The EU must survive because it is really about peace. Peace in Europe."

We agree that there is such a thing as necessary empires.

KORČULA IS INSEPARABLE IN my mind from Fitzroy Maclean, the brave, dashing, cool-as-ice, and indefatigable Highland Scottish gentleman who parachuted into the hills of Bosnia in September 1943, lived among the Yugoslav partisans, and got to know Tito on a daily basis better than any other Westerner before or since. Up until Maclean's foray, Churchill's government was still unsure about the political direction of the partisans. They were a mystery. Maclean convinced his government that Tito's resistance army was "infinitely" more important than generally supposed; that it was "very definitely" under Communist leadership; and that British support would help considerably in its fight against the Germans. But whether Britain helped the partisans or not, "Tito and his followers would exercise decisive influence in Yugoslavia after the liberation." All this would prove accurate.

So would another insight of Maclean's. At their first meeting, slugging plum brandy with Tito almost immediately after he had landed by parachute, Maclean observed that Tito was not like the Soviet Communists he had come to know while posted to Moscow. Tito "seemed perfectly sure of himself; a principal, not a subordinate." That attribute would turn out to be crucial in Yugoslavia's break with Moscow some years later, which led to its adoption of non-alignment.

But first Maclean had to get to the coast from the interior, in order to arrange for supplies to come to the partisans from Italy, where Mussolini had just been toppled. That meant hiking down from the wooded Bosnian countryside into the "gray rocks and crags" of Dalmatia. And thus Maclean came to sunlit Korčula, where near the "ancient circular tower, emblazoned with the Lion of St. Mark," he "noticed with pleasure, one extremely pretty girl." Later some Roman Catholic nuns "pelted" him with flowers. Small pleasures, but great under the circumstances.[35]

BEFORE DAWN THE SEA looks like glittering tar as the car ferry lumbers across the Pelješac canal taking me back to the mainland. Yet by the time we reach the opposite shore the water has already turned color, reflecting back the overcast clay sky. The bus then meanders south at the edge of bearded limestone hills and cliffs until we reach Dubrovnik by mid-morning. The olive trees along the journey are mesmerizing. They remind me of the first olive trees I ever saw as a young traveler in Spain and Tunisia, proof-in-landscape of North Africa's essential unity with southern Europe. The sea—still and fiery now as sunlight peeks through the clouds— has the flat, knife-edge perfection of Saturn's rings.

Dubrovnik is announced by a sprawl of new housing construction: this is different from how I remember it in the late 1990s, a blissful time after the war ended but before the local tourist boom. But now the old walled city suddenly appears before me, and with the cruise ships having stopped service for the season, it looks as isolated, dramatic, and inspiring as ever. I think of the Maritime Museum built into these massive walls that I have visited on a number of occasions, with its magnificent model ships and maps, maps, maps! It makes all the history I have read come back to me.

———

DUBROVNIK—A SERBO-CROATIAN TERM THAT may refer to
nearby oak forests—was not even the exclusive name of this city
until the twentieth century. Before that, for roughly a thousand
years, it was the independent, Roman Catholic seafaring republic of
Ragusa. (The word "argosy" means "ship of Ragusa.") After World
War I, the government of the new Kingdom of Yugoslavia officially changed the name to Dubrovnik because Ragusa sounded too
Italian, though the name is putatively Illyrian. Ragusa fought off
Saracen sieges and, with the passive encouragement of Spain and
the Vatican, constantly escaped the dominating grasp of the Venetian, Habsburg, and Ottoman Empires, playing each off against
the others. Ragusa, a true historical "miracle" in Rebecca West's
description—a tributary of the Ottoman Empire yet perceived by
many as an independent Christian state—was the gateway to Asia;
where caravans began their five-hundred-mile overland journey
through Montenegro, Kosovo, Macedonia, and Bulgaria to Constantinople and beyond. There was even a Ragusan colony in Goa,
on India's Konkan Coast. Ragusa's naval might ensured that it
owned warehouses in every major Mediterranean port from Tunis
in North Africa to Acre in Palestine. There is a map in the Maritime Museum that shows every coastal town along my own Adriatic route with a Ragusan commercial depot in the twelfth and
thirteenth centuries. Only after the Napoleonic Wars did Ragusa
succumb to Habsburg domination.[36]

To label Dubrovnik as lying between East and West does not
come close to capturing its nerve-racking geopolitical reality. While
its cultural and artistic veneer was certainly Venetian, in terms
of politics, economics, and culture, predominantly Serbo-Croat-
speaking Dubrovnik straddled the border between the Roman Catholicism of the West and the Byzantine Orthodoxy of the East.
Diplomatically, it balanced the Venetians, Hungarians, and the
Normans of the West with the Byzantine, Serbian, and Bosnian

monarchs of the East. The Ragusan patriciate itself was split between pro- and anti-Ottoman elements. (So much is known about early modern Dubrovnik! The University of Sydney academic Zdenko Zlatar actually lists the members of the Senate in 1611–1612, labeling them according to their various factions.)[37]

Medieval Dubrovnik's original and recurrent problem was that the Byzantine Empire proved a "somewhat unreliable protector," explains British expert Robin Harris in *Dubrovnik: A History*. "Consequently, the Ragusans [early on] had to reach their own arrangements with their neighbors in order to preserve their security," something that Byzantium accepted, "as long as its ultimate sovereignty was still recognized." Ironically, Dubrovnik further honed the arts of survival as a result of the limitations placed on it by Venice, which restricted its maritime commerce and thus forced Dubrovnik to develop its overland trade in the Slavic interior. The republic became both a Mediterranean and a Balkan power. This overland trade was helped by the fact that Venice, nevertheless, protected Dubrovnik against Serbia. While Venice wanted to keep Dubrovnik in check, it nevertheless required Dubrovnik's survival for the sake of *La Serenissima*'s own Adriatic security. Again, amoral geopolitics did allow for a semblance of peace, and was therefore preferable to the self-righteous excesses of religious war. And nobody played this game better than the Ragusans.

In the mid-fourteenth century, when Hungary got the better of Venice in a series of military hostilities, Dubrovnik quickly took advantage of the doge by forcing him to grant it more civil and commercial liberties. At the same time, Dubrovnik moved diplomatically closer to a victorious Hungary, in return for the protection of this new rising power in the Adriatic. And as Ottoman power rose in the fifteenth century, Dubrovnik maneuvered to get the Catholic powers of Europe to grant it permission to trade more in the Muslim lands. A "Slavic Athens" intense in its self-defining and liberal Catholicity, Dubrovnik, however, kept its political distance from the papacy.

Later on, in the sixteenth century, as Ottoman power reached its zenith and after Dubrovnik had become an Ottoman tributary, a nevertheless disinterested Dubrovnik became the conduit for East–West trade, and refrained from military actions on any great power's behalf. Thus did this city-state preserve its neutrality. Catholic Ragusans, for the most part, because of their realism—abetted by a sensitive geographical position—looked down upon the fervor of the Counter-Reformation wars of the sixteenth and seventeenth centuries against the Muslim sultanate.[38]

A Frenchman who visited Dubrovnik in 1658 said this about the Ragusans' unparalleled cynicism in international relations, something so necessary for their survival: "The Turks they fear; the Venetians they hate; the Spaniards they love, because they are useful; the French they suffer because of their fame; and foreigners they spy on very much."[39]

Dubrovnik is an illustration of how statecraft is often a matter of the lesser evil, for only by accepting that fact can an outnumbered people defend itself. Social order guaranteed freedom. A rigid caste system divided nobles, commoners, and workers: "the very impossibility of a commoner joining the patriciate's ranks probably made for a certain acquiescence and so stability," Harris writes. With thirty-three noble families in a population said to number in the tens of thousands in the fifteenth century, Ragusa constituted a Venetian-style corporatist leadership in which few dominant personalities emerged. The rector, in the spirit of the doge, was elected for only one month and could be reelected only after an interval of two years. During his month in office he was held prisoner in the palace except for ceremonial appearances, when he wore a black velvet stole over a red silk toga. It was a system made for Machiavelli: Ragusa's progressive, Whiggish-style government was a perfect expression of the famous Florentine's principles, those of a cold, aristocratic realism in service only to self-preservation.[40] The result was a free republic that endured throughout the medieval and early modern eras: celebrated by the Byzantine-Gothic-Renaissance art and architecture encased within its fifteenth-sixteenth-century walls.

IT IS A COLD early winter evening and lamps illuminate the battlements of Dubrovnik. I walk over a drawbridge and inside the Ploče Gate, a statue of Saint Blaise—Dubrovnik's patron saint—guarding me overhead in an alcove. I find myself inside a towering gorge: city walls almost grazing my shoulder on the left and the walls of the Dominican friary almost doing likewise on my right. Then the view widens into a plaza framed by the Gothic and Renaissance Sponza Palace and a fifteenth-century fountain. Extending from the plaza, as if into infinity, is the Stradun, Dubrovnik's main promenade of polished flagstones, glittering like glass in the floodlights. Built after an earthquake in 1667, it is lined with identical baroque arches: a linear time pageant out of a Canaletto cityscape. I wander off into staircased alleys and into stores and intimate neighborhood bars with gilded pictures bespeaking a deeply evolved urbanity. Outside, almost every time I look up I see a statue of a saint, usually Saint Blaise, cradling a model of Dubrovnik in his hand, as if ready to step off the top of a church and into the air, mingling with the crowd.[41]

In the Rector's Palace, amid gilded mirrors and blue-and-yellow Neapolitan faience, I look at the portraits of Ragusan noblemen, with their Italian and Slavic names. Their calculating expressions bespeak a monastic conformity. Between October and December 1991, and again in May 1992, when Serb shells rained down on the old city, the late medieval walls and seventeenth-century flagstones, particularly along the Stradun, which had been financed by these crafty entrepreneurs, absorbed many direct hits and shrapnel with remarkably little blemish.[42]

In 1998, I took a walk along the top of the fortress walls to assess the damage from the bombardment. I looked over hundreds of thousands of clay roof tiles, expressing what Edgar Degas called "the patient collaboration of time." Like fossils impressed on stone, the roof tiles formed a record of the seasons: cold, wet winters and

scorching-hot summers, creating a patchwork of the most haunting, subtle hues. There were chestnuts, ochers, glowing siennas.
Given enough decades, the tiles turn the color of bleached bone and
from a distance seem yellow almost. Yet, following a moment of
unparalleled splendor, I looked closer at the roofscape. Many tiles
were new, so that blotches of tomato red marked the areas where
Serb shells had hit.[43] Decay is beautiful, and the 1990s violence had
extinguished it.

Dubrovnik as I have experienced it over the decades exudes
eclecticism, as all my memories of the place coalesce. I enter the
museum of the Dominican friary, where neither a brass-cast flagon
from fifteenth-century Nuremberg nor a sixteenth-century Flem-
ish diptych of Christ and the Virgin seem out of place surrounded
by the art of Slavic, Hungarian, and Italian masters, including an
angel by Titian. The Dominican church, with empty white walls
distinguished by the most elaborate Gothic portals, is like many I
have seen in Italy. The fourteenth-century Romanesque cloister of
the Franciscan friary is yet another landscape experience more
Mediterranean than Balkan: a stone fountain in the midst of a luxuriant garden with a simple lemon tree. Alleyways are steep and
sun-swept mazes are graced by orange blossoms and drying laun-
dry.[44]

Also, on a previous visit, I headed for the old city's produce
market beside the cathedral, with a triumphant statue of the early-
seventeenth-century poet of the Counter-Reformation Ivan Gun-
dulić, in the center. At one vegetable stand a buxom woman wearing
an apron opened a bottle of brandy flavored with medicinal herbs
and poured me a capful, then handed me a juicy fig. It was nine in
the morning and the brandy seeped into my head and chest like
perfumed fire. She smiled. Every day, a few minutes before noon,
the rooftops surrounding this market suddenly fill with pigeons,
who wait motionlessly until literally seconds before the cathedral
bells peal, when they fly off in formation.[45] When I return years
later, the same miracle ensues.

KOTOR, PODGORICA, TIRANA, AND DURRËS

—

The Heart of Europe?

As the bus crosses the border south from Croatia into Montenegro, I am passing through subtle political and cultural gradations. I am still in the former Yugoslavia but I leave the European Union behind, even though the euro circulates in Montenegro, which, like Croatia, is a member of NATO. Montenegro, which formerly used the Cyrillic alphabet, is far into the process of switching over to the Latin one.

Yet the change is dramatic. The towns are shabbier, less manicured than in Croatia, with faded signage, rusted iron roofs, and overgrown lots amid the palm trees and hotel advertisements. I am conscious of a drop in living standards as I enter a country historically marked to a much greater degree by the Ottoman Empire and the Eastern Orthodox Church than Habsburg-inspired Catholic Croatia to the north. There are mean, half-finished apartment blocks, with clothes drying next to satellite dishes, that remind me of the scarred tenements in the Caucasus and Central Asia in the late 1990s. Expensive yachts packed tightly together float not far away from derelict yards, even as a vast sprawl of new and unregulated construction undermines the scenery: indicators of high levels of corruption coupled with weak institutions.

The old town of Kotor lacks the scrubbed and polished look of the walled Adriatic masterpieces of Croatia. Kotor is not quite yet a boutique-lined shopping mall to the degree of Split and Dubrovnik. The alley cats are scrawnier. From a table in the old town's most expensive restaurant I see bedsheets drying on a line beside a lovely, time-blackened archway and lintel. Deep inside a bay, there is an indefinable remoteness about Kotor, the smart pubs and wine bars notwithstanding. The air of the caravanserai haunts the gloomy alleys. I've gone back in time a bit. Meanwhile, the lofty peaks rise above the mist like cathedral spires, and are reflected in the mirror of the great bay.

KOTOR IS ACTUALLY WHERE adjectives fail. It is as though the bay, which has the proportions of a Norwegian fjord, carries you into the yawning interior of a vast and undiscovered continent, with its relentless mountainous eruptions. Yet the colors on a sunny day can be hot and intimate; this is the Mediterranean still. The small but majestic Catholic Church of Our Lady of Remedy, halfway up a steep mountain and eaten away by the centuries, lends the whole picture coherence.

Kotor, the former Italian Cattaro until after World War I, sits within the mystically winding Gulf of Kotor at the foot of the 6,000-foot Mount Lovćen and its secondary peaks, whose imposing shade obscures the old town's narrow streets. Even more than the other walled cities of Dalmatia, Kotor, which is open to the Adriatic yet accessible to the heart of the Balkan interior, has been a register of early modern and modern conquerors and their imperial forces that occupied it: Turks, Venetians, Austrians, French, Russians, and British. Long before all that, in Late Antiquity and afterwards, had come Ostrogoths, Byzantines, and Saracens to this idyllic spot, with the rule of medieval Bulgarian and Serbian dynasties thrown later into the interminable mix. But Kotor's ultimate historical personality may be that of a quasi-independent Dalmatian city-state, with an identity all its own, separated politically and psychologically from the dark fastnesses of the Montenegrin hinterland.

In Kotor I feel slightly disoriented. I sense the East in its distinct friendliness—in the way that strangers intrude on you in restaurants with personal questions—and in the stark visual effects of corruption coupled with the dusky mystery and distinct aura of antiquity of the Orthodox churches, marked by their imposing iconostases and priests swinging incense censers. Such thoughts tempt essentialism, I know. But these, I believe, are more than first impressions. The statistics concerning per capita income that foreign ministry officials provided me in Slovenia, as well as the rankings on the United Nations Human Development Index, point directly to a drop in living and governmental standards as one travels from north to south in the former Yugoslavia. And after all, despite the patina of globalization, there is still such a thing as the East, just as there is such a thing as the West.

Of course, it is far more complicated than that. In a local museum, for example, Balkan costumes stand adjacent to Venetian mirrors and other Italianate furniture. Yet we know that Denmark and Germany are quite different from Iran and India, which means that a traveler crossing the Eurasian landmass must notice changes along the way from northern Europe to the Near East and the Asian subcontinent, however more diluted these changes become in our age of globalization. To travel means to face up to constant minute comparisons between one place and the next (however imperfect they may be), which ultimately helps reveal the how and why of geopolitics.

For example, whereas 86 percent of Croatia's population is Roman Catholic, 72 percent of Montenegro's population is Eastern Orthodox. Years ago, a leading Romanian philosopher, Horia-Roman Patapievici, told me that Orthodox countries—Romania, Moldova, Russia, Serbia, Montenegro, and so on—have had a particular challenge developing a public style based on impersonal rules, since "Orthodoxy is flexible and contemplative, based more on the oral traditions of peasants than on texts."[1] The British journalist Victoria Clark notes in her book about Eastern Orthodoxy that it is a world where personal relationships matter much more than institutions.[2] Indeed, the last time I checked, in every case, Orthodox countries in Europe scored below their Protestant and Catholic counterparts in terms of perceived institutional transparency, and in almost every case in terms of per capita income.

Eastern Orthodoxy, as many observers have noted, has had a less contentious relationship with Islam inside the Ottoman Empire than with fellow Christian Catholics beyond it. For the Muslim Turks often treated Eastern Christians better than Western Christians (Catholics and Protestants) treated each other, so that Orthodoxy forms a part of the Ottoman inheritance in a similar way that Islam does; and Montenegro (along with Albania) forms a frontier of the Orthodox world, whose heartland remains in Greece and Russia.

Indeed, Eastern Orthodox Christianity constitutes the world of the former Byzantine Empire (before the arrival of the Ottomans) and its Slavic shadow zones to the north. Though I encountered the artistic and spiritual remnants of Orthodoxy in the churches of Ravenna on the other side of the Adriatic near the beginning of my journey, it is in Kotor where I encounter it as an active religion. I first became besotted with Orthodox churches and monasteries in the West Bank in Palestine in the 1970s, and in the 1980s I lived for

some years in Orthodox Greece. Standing in a near-empty Orthodox church in Kotor one morning, a lone priest walking around
with a censer—the smell of incense igniting a palpable sense of
heaven—some of my most cherished memories of Greece and the
Middle East return: memories of other lone priests chanting and
swinging incense, even if there was no congregation present; no
pews or chairs since in Orthodoxy there is generally no nave, only a
central space under the dome for people to stand, creating an unin-
hibited informality under the glow of iconography—art that allows
heaven and earth to meet.

And memories of course mean books, specifically *The Orthodox
Church,* a deeply *lived* and erudite volume I picked up in Athens
more than half a lifetime ago by Timothy Ware, or Father Kallistos
as he was renamed upon his conversion from Anglicanism to Orthodoxy in 1958. Whereas all Western Christians, Catholics and
Protestants alike, Father Kallistos explains, have been influenced
by "the Papal centralization and the Scholasticism of the Middle Ages, by the Renaissance, by the Reformation and Counter-
Reformation," Orthodox Christians have known practically none
of this: "they have only been affected in an oblique way" by the
civilizational upheavals that created the idea of the West following
the close of antiquity. And whereas the Catholic Church is unified under a pope, the Orthodox world is more an assemblage of
"independent local Churches" that are "highly flexible" and "easily
adapted to changing conditions." Thus, while the Orthodox world
claims universality as the original "true belief" about God, in practice it has become associated with ethnic nations and regimes, good
and bad. This is in part a doleful consequence of Ottoman rule,
which granted Orthodox churches political privileges as represen-
tative of their national groups, and so opened the clergy to ambition and influence-peddling.[3] Eastern Orthodoxy, therefore, for
reasons of doctrine, history, and geography (each one nurturing the
other), helps frame the transition from Western Europe to the Near
East.

"But what is Europe then?" Miro Djukanović, a local tour guide and intense student of Balkan history, challenges me one morning at a café in Kotor, taking long drags of a cigarette, snapping his fingers, and smashing his palms together with passion. "Europe, I'll tell you, is Orthodox as well as Catholic and Protestant. Kotor is the kernel of Europe every bit as much as the cities of northern Italy," he says. "In the fifth century we were a seat of a bishop. We had the Ten Commandments, while northern Europe struggled still with barbarism. Here you have Catholicism and Orthodoxy like inter-locking gears. Both halves of Christianity are within these city walls." His point is that if Europe were to stop at Montenegro, leav-ing out the much larger Orthodox nations of the Balkans, especially Greece, then Europe would be lost utterly. "The history of Europe is a search for undiscovered beauty," the beauty of an idea of unity, which so far eludes it, he suggests.

I recall how Yale history professor Marci Shore found the ideal of Europe in an indoor market as far east as the port of Odessa, where musicians from the local philharmonic were playing Beethoven's "Ode to Joy"—the anthem of the European Union—amid the "scal-ing of whitefish and cleaning of mackerel gills and weighing of an-chovies . . . drowning, for a moment, the voices of Putin's sirens" in the midst of the 2014 Ukrainian Revolution.[4] Because Europe, in order to survive, should mean more than a specific geography, it can-not be too strictly limited by geography, and so must try to reach out to its shadow zones.

THE JOURNEY FROM KOTOR to the Montenegrin capital of Pod-gorica takes you south along more dizzying, blazing-in-sunlight, enigmatic seascapes. The Adriatic is not the Aegean with its inces-sant mental associations with Greek mythology; nor is it the infi-nitely vaster Indian Ocean with its life-giving monsoon winds and suggestions of seafaring Islam. Rather, here are associations of so many different cultures and histories—with all the classic divisions of East and West—that there is only awe at the porousness of categories.

Suddenly I head inland, and Montenegro erupts, peak after stormy peak, igniting memories of the ruggedness of Yemen and the cold beauty of Switzerland: an infernally divided, mountainous redoubt of only 630,000 people that, as small as it is, unites the Mediterranean with the Balkan heartland, and because of its geography and blood feuds proved nearly impossible for the Ottoman Empire to rule.

Montenegro's twenty-first-century independence was not decided in the 1990s wars of the Yugoslav succession, but in a peacetime referendum held in 2006 that resulted in its leaving the federation with Serbia. In fact, Montenegro and Serbia share a long, somewhat ambiguous, and storied history. It has been a relationship that at times has divided Montenegrins among themselves. The greatest poem of the Serbian language, *The Mountain Wreath*, which marked a pivotal break with the Ottoman Empire and inspired generations of Serbs to fight against alien rule, was written by a Montenegrin, Prince Petar II Petrović-Njegoš, in 1846. Stefan Nemanja, the father of the great medieval dynasty that transformed the Serbs from "disparate tribes into a people," was born in Montenegro. And when the Ottomans finally established a tenuous hold over these Serbian territories, it was the warriors clustered near Mount Lovćen (the "Monte Negro," *Crna Gora*, or Black Mountain) that held out the longest against them. "Montenegrins came to view themselves as the Serbian Sparta," writes the British historian and journalist Tim Judah.[5] And so, the referendum result in 2006 was not about leaving Serbia so much as about leaving behind Serbia's problems, which included the diplomatic wrangle over Kosovo's independence and the legal drama about bringing Serbian war criminals to justice in the Hague. Free of all that, Montenegro, with its strategic Adriatic location—once one of the fault lines between the Venetian and Ottoman Empires—could more credibly apply for NATO and European Union membership.

Yet Russia, too, so many of whose ports are ice-blocked during the long winter months, covets Montenegro's warm-water perch on the Adriatic that is almost within reach of Italy. Russia's interest in Montenegro is also wrought by Russia's considerable history of cultural and linguistic ties to Serbian-speaking territories, to its economic investments here, and to the fact that this beautiful Adriatic resort has become a playground for Russian organized crime.[6] By some accounts, Russians own 40 percent of Montenegro's real estate, while a quarter of all tourism here is from Russia, and the casinos and marina project are designed for the Russian "mega-rich" with their "super-yachts," whose money "is of murky provenance to say the least," says Croatian-born, Washington-based analyst Damir Marusic. NATO officials are aware of all this and still welcome Montenegro into the Western alliance. With Croatia and Albania already NATO members, admitting Montenegro closes off the Adriatic to the Russian military.

Moreover, as NATO's thinking goes, membership will put Montenegro "on the path to eventual virtue," by helping its entry into the European Union, which has its own onerous standards in terms of legal and financial reform. Montenegro's split personality between East and West is perhaps best mirrored in its ethnic and political divisions over NATO membership: ethnic-Bosniaks and -Albanians here have supported it, while Montenegrins themselves support NATO only half-heartedly, with ethnic-Serbs opposed to joining the Western alliance.[7] This small and, to many, obscure country will continue to be a manifestation of the strategic East-West rivalry that will help determine the fate of Europe.

I ARRIVE IN PODGORICA and have never felt as far from the Mediterranean as I do here, barely an hour from the sea. Having changed its name a number of times through history, and known as Titograd during the decades of socialist Yugoslavia, Podgorica has a rather vague sense of *place*. Under the rainy winter sky, the city is ashen, angular, with pizza and kebab joints and the intermittent casino. There are some old brown Ottoman-era buildings with grimy red clay roofs, cheap modern architecture that evokes the design failures of the 1970s, and some glitzy new buildings. The lofty, snowy slopes in the distance remark on the impossible terrain that has made Podgorica the isolated city that it is. My hotel room has that chrome and brownish functional look that harks back to the socialist era. What a difference from the edgy, Viennese-style elegance of Ljubljana and Zagreb at the other end of the former Yugoslavia!

I once took a bus from Titograd to Sarajevo in November 1989, but while I have a vivid memory of how Sarajevo had already deteriorated in the five years since the 1984 Winter Olympics, I have little memory of Titograd, which even today resembles any number of big towns of the bleak Anatolian interior more than it does any place in Central or Western Europe. It is a quiet Sunday and lump-ily dressed people wander about, many of them taking furious drags on cigarettes. Roma girls chase aggressively after diners exiting from Pod Volat, a locally famous restaurant serving Turkish-style food in the old town square. I sit in a vast and mostly empty café listening to piped-in music from *The Godfather*. But I also observe state-of-the-art traffic lights, neatly cut hedgerows lining the bou-levards, bicycle paths, polite drivers, elegant signage, and brand-new taxis with the drivers using their meters, so that getting around is always easy. Within the first hour here, even though my introduc-tion to the place is merely visual, and thus superficial, I already know that the story in Podgorica is complicated. Something is hap-pening here.

A MIDDLE-AGED WRITER, who comes to Montenegro often from an adjacent country, informs me soon after I arrive:

"The real issue here is the security problem on account of the cocaine wars between gangs located in the suburbs of Kotor. This is

a function of the corruption, the nepotism, and the weak government institutions. Whoever runs the casinos runs Montenegro, so
you don't ask who runs the casinos. Criminal networks flourish at
the same time as the building of resorts near the Adriatic. There is
money here, I mean. Without the clans there is no mafia, but without the clans there is also no tradition. If you don't hire your relatives, you're a bad guy. Everyone privately cries for Tito. They want
him back. Under Tito, there were almost no gangs, no rapes, much
less drugs, more safety, more security, dignity to life. You didn't have
to worry about what could happen to your kids like you do now.
People were not so rich and not so poor as today. And so what if you
couldn't vote every few years."

With the exception of Slovenia, safely tucked inside Central
Europe, this is the refrain that I have heard throughout the former
Yugoslavia where the rule of law has sunk shallow roots and thus
atavistic allegiances thrive. Of course, this is all a legacy of Communism, which Tito himself inflicted upon everyone. Except that
in Montenegro I have reached a geographical juncture in my
travels—far to the south and deep in the mountains—where the
ethnic politics I observed in a place like Croatia has deteriorated
into (and been replaced by) outright criminality.

This place is really fragile. Because of that, I find that I constantly need to talk to people. I am becoming less of a traveler and
more of a journalist as I head south.

ANDRIJA MANDIĆ, AT THE time of my visit in 2018, is an opposition leader from a political party in Montenegro that is sympathetic
to Moscow, who has been indicted for an alleged pro-Moscow coup
attempt in 2016. He is burly with white hair, in business casual attire except for the jeans. His expression oscillates between suspicion
and friendliness. He is clearly nervous and says that he knows I will
write bad things about him. He greets me in a drab, threadbare
room that could have belonged to the Communist era except that

instead of the pictures of Marx and Tito there are now a Byzantine icon and a painting of Black George (the original Karageorgevich), a nineteenth-century Serbian revolutionary leader against the Ottoman Empire.

He explains that "for the last thousand years we have constituted an Orthodox Christian civilization, though we were occupied for a long time by the [predominantly Muslim] Ottomans. We are Byzantine, and the successor to Byzantine Constantinople was Moscow, the Third Rome. The father of *Sveti* [Saint] Sava, the founder of the Serbian Orthodox Church in the early thirteenth century, was born here. We are spiritually part of the Serb nation, in terms of our church, language, and customs. Geographically we are the western outpost of the East, but also an eastern outpost of the West. We should be politically neutral, in other words. But our government has taken decisions against the people, decisions which are not sustainable—it joined NATO and recognized [ethnic-Albanian] Kosovo. But NATO means nothing to our people, and we mean nothing to NATO. Our military certainly does not help NATO. All NATO cares about is our strategic location on the Adriatic."

"But isn't this all that Russia cares about, too, Montenegro's location on the Adriatic?" I ask.

"Russia is weak. It can't even defend completely its own borders and seas."

That is exactly how Vladimir Putin would put things, I think to myself: an emphasis on blood and ethnic nation, while professing innocence and weakness in the face of NATO aggression. In fact, Mandić does tell me he is in favor of Montenegro joining the European Union, since only if all the Balkan countries are within the EU can their border issues stemming from overlapping historical claims be resolved. But this, too, is not unreasonable from a Kremlin perspective: Putin does not demand ideological purity, he does not want to re-create the Warsaw Pact; he wants only a soft zone of imperial-like influence in Central and Eastern Europe, and so having a state sympathetic to Russia inside the European Union has its advantages. Didn't Mandić say that he wants Montenegro to be neutral? Moreover, precisely because of the institutional weakness and geography of southeastern Europe, officials in Brussels have made it clear that EU membership must be preceded by NATO membership. Brussels knows that to absorb these countries is a historical process in itself, not a matter of one decision. So Mandić's position against NATO is a nonstarter. But he is indicative of a not inconsequential strand of public opinion here, as future elections here would show.

Indeed, as I've said, the legacy of Communism is criminality and weak institutions, and because improvement takes decades and not years, there is a yearning for a return to the bosom of the ethnic nation on one hand and a return of Tito on the other. Democracy must play the role of the long-distance runner in this struggle.

MILO DJUKANOVIĆ, A SILVERY-HAIRED, six-foot-five-inch politician, has been both prime minister and president, holding just about every top-level post in the country for almost a third of a century. He balances the West off against Russia. The product of a pseudo-democracy, he has faced the dilemmas of the dictator that he has almost been: in power so long in such a murky, weakly institutionalized system that if he returned completely to private life he might well and deservedly be prosecuted for corruption. A truly historical figure in post–Cold War Montenegro's short history, he has been defined as the shrewdest of manipulators, "always playing 4-D chess with geopolitical standoffs."[8] Originally a close ally of infamous Serbian leader Slobodan Milošević, Djukanović deftly switched sides to join the West in the 1990s, just as the war began to turn against Belgrade. In a very small sense, he defeated Milošević. And as Putin began to ratchet up tensions with the West in the 2000s, this self-styled Putin of Montenegro later made himself into an enemy of the Kremlin, so that the West forgave Djukanović's increasing autocratic tendencies at home and his background as an alleged cigarette smuggler, connecting Italian and Montenegrin criminal networks. Indeed, the alleged Moscow coup attempt here supposedly targeted Djukanović himself, at least to hear him tell it.

Djukanović is dressed in expensive business casual attire when I meet him, his top shirt button open. Every hair on his head is combed in place. There is a sleek cheetah-like quality to this Balkan strongman. His face is immobile as I introduce myself in his office. After a few moments, he suddenly becomes animated and is unstoppable as he leans into me, only a few inches away. His thoughts appear quick, so that speech itself frustrates him.

"The region is deteriorating. After the fall of Communism, the EU, [U.S. Secretary of State James] Baker were optimistic. They wanted to welcome Yugoslavia into the West. Why do I recall this? Because while the international community was constructive, we were not. Then came the horrors of the war. After Dayton [the December 1995 Bosnia-Herzegovina peace agreement] we had another window of opportunity. Again we did not take it. Bosnia today is dysfunctional. The pre-Dayton dilemmas are returning. Serbia and Kosovo are the same. [North] Macedonia is deadlocked, though improving a bit. So we had war, lost opportunities, and now a third stage: a faltering vision of a United Europe, while the United States was increasingly absent. We saw the United States [under Donald Trump] question the European-Atlantic alliance in the face of a newly refreshed Russia. Russia does not consider the Balkans a priority. It has its sights set on destabilizing Europe as a whole. Yet we are fragile because of our own particularities. You see, there is a strong pro-Russian sentiment here. So, with little effort from Moscow, we are the object of Russian artillery, so to speak.

"Let me be blunt," he goes on. "We need NATO. We have no second thoughts about negotiating for membership in the EU. We know all about the EU's weaknesses. But we see no alternative. The EU offers the only solution to the successive imperialisms [and instability] that have dominated our weak and divided region. Europeans and the Americans have now let Putin inside. And the Russians are not the only players here. The Turks and the Chinese are also gaining ground. The Chinese want to build a road from [our Adriatic port of] Bar north across Montenegro to the Serbian border [as part of their new Silk Road system]."

"The Chinese," I interject, "like the Russians, are not democratic, and could be a bad influence."

He frowns in agreement. "Europe, the EU, even with low economic growth, is something for us to emulate. Otherwise, our democratic prospects are bleak."

"Did the EU, after the fall of Communism," I ask, "underestimate the depth of the problems in this part of the world?"

He frowns again, agreeing with the supposition.

As intensely focused as he appears in our hour-long conversation, as I shake hands to say goodbye, he looks over my shoulder to an advisor, and immediately seems concerned about something else, forgetting me already. He was the president of the ruling Democratic Party of Socialists, so he was still in power behind the scenes at the time of my visit, even though he was not prime minister. In a country as bureaucratically fragile as this, he must deal with levels of stress that might immobilize the average Washington politician.

A few months later he would again become the country's president. Politics here is tumultuous, and would change again and again in the years following my visit. But what would remain the same was the dilemma of a rugged and mountainous country in a far-off corner of Europe, where even the pro-Western forces were allegedly gangsterish and corrupt.

"I HAVE BEEN A MEMBER of four national parliaments in Montenegro," Ranko Krivokapić explains, "those of Tito's Yugoslavia, of Milošević's Yugoslavia, of the independent Serbian-Montenegrin state, and finally of independent Montenegro. But the same party has often been in power here: the Communists, who renamed themselves the Democratic Party of Socialists, which is Djukanović's party." Krivokapić, who is also exceedingly tall and expensively dressed, was actually the party leader under Djukanović, but broke with Djukanović after condemning him for corruption. We meet in a crowded, noisy café in Podgorica frequented by young people, a refuge from the pouring rain.

"Djukanović, whatever he tells you, has no beliefs, only positions," Krivokapić claims. "He rules Montenegro like an owner, not like a politician. It doesn't matter what he may say publicly about the West and the Russians, if you are encouraging a corrupt system like he is, you are in the final analysis compatible with the Russians— even if the Russians might have preferred someone else, even more compatible. And the Russians know it. Without clean government, without the rule of law at home, without the normal rotation in power of parties and rulers, we in Montenegro are moving into the camp of the Russians, no matter what our professed positions about NATO are. It is similar in Kosovo and Bulgaria. In this part of the world, the direction of money-flows are much more crucial than Western values. Without real democracy, the Russians must win."

And he adds: "Russian influence in the Balkans was the knife in the stomach of the Ottoman Empire. Now Russian influence in the Balkans is the knife in the stomach of the West."

There was only one time in modern history, actually, when the western Balkans as a whole (from Slovenia to Macedonia) were truly free from an outside imperial power. That was during the Yugoslav kingdom and then under Tito, who survived not only by creating a police state, but also by granting his people comparatively more freedom than existed in neighboring Communist countries. "Tito is still the most popular politician in the western Balkans," Krivokapić exclaims, talking loudly above the music.

The dilemma is classic. Order must come before freedom, but once order is affirmed, the immediate challenge is to make order increasingly less overbearing. Montenegro is in the midst of that struggle. Djukanović wants the West to have more influence here, but he doesn't know how to survive except by ruling in the way that he does. Boban Batrićević, a local historian, tells me that Djukanović rules as he does because institutions here are so frail. And that frailty is a consequence of a "tribal, clannish system," itself the upshot of a "mountain landscape, the historic fear of the Turks, and the tradition of both warriors and herders." Thus Montenegro, despite its rich medieval identity, has had difficulty building a modern state. "We have to change ourselves," Batrićević says. "We cannot wholly rely on the West."

As it stood at the time of my visit, Montenegro was the only country in former Communist Europe that never had a democratic transition. "Even in Belarus and Russia Communists have been out of power for at least one electoral cycle," noted Gordon N. Bardos of Columbia University's Harriman Institute.[9]

IT HAS BEEN RAINING hard for days now. The sky is somber. I wake up in my luxurious but grim and alienating hotel room in Podgorica, full of personal worries. At home in the countryside in western Massachusetts, far from the city, one email can darken or brighten my mood much more than if I were immersed in city life, always with other people, always in the flow of sensations. Traveling alone in the winter in a place like Montenegro, the effect of just one email is that much more extreme.

Of course, this is a problem of traveling alone for weeks at a time in my mid-sixties with a family far away, often busy writing in the dawn hours, and meeting people the rest of the day—but also of long hours with nothing at all to do. I am as prone to loneliness as anyone. And loneliness encourages depression and pessimism, leading to questions about the very purpose of what you are doing. My yearning for solitude and my determination to travel alone has failed. It worked at the beginning of my journey in Italy, but it doesn't work here. Here, unlike Italy, there is much less of an accretion of art and architecture to both occupy and distract your mind.

Here, where the deposits of urban civilization are so much slimmer—and the state weaker—geopolitics takes over.

So I worry that the book I am writing fits no category. It is not military strategy, political science, original archival history, conventional long-form journalism, traditional travel writing, memoir, or literary criticism. After all, what does the poetry of Ezra Pound have to do with the current position of the West and Russia in Montenegro? True, as I've already maintained, the study of geopolitics may benefit from a return to terrain that is the province of old-fashioned travel writing. *But really?* I ask myself. *Have I taken it too far?* My only justification is that a ramshackle amateur may catch things that the specialists miss, and that by linking together disparate subjects I can shed fresh light on some of them as part of a self-inspired liberal education.

In his travelogue about Germany, *The Bells in Their Silence*, Smith College professor and literary critic Michael Gorra explains how he "enacts a dialogue between my hours in a library and the ones I passed on the ground itself, and I've skipped over those travels that didn't push me toward some sustained textual encounter."[10] That is to say, Gorra's book is a series of awkward and beautiful digressions, as when he uses a visit to the city of Munster to transport himself, by way of one book and another, to ultimately arrive at Italo Calvino's *Invisible Cities* (1972), in which Marco Polo describes to Kublai Khan the metaphysical character of the places through which he has traveled. Yet it all hangs together. Will my book, too? I really wonder.

And what will it reveal about me? For society gets to define us differently from how we define ourselves.

To special-plead for a moment, as in the cases of so many people, I am not what others sometimes say I am. And I don't mean only the bad things. For example, I am not brave. I was always terrified in war zones, writing away in my notebook while my stomach churned. I could never have been a war photographer, a profession where real bravery is required.

I travel to recover my sense of self, to be alone with my contradictions, to know tangibly how they are not really contradictions, at least not to me. I wrestled with them explicitly in an earlier travel book, which one reviewer was kind and perceptive enough to diagnose rather than praise outright.[11] Of course, I am not at all unique. We all are obsessed with self and want therefore to be understood. That is the postmodern condition. And so we expose ourselves on social media and then complain when we are misinterpreted.

Postmodernity is about the individual who wants to separate himself from the mass, even as his thoughts are often prepared by others who think for him, so that, counterintuitively, he lacks the very inner life he demands and thinks he has.

As with individuals, similarly with states.

The modern state, with its public schools, mass conscription army, and uncomplicated, one-dimensional patriotic loyalty, has been inexorably eroding in our era. People are more and more like Noel Malcolm's Brunis and Brutis—cosmopolitan, that is, complex in their identities, comfortable with their contradictions.

The Adriatic basin is a monument to such complexity. The metamorphosing of borders, identities, and loyalties has been going on here for thousands of years, with the crumbling and devolution of political communities followed by their aggregation into new and larger forms. Political identities and linguistic traditions have both combined and overlapped here. Who is to say that the port cities of Slovenia, Croatia, and Montenegro will not again one day be independent city-states, perhaps part of a new federation to be called— *who knows?*—"Yugoslavia," merely the land of the South Slavs, a word that early in the twentieth century once carried elements of hope and idealism before the wars of the end of that century. This original seed of hope is how I know that Montenegro is not necessarily doomed.

After all, the Adriatic is nearby. So is Central Europe. Koper and Split and Dubrovnik and Kotor are also part of this European world: much like a person with multiple passports, so common these days. The trick is how, despite all these layers of identity, to nevertheless retain a sense of belonging, rooted ultimately in a particular place.

THE MORNING OF MY departure from Podgorica I suddenly get a call from the Montenegrin foreign minister, Srdjan Darmanović. He can see me at my hotel at 8:30 A.M. for a few minutes. I have been leaving messages with him for days to no avail. Such last-minute meetings are common. And this one lifts me out of my depression. Because of Montenegro's smallness and isolation, it is relatively easy to meet high officials. I am truly a big fish in a little pond.

Darmanović is a think-tank academic, not a politician, and so refreshingly lacks the charisma of Djukanović and Krivokapić. But he covers similar themes. He tells me over coffee that "it is not easy being an Orthodox country with an authoritarian past, making it natural for Russia to have friends here. That's ultimately why American leadership will be required in the Balkans and Europe at least in my lifetime. But it was only after Ukraine," he goes on, "that America realized what is really going on in this part of the world." Then he makes a reference to the alleged coup attempt by Russian interests in Podgorica in 2016.

Still, he is not a pessimist. "Montenegro has been part of several different countries in my lifetime," he explains. "Almost every change was caused by some geopolitical cataclysm. But now for the first time we are well settled. Joining NATO, we finally found our way inside the West, and we are striving for EU membership. We have a direction. We stayed out of most of the bloodshed of the 1990s. And as for the region, you can't win an election in the Balkans these days without advocating EU membership. While populism is new in Western and Central Europe, and thus has a certain dynamic, it is old and tired here, linked as it is to the various Balkan nationalisms. That is the hope."

CROSSING FROM MONTENEGRO TO Albania, I officially leave the former Yugoslavia behind. Yet, because of the ethnic rivalry between the Serbs and the Albanians, both provoked and made more complicated by the heavily ethnic-Albanian region of Kosovo located inside historical Serbia, the geopolitical issues of the former Yugoslavia are with me still.

I was last in Albania in 1990, during the collapse of Communism in Europe. I recall oxcarts driven by soldiers with shaven heads, clogging cratered roads; gangs of women, wearing smocks and kerchiefs, with scythes and shovels over their shoulders, plodding back from grain and tobacco fields; apartment houses built of corrugated metal and badly mortared bricks, surrounded by barbed wire and concrete bunkers. "Every man-made object—the rough cakes of soap, the water taps, the door handles—manifested a primitive, just-invented quality," I wrote at the time. I remember a crowd gathered around a kiosk to look at an exhibition of safety razors, the kind my father used when I was a little boy in the 1950s.[12]

The change since then is disorienting. Immediately after the border post I am on a new road with new gas stations, guardrails, and safety markers. Amid fields of rubble are recently constructed and landscaped buildings. Police stand around wearing smart uniforms. Neat farm fields are bordered by young poplars with a Catholic church tower nearby. Jagged icy peaks, as amazingly steep and sudden as the Karakorams in northern Pakistan, loom cloud-girdled in the distance.

After an hour of driving I enter Shkodra. A horse attached to a refuse cart feeds beside a postmodern building where an Italian bank is located. There are ranks of old rusted bicycles adjacent to new motorcycles. People crowd the streets properly dressed for winter, but in the styles of black-and-white photographs. I see a handsome and rebuilt Ottoman mosque with rocket-like minarets, from where at noon I hear my first Muslim prayer call since beginning my journey. The haunting croon pierces my hotel room, situating me at a northwestern edge of an empire that once stretched eastward to Mesopotamia.

The hotel lobby is like a garish emporium and nightclub, overdone in splashy reds and gold paint that evoke Russia. The restaurant has an Italian menu. The chandelier is cheap and so large it could crush an elephant. My room is decorated with brocade and lacquer, in a Greek-cum-Balkan style. Whereas Podgorica was dreary, Shkodra on first contact is gaudy. The place has a Klondike feel. Just as slivovitz replaced limoncello when I crossed from Italy to the former Yugoslavia, now that I have passed from the former Yugoslavia to Albania, rakia has replaced slivovitz: each drink successively stronger and harsher than the one before it as I head south.

After lunch, I leave my hotel and—since it is only raining lightly—take out my umbrella and go for a long walk through town. Suddenly I am struck by the normality of Shkodra. The center is a beautifully laid-out network of pedestrian streets lined with cutting-edge signs over new stores. A giant kiosk is crammed with serious books. The parents with children often look like middle-class people the world over. Young men and women fill up the handful of up-market cafés: again, no different in appearance and expression than the young everywhere. And after lunch they promptly desert the cafés and return to work. As usual, the women are more stylish and look a bit more evolved and integrated into the global cosmopolitan world than the men. Everyone has a smartphone. The world of my first visit three decades ago appears ancient—and I haven't even arrived in the capital of Tirana yet. Of course, there is the corruption, the rackets, the gangs, and the dirty politics, of which I have heard. The profusion of high-performance cars in this provincial town attests to it. But progress anywhere can be uneven, particularly in a backwater of the Ottoman Empire that saw only a century of Venetian rule in the fifteenth century, with little tradition of grounded urbanity to draw upon.

———

EDWARD GIBBON DESCRIBED ALBANIA as a country "within the sight of Italy" that was, nevertheless, lesser known and less accessible than the interior of a barely explored continent—owing to a high and rugged landscape that confounded any notion of central control. In early antiquity, the area of present-day Albania was inhabited by tribes of Illyrians, an Indo-European people who may have ranged as far north as the Danube, and in the south of Albania were mixed in with Greek settlers. Over time these Illyrians became known to their southern neighbors as Albani, and their language as Albanian, a tongue quite different from the Slavic languages or Greek, and yet so beautifully ancient when you hear it. By the late third century B.C., the Illyrians were close to becoming the dominant power in the Adriatic, something that alarmed the Romans, who conducted substantial trade with Greece and the Greek settlements in Illyria. Thus, in 229 B.C., the Roman fleet sailed from southern Italy to conquer Illyria. This would be the first of a series of military strikes that would extend Roman rule over much of the Balkans.

At first, Rome created three provinces from north to south: Illyricum, Macedonia, and Epirus.* Interestingly, this very roughly corresponds to the current national groupings of Albania, Macedonia, and (northwestern) Greece. But the key element through much of this history is the subtlety of constantly shifting boundaries, rather than hard and fixed separations. To wit, in the late Byzantine era (the thirteenth century) there would come to exist the Despotate of Epirus, which extended from what is now central Albania to the Gulf of Corinth in southern Greece—sprawling, that is, over what is now four countries (Albania, Serbia, Macedonia, and Greece). And whereas at first there was a Roman and Byzantine

———

*   A few of the most notable Roman emperors were of Illyrian origin: Aurelian, Diocletian, and Constantine the Great.

overlay in this region, in Late Antiquity and the early Middle Ages there would be a Slavic one, as Slavs arriving from the east forced the indigenous inhabitants of Illyria deep into the highlands. The geographical theme was often of many principalities existing within large and weakly governed empires.

In the tenth century, the Bulgarian Empire, expanding westward, actually extended its reach to the southern tip of the Adriatic, remaining on Albanian territory for almost two centuries. Then the Normans, coming eastward, besieged the Albanian coastline. These East–West pressures crystallized in the schism of 1054, when Christianity split into Eastern and Western halves, with southern Albania becoming Orthodox and northern Albania becoming Catholic. Later the coast, centered on Dyrrachium (later Durazzo, and now Durrës), fell under Venetian control.[13] Remote Albania, barely thought of in our own era, was a seismograph for geopolitical forces coming from both Europe and the Near East.

The Ottoman Empire consolidated its hold over Albania in 1417. This locked away Albania within the confines of the Near East until, one might argue, 1989, when Communism—a Western ideology in the service of an Eastern-style despotism—finally collapsed. Yet, the Ottoman consolidation was often relative, and low-level warfare between the imperial authority and powerful Albanian clans became a feature of life in this impossibly rugged landscape. The most important of these anti-Ottoman warlords was Gjergj Kastrioti, born around 1405 to a prominent clan leader and famously known as George Skanderbeg. Delivered as a hostage to the Ottoman court in Edirne (Adrianople) and converted to Islam, he acquired the name Iskander (Turkish for Alexander the Great) and the rank of bey, thus Skanderbeg. After the Ottoman defeat at Nis (in southeastern Serbia) in 1443, he deserted the Ottomans, returned to Albania, forsook Islam, and embraced Orthodoxy. For almost a quarter century until his death, helped by the Venetians, Skanderbeg led the Albanians in a succession of campaigns against much larger Ottoman forces. Because Venice, as usual, balanced between resisting Ottoman expansion and trading profitably with the Ottoman Empire, it did not (to say the least) prove a steady ally for Skanderbeg in central Albania. Therefore, he had to rely on his own men, an irregular army not propped up by any foreign power, and yet he managed to hold back Mehmed the Conqueror's emerging world empire. Skanderbeg's coat of arms, a black double-headed eagle of the House of Kastriota, became first a symbol of resistance against the Ottomans and later the basis of the Albanian national flag. The idea of a modern independent Albanian state can truly be said to have begun with him.[14]

By the eighteenth century the ethnic-Albanian territories, divided among Catholics in the north, Muslims in the center, and Orthodox in the south, all existing within clans and tribes, had settled into a status (especially as the Ottoman Empire declined) of being "by far the most backward parts of Europe," writes British historian Miranda Vickers. (And by Albanian territories we mean not only present-day Albania, but the historically Albanian-inhabited regions of Kosovo and Ohrid.) Ironically, as Vickers explains, the very close identification of so many Albanians with their fellow-Muslim Turks, who had converted the Albanians to Islam and whose empire provided protection against the Orthodox Slavs and Greeks, inhibited the development of a national consciousness in the nineteenth century.[15]

Vickers's *The Albanians: A Modern History* precisely captures the story of an ancient people that have miraculously survived inside a weak state of debatable borders—coveted by both hostile neighbors and great powers because of its geographic position. As Europe in 1912 hurdled toward two Balkan wars, to be followed by World War I, Italy, Serbia, Montenegro, and Greece all endeavored to violate Albanian territory, even as political order there disintegrated. Albania's tragedy was that it was a historical nation without being an institutionalized modern state, while it also guarded the entrance to the Adriatic, so that everyone wanted a piece of it.

It was the first Balkan war that helped force a national consciousness upon Albanians, in order to defend themselves against Balkan neighbors whose own national identities had developed earlier. Albanian independence was proclaimed in 1913 mainly because the Ottoman Empire had simply become far too weak to hold and maintain it. Yet violent territorial incursions from Serbia and Greece persisted. To help stabilize the situation, Albania did what other Balkan countries had done: import a German king, Wilhelm, Prince of Wied. But his control would never extend much beyond Durrës, a city halfway down the country's Adriatic coastline. He abdicated in 1914 and the country fell again into chaos and dismemberment, with Serbia now the chief outside instigator. The post–World War I peace agreement awarded the ethnic-Albanian areas of Kosovo, Macedonia, and Epirus to Serbia and Greece. Albania ended the decade of war a devastated nation, where postwar governments would fall one after another, as corruption and abject illiteracy fundamentally undermined stability. Yet it survived.

In 1925, Ahmet Zogu, heir to the leadership of the largest Muslim tribe in the country, set up what in Vickers's words "was an authoritarian and conservative regime, the primary aim of which was the maintenance of stability and order."[16] In 1928, he proclaimed himself King Zog. But the influence of a newly Fascist and expansionist Italy kept growing, even as Zog created his own problems by overreacting at times to internal dissent. A decade later Italy invaded and occupied Albania, and King Zog's short-lived dynasty fell. Zog did further encourage the beginnings of a national consciousness, though it remained underdeveloped.[17]

So, as in the days of the Ottomans and other occupiers, the clans and subgroups of the Albanian hinterlands (Tosks and Ghegs in the most general sense) remained a law unto themselves, and Italy's occupation of the early 1940s was restricted to the coast and major towns. Nevertheless, Fascist occupation had the effect of helping to stimulate the birth of the Albanian Communist Party. Like national consciousness itself, Communism had come late to Albania relative to other Balkan nations, and was aided by Yugoslavia, the comparatively powerful, multiethnic federation next door that had, under Josip Broz Tito, at least temporarily subsumed ethnic-Serb ambitions in ethnic-Albanian Kosovo (though this would not last long). It was actually the Yugoslavs who appointed Enver Hoxha, the son of a Muslim landowner, to lead Albania's Communists in 1941. As Nazi German occupation followed that of the Italians, the situation of Hoxha's Communist partisans in Albania would be analogous to that of Tito's in Yugoslavia: fighting both local nationalists and foreign occupiers.

Both Tito and Enver Hoxha were unique among Central and East European Communist leaders. They were charismatic guerrilla fighters in their own right, who did not really require the Soviet military to liberate their countries from the Nazis. In other words, they were not the dull, unoriginal functionaries that the Soviets would install elsewhere in Communist Europe to help police their empire; thus Tito and Hoxha were in comparatively strong positions internally, enabling them to eventually chart their own paths outside the Warsaw Pact. (They were also helped by having no land borders with the Soviet Union.)

While Tito, a half-Croat, half-Slovene, with roots in Central Europe, would opt for a more liberal version of Communism, though still clearly remaining an autocrat, Hoxha, from a more backward and isolated country, would go in the other direction, towards a Maoist-style autarky, like in China during the first decades of Communism there. Of course, nasty and complex rivalries between the two Communist parties, and their differing attitudes towards the contested region of Kosovo, would play a role in how they both evolved. But Albania's utterly repressive form of Communism cannot be divorced from the country's historic isolation and lack of development: an isolation that Hoxha's actions would only deepen as the Cold War went on. Hoxha's ultimate policy aim during his decades in power was that of "mere survival," as Vickers puts it.[18] And thus as the Cold War drew to a close, Albania, having denounced in succession Tito's Yugoslavia, Soviet Russia, and Maoist China, found itself completely alone. It was as though the experience with Communism had only intensified the most tragic element in the country's long history.

Few capture this reality better than Ismail Kadare, born in 1936, the country's most celebrated novelist, periodically mentioned for the Nobel Prize in Literature. Without being a dissident outright—something impossible in Hoxha's Albania—Kadare was a consistent regime critic in the philosophical sense. I remember reading his novel *The Concert* in 1994 and reviewing it for *The New York Times,* after it had been published in English, and becoming fascinated with how Albania's successive breaks with Tito's Yugoslavia in 1948, with Khrushchev's Soviet Union in 1961, and with Mao's China in the early 1970s were the only distinctive time pegs in an otherwise monotonous and monochrome existence for average Albanians. By injecting high doses of tension and intrigue into the society, each diplomatic crisis led to extramarital affairs, divorces, and all manner of romance and reversals of personal fortune: it enriched lives, in other words. Nothing else did, it seems.[19]

Because the decades of Communist autarky only further decimated the already weak polity, the 1990s saw massive corruption and bouts of anarchy undermine an embryonic democratic system that was buffeted by social upheaval, as masses of people deserted the countryside and rushed into the cities.* But near the end of the second decade of the twenty-first century, a more nuanced picture began to emerge amid dramatically higher living standards among part of the population, and a commercial transformation and revitalization of the cities. Albania had joined NATO in 2009 and was possibly on a path toward membership in the European Union. It had avoided ethnic and religious conflict and had proper, peaceful

---

* In Robert Carver's *The Accursed Mountains,* Albanian peasants "bellowed and thumped" on the table, telling the author how post-Communism had destroyed their lives by ending agricultural subsidies to the villages, while cheap food poured in from Greece, produced under the European Union's own subsidies (London: Flamingo, [1998] 2009), p. 36.

relations with its Balkan neighbors—no mean feat considering the epic and bloody past.

Nevertheless, organized crime and endemic corruption had become major elements of daily life. Albania, as I write, is still a deeply divided and weak democracy. An opposition leader has accused the government of promoting "narcotraffickers, pimps, even killers as Members of Parliament." The U.S. State Department and Europol have declared Albania the largest producer of cannabis and the key gateway for heroin into Europe. In 2016 Albanians "came second only to Syrians as asylum seekers in Germany and France. More than 42 per cent of the population live on less than $5 a day," reports Besart Kadia, executive director of the Tirana-based Foundation for Economic Freedom.[20] While the long, historical ages of extreme isolation have receded, Albania remains a world removed from Italy, less than fifty miles to the west across the narrowest point of the Adriatic.

Albania and Montenegro both are, in developmental terms, places where Europe ends and also begins. Geographically they are unquestionably part of Europe, even as their mountainous topographies have tempered the influence of the Mediterranean. Moreover, historically and culturally they have been mightily shaped by the long centuries of often weak rule by the Ottomans, whose imperial footprint was planted mainly in the Near East. These are in many respects Europe's borderlands, which Europe cannot disown. If Europe makes any claim to universal values, it has no choice but to find a way to spiritually incorporate these two far-flung outposts of imperial Venice.

TAKING AN HOUR TO sip an espresso in a café in Shkodra, I recall that it was from this town that Edith Durham, the daughter of a London surgeon, launched her travels through the mountains of northern Albania in 1908. It was clear to her that Albania was still part of the "Near East" and "Turkey in Europe," as it had been since

the late sixteenth century.* Her book *High Albania* is an anthropo-
logical document on the absence of government and its resultant
Hobbesian "tyranny" of blood feuds—on "the tribal instinct and the
call of blood," as she puts it. There is also much about folkloric dress,
on the status of women, on the meaning of gravestones, the "semi-
tones" and "fractional tones" of Albanian singing, all accompanied
by vivid sketches, for she was an accomplished artist as well as a
writer.[21]

Durham's book is also a monument to her strong character and
prodigious talents. Her descriptions erase the decades and centuries
and make you feel that you are right there. Here she writes leisurely
about a house that was more like a cave, and both "majestic and
primeval" for it:

> It was a vast room—so vast that, though stacked with
> goods, the twenty-seven persons in it only made a tiny group
> at either end. Far away at the great hooded fire the women,
> silhouetted black against the blaze, were making ready the
> midday meal.
>
> The red flare danced on the smoke-blackened rafters. . . .
> Rudely painted chests . . . containing the belongings of the
> family, were piled and ranged everywhere. Arms and field
> tools hung on the walls and from the tie-beams on wooden
> hooks. . . . An indescribable jumble of old clothes, saddles,
> bridles, cartridge belts, was strewn over all in wild confusion.
>
> The bedding—thick sheets of white home-woven felt,
> pillows of red cotton, and plaited reed-mats—was stacked on
> the chests. . . . Dried meat hung from above . . .[22]

The capacious detail never lets up, especially as she evokes ramshackle dirt shanties that, nevertheless, after hours of walking,

---

* Indeed, she talks often about the *medjliss*—Arabic for "council"—a traditional gathering that takes place in Albania, just as it does at the other end of the Ottoman Empire in
Mesopotamia.

drenched and exhausted, "warmed and . . . revived me." Even when I was young and traveling through central Tunisia, Afghanistan, and Pakistan in the 1970s and 1980s, I had not half the stamina and enthusiasm that she had, though she was already forty-five at the time of her journey. She could lose her already meager toiletries on the road without it affecting her spirits. She grasps that the quality of the written product depends on being able to put up with a bit of dirt. And yet to do so can, at times, be almost a moral struggle. She writes about sighting Podgorica from just over the border in Albania, with all the creature comforts it promised:

> Podgoritza! I thought of the Hotel Europa—it seemed a little heaven below.
>
> I was drenched with sweat, dizzy with heat . . . and very little sleep. Why suffer torture in an aching wilderness when Podgoritza would receive me joyfully? . . . But I could not show my face in England and say the North Albanian mountains had beaten me in six days.[23]

And thus she goes on, later to find a dark and dusty hovel of a church where a humble meal of rakia and fried eggs would revive her. I myself might already have given up.

IN THE 1990s, the English writer Robert Carver began his own intrepid, Durham-like travels through the wilds of Albania, inspired by a meeting in London in 1991 with Patrick Leigh Fermor, who told him that Albania is where he would head were he still young. Though the period immediately after the fall of Communism was technically democratic, Carver describes the Albania of the early post Cold War as hovering between autocracy and anarchy. Tirana at the time, he observes, was an armed camp with police, special forces, and the armed units of the ruling political party nervously fingering their shotguns, assault rifles, and bazookas in the streets. Carver writes: "What could you say about a culture where . . . everyone stole and was proud of it; where girls were kidnapped at fifteen and sold into prostitution; where lying was normal and the government stole more than anyone else? Where people trafficked in guns, drugs and false identity papers, and went to richer countries deliberately to rob and pillage?"[24]

But that was *then*, I tell myself, and even *then* it could not have been the whole story.

THE ROAD FROM SHKODRA south to the capital of Tirana is a panorama of construction, interspersed with rust and dereliction: a typical post-Communist tableau. There are piles of rocks, old tires, and refuse heaps beside glitzy new restaurants and nightclubs, standing literally in the middle of nowhere. The breakneck development yields a pervasive ugliness while mournful snowy winter massifs stand in the background. Closer to Tirana, after ninety minutes of driving, are kitschy resorts next to bare fruit orchards. The sun peeks through for the first time in a week, making some of the mountain vistas look as lovely as Switzerland. Then come miles of sleek new office blocks, pulsing video advertisements, and massive traffic congestion on an excellent road. The global world has seeped in. It goes on like this for miles. None of this construction was here in 1990, when I last visited. I recognize absolutely nothing from that time. Finally, as I approach downtown Tirana, there are mini shopping malls and cafés where everywhere, as in downtown Shkodra, people simply look ordinary. Skanderbeg Square, where in 1990 I observed gangs of young boys harassing passersby and stepped into an old barbershop to get a shave, now is plied by new buses and young people riding on bicycle paths. A nearby mosque, the snowy mountains, and the air that betrays the clarity of the Adriatic not far away, provide me with only suggestions as to where exactly I am. Albania, that is, reminds me of no other place where I have ever been. It has become a stage set for a normal country, except that it really isn't.

"Every new building you see is dirty money," the first Albanian friend I meet, a young academic, tells me. "Here you still find the refuse of Stalinism on the Adriatic, which, after the most oppressive system in Communist Central and Eastern Europe collapsed, has bred a generation of sheer criminality. There are still no working institutions," he continues matter-of-factly. "The political parties, the politicians are all implicated. The more brutal the system, the worse and more deeply entrenched is the corruption afterwards."

Later, Remzi Lani shows up for coffee at my hotel. He is the director of the Albania Media Institute. At sixty he is handsome and distinguished, a true classical liberal. "More Albanians believe in NATO and the EU than believe in God in this predominantly Muslim country. They know that it is probably the EU that can begin to clean things up. It's unfortunate," he goes on. "Albania is the only country in the Balkans without a Plan B. Serbia's Plan B is Russia, Bosnia's is Turkey, and so on. For Albania, the EU is the best destination, partly because we are so much more corrupt than the others. We don't debate Russia, NATO, the U.S. The big things all the politicians agree on. It's the small things that eat our politics up alive."

"Could that be a factor of mountainous isolation where the clan tradition is even stronger than in Montenegro, with historical enemies on all the borders?" I ask.

He agrees, saying that Albania does not really have Italy and Greece as neighbors, but its neighbors are the poorest and most corrupt part of Italy, Puglia, and the poorest and most corrupt part of Greece, Epirus. "We are thriving in terms of our civil liberties, and failing in terms of political culture and the rule of law."

The failure of the Albanian political class since the fall of the Stalinist regime is natural, I tell Lani. The first generation had to fail, since it had no role models at home and no lessons learned to fall back on, after four and a half decades of the most brutal, murderous Stalinist system anywhere. (North Korea not excepted, since at least in North Korea there has been more social discipline than obtained in Hoxha's Albania, as Lani informs me.) The pyramid schemes that wiped out people's savings in 1997 and caused anarchic violence were the culmination of unplanned, hurried development without institutional safeguards. The very fact that the country has recovered so well is testament to the resilience of Albanians themselves and the sheer, never-ending process of history, I tell Lani, as well as myself.

I GO FOR MY first extended walk in Tirana. I immediately notice the postmodern glass skyscrapers with lots of local banks. "All are houses of mafia, of cannabis, of laundered money; only such can build these new monuments," another friend informs me. I see old monuments, too, within a few steps of my hotel. There are the headquarters of the World War II–era Fascist Party and the Cold War–era Communist Party, with a remnant of the Berlin Wall on display, a gift of the German government. Deserted and graffiti-scarred bunkers edge the house of the Communist-era prime minister, Mehmet Shehu, who committed suicide in 1981. (Or was he killed by Hoxha?) There is the great new mosque built by the Turkish authoritarian-style leader, Recep Tayyip Erdoğan, who wants to re-create a new Ottoman Empire of sorts. The pyramidal structure that once housed a museum dedicated to the life of Enver Hoxha is now closed, rusted and defaced by graffiti. On the same block as Shehu's house and the party headquarters are cheesy and expensive boutiques, signifying the new idols, the new ideology. All of Albanian modern history is right here. The changes have been monumental, but they have not been deep. For everything has—in a certain peculiar sense—remained the same. The abuse of power is not as stark and physical as it once was, with killers and killed, but the improvement has been stylistic more than fundamental.

ALBERT RAKIPI IS THE director of the Albanian Institute for International Studies. He is another civil society intellectual, with rounded glasses, clipped gray hair, and a half-undone tie with a sports jacket. "We have had the same leadership for thirty years," he starts with a whisper, "the same political culture. Of course, we have institutions, political parties, but nothing works. In terms of the mentality and the inner workings of the psyche, too little has changed since Hoxha's time. Instead of killing you, now they just put you in prison; or they put you out of work, or forcibly buy you out with licenses. In Albanian society, there is loyalty only to the family, to the clan, to the village. In Albanian politics you give blind loyalty, or you are simply expelled from the party. Stalinism, Communism are both dead. But the behavioral metaphors of Communism live on.

"We are only one hour by plane from Rome," he goes on in a very low voice. "Yet here the jet age is irrelevant; geography still rules." He then talks of Ottoman-era tribal anarchy begetting political incoherence, in turn begetting Stalinism and finally criminal capitalism. "If only in a small way, nearly everyone in Albania is involved in some illegal business or other, because the state has never really existed; only clientelist networks have. For example, in Europe, Serbia is seen as a state with weak institutions. To us, Serbia appears like a strong state."

In passing, he talks about Ioannis Kapodistrias, the early-nineteenth-century Greek statesman, who envisioned Greece eventually becoming like France, despite hundreds of years of Ottoman rule. Kapodistrias wasn't naive: he simply had a direction in which to orient Greece. In the early twenty-first century, Greece is still far behind France. Nevertheless, with all of its upheavals and political weakness, Greece has certainly dramatically evolved in a positive direction. That is how, I realize, one must approach Albania.

IF POST—COLD WAR ALBANIA has a historic figure, it has been Sali Berisha, former president and prime minister, who before the fall of Communism was a highly placed medical doctor and then a leader in the struggle against dictatorship, before becoming dictatorial himself in his years in politics. We meet for lunch in a private room of a boutique restaurant, first opened by a notable businessman under King Zog, whose imposing, touched-up photograph with his dog graces a wall. Seventy-three at the time of our meeting, Berisha is white-haired with a well-structured face, formally dressed, and blessed with the genius of personality that defines a sharp intelligence merged with an animal, human force. He launches into a narrative that covers the most heroic part of his own political life, the part where he likely has the fewest regrets.* His style is both didactic and commanding. It seems as if he is speaking to a crowd.

"The enemies of Communism were the former elites, their families, and their friends. The supporters of Communism were the criminal elements, the indoctrinated true believers, and the massive, silent majority of conformers. It took me years to journey from being a conformer to discovering my own dignity. After all, I had my family to protect. It was 1988 already. As a doctor, I knew that the peasants were dying of starvation and disease, pellagra in particular. [Ramiz] Alia, who succeeded Hoxha [as Communist Party leader], wouldn't even let a peasant own a pig. At this time I had heard of [Andrei] Sakharov in Russia, and of the Polish dissidents." Berisha then called publicly in the late 1980s for pluralism and a market economy, "even though I knew zero about a market economy, I just knew that people were starving.

"You see," he continues, "we were the only country in Eastern Europe with four levels of dictatorship. One, we were Communist. Two, we had the cult of personality of Enver Hoxha. Three, we suffered worse misery and worse starvation than even in [Nicolae] Ceauşescu's Romania. Four, we were in total isolation, psychological and physical. Again, much worse than in Romania." He then describes the "barbaric beatings" of students in Skanderbeg Square by the regime in December 1990, already a year after Ceauşescu had fallen.

---

* In 2021, his family was sanctioned by U.S. authorities for alleged corruption.

After the Communist regime fell, "for us, the first generation of politicians, it was like building from scorched earth. At the time, the per capita income in Albania was comparable to only certain African countries; now it is over $11,000.* Urbanization has been one of the most dramatic in the world because the Communists left behind a countryside with literally no means of life. As for the rule of law"—he grimaces—"that will take another generation, or two." *In other words, never,* I thought. Because of historical, economic, and geographical forces, Albania was trapped for this period of its history into being for Western Europe what Mexico and Central America have been for the United States: a wellspring of contraband and corruption.

But Berisha recovers his composure and adds, with a hint of complaint, "Isn't loaning money that is several times more than what a bank has in deposits a form of corruption—a pyramid scheme—as banks in Europe did during the Great Recession in the last decade?"

"It was," I tell him. "But it occurred at a much higher stage of capitalism than exists in Albania, and often led to real consequences for the banks."

Our discussion proceeds to regional geopolitics.

"The biggest problem in the Balkans," he explains, "is Albanophobia," the fear of Albanians, because of their relatively high birthrate, their poverty, and their corruption. "You find Albanophobia in Serbia, in Macedonia, in Greece, and in Montenegro even. Albanophobia is all that remains of the Balkan tinderbox." It is the essence of the dread of Muslims in the region, he means to say, and is therefore related to the dread of the Bosnian Muslims by the Serbs. So the Balkan problem, such as it remains, is now part of a global problem regarding the relationship between Muslims and the West.

---

* Albania ranked 124 out of 229 countries at the time of our conversation, according to the CIA World Factbook.

———

AFTER MEETING BERISHA, I go on a journey. In under an hour I am in the port of Durrës. I remember from my visit in 1990 the amphitheater of Roman Dyrrachium, once the greatest city on the Adriatic's eastern shore. It marked the beginning of the Via Ignatia, the great Roman and Byzantine highway that connected the Mediterranean by road eastward across the Balkan peninsula to Constantinople and beyond. In 1990 there were heaps of garbage, a wall used as a public toilet, and other forms of desolation by the amphitheater. The nearby shops were generally those of tailors and cobblers. A Byzantine church apse is part of the ancient complex, with mosaic tiles depicting an angel. I remember back then admiring the loving care of the antique, wafer-thin brickwork, since everything in the streets around it was of an inferior construction standard.

Now everything has changed, and not completely for the better. The amphitheater lies adjacent to a landscaped square, punctuated with palm trees, and a rash of construction. There is a gleaming archaeological museum with exquisite displays and labeling. I climb to the top of a round Venetian tower. Directly in front of me is the Adriatic and the modern port of Durrës with its gantry cranes. To my right are the sixth-century walls of the Byzantine city. And to my left I see a large remnant of another ancient wall that heralds the Via Ignatia itself. It lies half hidden inside what looks to be the garage entrance of a hideous new "tower of mafia." In fact, this whole area, which should all be an archaeological park, is defaced by unwarranted, unregulated construction. The Via Ignatia is now the Via Cannabis, as an Albanian source told me, with drugs traveling from the Near East westward to Mediterranean ports.

Of course, there is NATO's presence here on the eastern shore of the Adriatic to consider, which, coupled with the growing Turkish influence in Albania, made me realize that Europe's geopolitical challenge is in one respect a question of defending three seas: the Baltic, the Black, and the Adriatic, with the Russian threat demon-

strably apparent in the first two seas, and the threat of Russian subversion, the influence of a rising autocratic Turkey, and finally
organized crime apparent in the third sea. For the Adriatic defines
the borders of Central Europe as much as the Baltic and Black Seas
do. After all, what was it that Churchill said in describing the division of Europe in his famous March 1946 speech?

> From Stettin in the Baltic *to Trieste in the Adriatic,* an iron
> curtain has descended across the Continent. Behind that line
> lie all the capitals of the ancient states of Central and Eastern
> Europe. [Italics mine][25]

Indeed, the Adriatic is more than a vital component of the Mediterranean. It is also a fault line of civilizations and ideological
systems, as well as being a key to Central Europe's geographical
identity. But let's not forget that Central Europe, at least in its ideal,
signifies a civil and moral space with a cosmopolitan spirit: threatened not only geopolitically but culturally by a combination of reactionary populism, drugs, corruption, the illegal traffic of migrants,
and Russian destabilization, often in the cyber realm. These various
forms of aggression are all of a piece, undermining the social fabric.
The new cold war, in the lowercase sense of the phrase, is simply
more complicated than the old one, and here at the start of the Via
Ignatia is one of its deceptively quiet epicenters.

THE CITADEL OF BERAT, to the south and inland from Durrës, is
where the great coastal plain abruptly meets the mountains. Because of the new roads, I am there in no time. The citadel is a chaos
of different patterns of stone, signifying a continued occupation
from early antiquity by the Illyrians to the end of the Middle Ages
by the Ottomans. Here, Byzantine churches and the remnants of
Ottoman mosques practically touch each other before a dramatic
cake-swirl of olive- and pine-imprinted hillsides, constituting the

ultimate concision of history: a prospect in which geography itself is miniaturized, with nearly each roadway a former trade route. The cultures of the Adriatic—that is, of Europe and the Near East, of Christianity and Islam—all come together at Berat, like in the maps of old-fashioned social studies lessons when I was a child.

In one of the churches is an eighteenth-century icon composed of tempera on wood, painted in the pure Byzantine style of savage beauty that bespeaks literal belief. In the icon, the Virgin Mary and the infant Jesus stand atop a monument that at its base delivers the water of life. The Virgin's hands are outstretched in benediction; on both sides of her are two mosques. The iconographer was obviously paying a tribute to the Muslim rulers. But the icon also evinces the religious tolerance of Ottoman imperial society, in which the Orthodox Church and its communities were protected inside an Islamic sultanate.

Before this icon, I feel a degree of culmination in my journey, with my certainty established that Europe must aspire to universal values, and yet be anchored to its local beliefs and cultures at the same time. This is not an original idea by any means, but it is one that I have palpably discovered, as a reality from Italy around the Adriatic to Albania. Berat is as much a compass point as Rimini, a nexus of routes and civilizations. There is no beginning and no end to Europe in a global world. There is only the constant struggle for tolerance and the rule of law, easier to forge in some places than in others, with Montenegro and Albania representing, perhaps, the most extreme challenges.

As for myself, I have been not so much a traveler as an introvert trying to be an extrovert, insisting on solitude but also recognizing the constraints it imposes, and thus forcing myself to meet people. A true traveler—a Durham, Leigh Fermor, Durrell, or Theroux—is an eruption of life, full of exuberance, who doesn't need to make appointments in order to have meaningful encounters. I can't measure up, but I am compelled to travel, nevertheless. How else can I ever truly arrive home?

CORFU

---

*The Archetypal
Refugee Experience*

SOUTHERN ALBANIA IS A BIBLICAL IMMENSITY OF PEAKS
ribbed with early spring snow. I arrive at the coast and notice that I
have passed an imaginary line in latitude. The blue water has that
lit-from-below quality that almost blinds with delight. I am within
the orbit of Greece. The colder Adriatic is right behind me. Here-
abouts begins the Ionian Sea.

From the sleepy port my memory from 1990 recalls, in the course
of the last three decades the Albanian town of Saranda has become
a cancer of cement. The ugly high-rises, some tiled like lavatories,
are practically stacked one on top of the other. The building materi-
als are shoddy. The few areas left bare are weedy lots with garbage.
Nowhere in the developing world have I witnessed such a lack of
government planning and unchecked construction. There is a quality of barbarism about it that goes beyond aesthetics. It is the Klondike capitalism version of early Soviet design. Despite the obvious

material progress, the Albanian struggle to erect a civil and humane state bravely goes on.

The ferries don't operate in the off-season and so I board a hydrofoil to cross the Iron Curtain of yore, from Albania to Greece. The trip lasts thirty minutes. The distance between Saranda and the northeastern tip of Corfu is so short, and the water so flat on this calm day, that one really can swim it. So narrow is this distance! From one shoreline you can see the houses on the other. Geography is so arbitrary, and yet its effect on human destiny is truly heartbreaking. For this is still a hard border. Modern states with their bureaucratic control mechanisms only reinforce geographical divides.

On the western side of this seaboard the rule of law, however weak in areas, exists nevertheless. On the eastern side the rule of law is that much weaker or absent entirely: a fact that must give hope to the Kremlin, even if these countries are members of NATO. Elections matter less than institutions in this regard. Thus, the Adriatic is still a sensitive barometer of the political strengths of East and West, and if the eastern shore is not incorporated into Europe, the disorder of Eurasia looms uncomfortably proximate to Italy, which has its own problems.

Europe does not have the luxury to wash its hands of these troubled states through which I have just traveled. Indeed, the Adriatic, at the heart of both the Mediterranean and the Central European worlds, constitutes a nervous geography that in the twenty-first century will have a geopolitical story to tell, the plot of which has yet to be written. Such are my thoughts as the hydrofoil passes through the breakwater towards the Greek customs station.

WHEREAS SARANDA IN ALBANIA bespeaks urban anarchy, Corfu Town astonishes with its potted flowers overflowing onto iron trellises against the Italianate and neoclassical facades. Here, thanks to both nature and the imperial rule of the Venetian doges, exists a more luxuriant and cosmopolitan version of Greece. The clay roof tiles, the blood-brown madder walls, and the towering, bone-charred Venetian fortress carry the earthen air of an archaeological ruin and thus suggest the basis of civilization. The parks flare with lavender almond blossoms in April. And the cafés are on an Italian standard, so that wealthy Russians and Britons both make Corfu one of their playgrounds.

Before sunset, on a weekday no less, the cafés and restaurants are absolutely jammed with people: grandparents, parents, and young children all together, the latter of whom noisily scamper around the tables while the fathers sip ouzo and the mothers nurse babies. *Family.* This is the true indestructibleness of Greece, despite economic depression and populism, and it is true of the Mediterranean in general, where the generations are not isolated from each other by technology and loneliness to the degree that they are elsewhere. There are no family scenes quite as poignant as Greek ones, where alcohol is not taboo, but something children grow up with and therefore do not abuse; nor is there quite the chicness of Italy or the sloppiness of the postmodern West. In the grounded stability of this evening crowd—where children go out with their parents to fine restaurants—I sense something eternal. And then, of course, there is the language, which, with its gyrating phonetic eruptions, is meant for the stage as much as its ancient counterpart.

Of course, there is another side to this romance, as a Greek friend, who is a specialist in economic crime, tells me over a drink here. The emphasis on (and the strength of) family can also lead to corruption, since family bonds have historically come before legal norms and other ethical boundaries. Modern Greece's tradition of a weak state—where services such as urban planning and garbage collection are feeble, and so too is tax collection—is partly traceable to the panorama I see before me on my first evening in Corfu Town. There has been an implicit bargain between government and people here since the mid-nineteenth century: *we will give you little but we will also take little from you.* Though the situation is not nearly as dire as in Albania or Montenegro, Greece remains arguably among the more corruptly governed states in Western Europe, though this has lately been changing.

"The weak state was a strategic choice," my friend tells me, and then he casually mentions the assassination in 1831 of Ioannis Kapodistrias, the brilliant and disciplined Greek diplomat with an international background, who consequently harbored no illusions about his homeland. Had he survived, he might—just might—have set Greece on a different path after independence.* It was the second time in my journey that I heard Kapodistrias's name mentioned as a historical-change agent. There are many reasons why things happen as they do. And many of them have nothing to do with geography.

I sit down for dinner. Corfu is quite familiar to me, even though my last visit here preceded my one to Saranda. Little here has been uprooted. The changes have been subtle. In fact, fifty years after my first coming to Greece, waiters at tavernas still invite me into the smelly bowels of their kitchens to choose my fish and meat. Customs hold firm. Don't ever think that an economic depression—as devastating as what America experienced in the early 1930s—has damaged Greece as much as almost a half century of Stalinism has done to Albania. Greece is something you can hold on to. It never did leave the Eurozone. It never did crumble into anarchy, as many had predicted a few years before.

Thus far I have been traveling through landscapes that I did not earn, that is, I bring no trained scholarship or linguistic skill to the task. Greece, at least, is a place where I have lived and worked as a journalist in an earlier period of my life, and therefore have some familiarity with. I met my wife in Greece. I was married here, and it was in Greece where my son was born. Returning to Greece is

---

* As the name suggests, Kapodistrias's family was originally from Koper, on the Adriatic in Slovenia, before settling in Corfu in the fourteenth century.

like coming home. It is like pushing open the front door of my house with my bags at my feet after a long journey. Because languages can be learned only with a vast amount of time and effort, further improving my Greek, as someone once said, will constitute my own struggle against mortality.

THE ISLAND OF CORFU is, and is not, Greece. It has been identified as much with the Adriatic as it has with the archipelagic Greek seaboard. Corfu, in a larger sense, constitutes a register of (and a meditation on) European history itself. The real beauty of this island is how it makes you think, in the most profound and analytical way. Vandals, Goths, Byzantines, Slav and Barbary pirates, Normans, Angevins, Catalans, Venetians, Ottomans, Russians, French, British, Germans, and Italians all conquered, reconquered, or raided this Greek island not because of its beauty, but because of its strategic location. It is the Gibraltar of the Adriatic.

And before all of that there was an ancient history.

The Peloponnesian War (431–404 B.C.), which engulfed all of Greece, had its specific origins (though not its underlying ones) in relatively minor conflicts involving Corfu (Corcyra) and Potidaea, which helped drive tensions between Athens and Sparta, the great city-states and empires of the age, to the breaking point. It was Corfu's rivalry with Corinth over Epidamnus (modern-day Durrës in Albania) that led Corfu to seek a military alliance with Athens. This blow to Corinthian prestige led Corinth, in turn, to seek an ally in Sparta, so that the system of interlocking alliances got out of control. Corfu is a caution for how small conflicts can unpredictably lead to big ones, and for all those who imagine wars as short, intense, and contained, without realizing what great demons they can unleash.

Corfu was also where the Athenian navy gathered for the ill-fated Sicilian Expedition that began in 415 B.C., and is described in the seventh book of Thucydides's *Peloponnesian War*. Athens was lured into Sicily by local allies, who were threatened by other Sicilian city-states loyal to Athens's rival, Syracuse, in turn an ally of Sparta, with whom Athens was fighting a war. The Athenian intervention began with just a score of ships and grew over time to hundreds of ships and thousands of troops, as Athens became more and more deeply involved on the far-off Sicilian mainland. The Sicilian Expedition, which lasted only a few years, ended with the deaths of 40,000 Athenian troops, of whom 6,000 survived to labor in the quarries of Syracuse and be sold into slavery. The American wars in Vietnam and Iraq have been compared to the Sicilian Expedition, whose opening scene is here in Corfu.

Cicero, that wily and eloquent political operator and humanist extraordinaire of first-century-B.C. Rome, met here for the last time with Cato the Younger in 48 B.C. Cicero was on his way back to Rome to seek Caesar's mercy. Cato was en route to Africa. Three years later, Cato, who led a revolt against Caesar in defense of the democratic ideals of the Roman Republic, committed suicide after marching across Libya and being surrounded by Caesar's troops in Utica, in northeastern Tunisia. Cato had locked the gates of Utica and evacuated his soldiers by sea before driving a sword through his own body, dying, in Plutarch's words, as "the only free and only undefeated man" in Rome.[1] Politics in the ancient world—and in some regimes today, in fact—was literally about life and death. It took courage and character that few politicians in the West today can even comprehend. How to imagine Cato the Younger?

But when we think of history in Corfu we think primarily of Venice, which required control of Corfu for its control of the whole Adriatic. Most of the stopping points of my journey would have been impossible—or more difficult—for Venice to hold without Corfu. It is Corfu that guards the sea at its narrow southern entrance, the Strait of Otranto, and thus helps give the Adriatic, in Braudel's words, its "essential characteristic" as almost an oblong lake. By the late fourteenth century, Venice headquartered one of its fleets of observation here, "to protect her pretended rights over the whole Gulf," writes nineteenth-century British historian and soldier Henry Jervis-White-Jervis. The Venetians called Corfu "Our Door," and had an emotional attachment to this island, the place where Venice lost thousands of men in sea battles against the Normans in the eleventh century.[2]

In 1571, "the Christian fleet," in the words of Jervis-White-Jervis, "consisting of three hundred sail, and carrying fifty thousand foot, and four thousand five hundred horse, under the command of the celebrated Don Juan of Austria, arrived in the harbour of Corfu." Soon, "having there obtained information that the Turkish fleet was off the Gulf of Lepanto [in the Ionian Sea], he followed them thither, and defeated them, in one of the most signal victories that have obtained a place in the annals of the world." Lepanto, fought on October 7, 1571, cost the deaths of almost 8,000 Christian soldiers, sailors, and rowers, with even more wounded, and with an even higher number of casualties on the Ottoman side. While the horrendous blood price is commonly thought not to have paid great strategic and diplomatic dividends (on account of the need of Venice and its allies to continue dealing with the Ottomans), Noel Malcolm points out that had the Ottomans not been defeated at Lepanto, the sultan might well have been able to take both Crete and Corfu, and thus, by holding Corfu, launch an attack on southern Italy itself across the Strait of Otranto.[3]

From 1814 to 1864, as a consequence of the post-Napoleonic peace treaties, Corfu and the other Ionian islands were placed under British rule, with the intent, according to Jervis-White-Jervis, that Corfu "should enjoy the municipal liberty which the Greek cities enjoyed under the dominion of the Romans."[4] That period of British rule, which was less constitutional and democratic than it seemed, lasted half of the nineteenth century: a very long time for a group of islands that are part of Greece geographically, and quite close to the mainland. It is another lesson in how geography is not altogether deterministic and has many conflicting stories to tell.

Just consider that in our day the northern and northeastern parts of Corfu have their British-owned villas and sensitivity to environmental preservation, while the equally beautiful southern part has been given over to breakneck package tourism.

I OWE MY DISCOVERY of the Jervis-White-Jervis book to the bibliography in Lawrence Durrell's *Prospero's Cell: A Guide to the Landscape and Manners of the Island of Corfu.* Durrell's first travel book, *Prospero's Cell,* is really a travel-in-residence book, written in the form of a diary, and thus was somewhat unusual for its time: the effect of a delicious landscape, language, and culture imprinting itself on a sensual and ravenous young mind. Though the diary is from the late 1930s, few were interested in an introspective, self-indulgent, and utterly romantic account of life on a Greek island during a world war. But as soon as the war ended, the book, published in 1945, "electrified a war-weary, color-hungry British public," writes one biographer. Indeed, Durrell consciously ignored the Spanish Civil War, the rise of Hitler, and the other horrors of the decade. He said that whereas politics was a subject "that dealt in averages," the artist was driven by "his self-isolation and the dislocation of the societal instinct." Thus, while politics was about understanding and shaping the attitudes of the common man, art was the opposite—it was about dealing with the exceptional. Art was solitude; politics, social engagement. Arguably, given the stakes in the 1930s, such an attitude was irresponsible (though Durrell would serve as a British diplomat during and after the war). And yet living in a white-washed house by a small and secret bay on the remote northeastern coast of Corfu, amid insects and a lack of plumbing, Durrell and his wife, Nancy, dedicated themselves "to art and literature and freedom," some of the very values that the war would soon be fought for.[5]

No one, perhaps not even Patrick Leigh Fermor (Durrell's good

friend), has ever so literally captured the supernatural effect of the
Greek landscape upon a visitor coming for the first time from the
West:

> Somewhere between Calabria and Corfu the blue really
> begins. All the way across Italy you find yourself moving
> through a landscape severely domesticated—each valley laid
> out after the architect's pattern, brilliantly lighted, human.
> But once you strike out from the flat and desolate Calabrian
> mainland towards the sea, you are aware of a change in the
> heart of things. . . . You enter Greece as one might enter a
> dark crystal; the form of things becomes irregular, refracted.
> Mirages suddenly swallow islands, and wherever you look the
> trembling curtain of the atmosphere deceives.[6]

It goes on like that. For Durrell, the Greek landscape is nothing
less than a living being, the eternal "Enormous Eye," as he calls it,
God's way of looking at the world, "like a lens fitting into the groove
of the horizon." And so, "our life on this promontory has become
like some flawless Euclidean statement," even as he admits that
Corfu is merely the Venetian "ante-room to Aegean Greece," whose
effect will prove to be more powerful and mathematical still. What
follows are pages of crystalline introspection, enlivened by an un-
matchable life force (the very thing that really unites Durrell with
Leigh Fermor)—about local saints, carbide fishing at night, Albanian smuggling, taking a bath in a natural cistern by the sea, among
so much else. Indeed, there are learned disquisitions about the olive
harvest and shadow-puppet theater, and a rich description of feasts
with a local count, who convincingly argues that Corfu is the real
setting for Shakespeare's *The Tempest*. Enjoying the bawdy fantasia
of Karaghiozis, Durrell is aware that the Greeks sitting nearby
might distrust his interest in the performing puppets, thinking that
in an oblique way he is, albeit good-naturedly, looking down on
them. His ruminations on the Greek national character—that of

the "downtrodden little man getting the better of the world around him by sheer cunning"—leads ultimately to an observation about Greek politics, which is "not the barren politics of abstraction and principles, but the warm cruel politics of the heart: hero-worship, the advancement of parties and personalities. In this alone we catch a glimpse of his [the Greek's] bitter dualism of the heart—an interior anarchy which will not let him rest."[7]

Seven years of living as a journalist in Greece in the 1980s and observing political parties that were less parties than passionate coffeehouse aggregations centered on charismatic personalities has demonstrated to me the essential accuracy of Durrell's admittedly broad judgment. Though Greece, like many countries, has been changing, as politics increasingly takes on both a global and a technocratic character.

"FEW COUNTRIES IN EUROPE have had such a harrowing and strife-torn recent history," begins King's College London scholar Richard Clogg in his *Short History of Modern Greece*.[8] Writing from the vantage point of 1978, more than three decades before the Great Depression–like collapse of the Greek economy—something itself tied to Greece's long legacy of institutional underdevelopment—Clogg identified the inheritances of Eastern Orthodoxy and centuries of Ottoman rule as making Greece distinct within the European Union, with the obvious exceptions of Bulgaria and Romania. In fact, the decisions to admit such a country into NATO and the EU demonstrated the very ambition of those two organizations—to both bridge and ignore the gap between East and West. For despite Greece's obvious strategic value, and despite the emotional pull of ancient Greece to the citizens of the West, the ambitious attempt to absorb this poor child of Byzantine and Ottoman despotism—not so much better off than Montenegro and Albania today—into the postwar alliance structure spoke to the universalism to which Western institutions aspired.

The variously shaded map at the beginning of Clogg's *Short History* shows the conspicuously artificial territorial conception that is modern Greece: expanding gradually, by war and other random contingencies, northward through the course of the nineteenth century and into the twentieth, roughly from a base in the Peloponnese, Attika, Euboea, and the Aegean islands, to eventually incorporate parts of Epirus, Macedonia, and Thrace by 1920. Greece, very much like Italy, is a great, blunt, and obvious fact of geography, history, and culture. And yet, like Italy, precisely because geography tells many contradictory stories, Greece's current borders, while declared by everyone to be unarguable, may in the fullness of time acquire a more subtle meaning.

We think we know Greece because of its famous association with Periclean Athens, the spiritual birthplace of the West. But the memory of classical Greece always distorted the modern reality. Clogg identifies the earliest seed of modern Greek identity with Georgios Gemistos Plethon, alongside whose tomb outside the church in Rimini I began this journey. For as the Ottomans were overrunning the Byzantine Empire—with Mistra in the Despotate of the Morea being one of the last remnants of Eastern Rome still standing—in the early fifteenth century Plethon stressed the link between the Eastern Orthodox Greeks and their Hellenic forebears, thus helping to forge an identity for the Greeks not wholly linked to religion, and encompassing the glories of antiquity.

But for centuries thereafter, Greece's only "window to the West" was Venetian rule in Corfu and the other nearby Ionian islands, even if Muslim Turkish rule offended Orthodox sensibilities less than rule by the hated Catholics of Venice.[9] Yet, in many respects, Ottoman rule was simply shattering and meant little more than a struggle for physical survival, in which many Greeks pinned their hopes on the Orthodox Russians to the north for their eventual liberation.

An indigenous uprising and the destruction of the Ottoman navy by the British, French, and Russian fleets in 1827 off the western Peloponnese gave birth to an independent Greece. But this eventually meant rule by a Bavarian prince, Otto Frederick of Wittelsbach, partly because the Western powers feared that the new chaotic state (in the wake of the heroic diplomat Kapodistrias's assassination) would otherwise fall under the sway of Russia. As it happened, the new state "was overrun with armed irregular troops," writes Clogg, stemming from internal divisions inherent in the ten-year struggle for liberation. Further delegitimizing this new and unstable state was the fact that it encompassed less than half of the Greeks who had been living under Ottoman rule.[10] This fact would lead to an irredentism lasting into the middle of the twentieth century, which went under the banner of the *Megali Idea*, or Great Idea, which was no less than a wild dream on the part of the Greeks to reconstitute the Byzantine Empire.[11] Anarchy hence became a feature of modern Greek life amid constant territorial disputes with the Ottoman Empire and Slav nationalists to the north. Emotions would frequently boil over in the course of the struggle to liberate Crete in the south and in the fear of losing Macedonia in the north.

After World War I and the dissolution of the Ottoman Empire, Greece attempted to annex the western edge of Asia Minor with its 1.5 million ethnic-Greeks concentrated around the great cosmopolitan city of Smyrna. The Greek army landed on the coast in 1919 and, deluding itself about Allied support, advanced inland almost as far east as Ankara, deep in the Anatolian interior. In 1922, the Turkish army counterattacked and literally drove Greek forces backward into the sea. Tens of thousands of ethnic-Greek civilians around Smyrna were killed and 1.2 million—practically the entire population of Greeks in Turkey—were made refugees. At least 100,000 ethnic-Greeks were marched into the interior of Anatolia, most never to be seen again. Two thousand five hundred years of Greek civilization in Asia Minor abruptly came to an end.

The 1922 *Catastrophe*, as it came to be known, destabilized Greek politics for decades, with several coups in its wake, as the refugees from Smyrna were resettled into an already poor nation whose population was only 5.6 million before the Greek-Turkish War. (Makeshift refugee encampments were to become a semi-permanent feature of Athens.) The population exchange, which also featured 400,000 Muslims being forced to move from Greece to Turkey, was "a grim cultural and geopolitical landmark," according to British historian Bruce Clark, in which international bureaucrats, working under the provisions of the Treaty of Lausanne that followed World War I and the Greek-Turkish War, provided a legalistic template for ethnic cleansing in twentieth-century Europe, for as the Ottoman Empire collapsed following World War I, a multicultural and traditional world—representing the last vestige of early modernism—gave birth to monoethnic modern states.*

The first truly stable government in modern Greek history emerged only fourteen years later in 1936—a military dictatorship under General Ioannis Metaxas, which against all odds would repel Mussolini's invasion into Greece from Albania. Metaxas's forces would reconquer for a time the ethnic-Greek part of southern Albania, known as Northern Epirus (around Saranda). Greek resistance against the Italians provided the Allies with their first real success of World War II, and thus inspired the forces of good when they were most needed. Alas, the Nazi occupation of Greece followed, its wanton cruelty over the entire country giving rise to a Communist resistance.

The end of World War II brought not peace but a civil war lasting until 1949, between the Communists and the ultimately victorious right-wing loyalists, which resulted in 80,000 dead and 700,000 internal refugees. Because of the brutality on both sides, particularly against civilians, Greek politics would remain polarized for decades,

---

*   Bruce Clark, *Twice a Stranger: The Mass Expulsions That Forged Modern Greece and Turkey* (Cambridge, MA: Harvard University Press, [2006] 2009), p. 19. Giles Milton, *Paradise Lost: Smyrna 1922; The Destruction of a Christian City in the Islamic World* (New York: Basic Books, 2008), pp. 372–73. Actually, the first example of ethnic cleansing in Europe in the twentieth century was in the 1912–13 Balkan Wars. See Mark Mazower, *Governing the World: The History of an Idea, 1815 to the Present* (New York: Penguin Press, 2012), p. 156.

divided between parties of the hard Left and the hard Right, so that a modern liberalism and a modern conservatism would find little room to emerge. Thus did Greece, abetted by its geography—as close to Moscow as to Brussels—become an ideological battle-ground of the Cold War.

Greece's Cold War years were marked by weak governments as well as deep, internecine political divisions, which were further aggravated by the independence struggle on Cyprus, with its consequent calls for *Enosis* (or union) of the island with Greece. (Of course, this itself was an echo of the Great Idea.) In 1967, junior officers staged a coup, toppling the Greek government in Athens. This led to a particularly brutal seven-year military dictatorship in which the Athens "Regime of the Colonels" bore greater similarities to those of the Third World than to any government in Western Europe. The Colonels' regime dissolved in 1974 after their failed political intervention in Cyprus led to a Turkish invasion and occupation of the northern part of the island.

It was only with the reestablishment of democracy in July 1974 under the conservative politician Constantine Karamanlis (who had returned to Greece from exile in France) that Greek politics began slowly—for the first time in history—to stabilize and achieve a modern, Western character. Greece, the birthplace of the West, finally reentered the West. This process was helped by the country's admission to the European Economic Community (later the EU) in 1981.

Like membership in NATO, membership in the EU and Greece's subsequent admission to the Eurozone represented purely political decisions on the part of the Western alliance. In fact, neither Greece's bureaucratic institutions nor its economy was ever up to the standards of core-Europe and the West. Yet, it was felt (if never publicly admitted) that leaving Greece outside European institutions, given the country's vulnerable geographical position and its long history of instability, would pose a greater threat to the West than bringing Greece inside them. As it turned out, the Greek variant of the Great Depression, in which the country was brought to its knees beginning in 2009 by widespread poverty, a dramatically declining GDP, and mass unemployment—leading to a far-left-wing government initially close to Moscow—was directly related to the country's abject lack of preparedness for the rigors of the Euro-zone. The Byzantine and Ottoman legacies of underdevelopment, while not determinative and always able to be overcome, still counted for something in Greece in the second decade of the twenty-first century.

TRULY, ATHENS IN THE immediate wake of Greece's Great Depression was, as I experienced some years ago, a tattered cityscape blackened with graffiti at the foot of the great classical monuments of Western civilization. Athens, surrounded by the sea and gaunt, pine-clad mountains under a melodramatic sunlight, remains spellbinding. Yet the graffiti, more oppressive in some districts of Athens than in any other Western capital I know, spoke of an anarchy and of a resistance to the state itself that many Greek commentators themselves have observed. Very few radicals elsewhere openly call themselves anarchists as they do in Greece.

A leading Greek journalist explained to me that for most of history, especially in Ottoman times—but also in ancient Greece—government was "intimate, personal, it involved only people you knew." For as always, there was the emphasis on family and close friends. Because the vast modern state as an abstract impersonal force destroyed that intimacy, Greeks rejected it. Eastern Orthodoxy didn't help, with its rejection of the material world's formal obligations beyond the clan and family in exchange for the promise of an otherworldly existence: something that, as a Romanian philosopher and friend once observed, burdens the entire Orthodox realm in Russia and the Balkans. To understand the mindset of the postmodern Greek anarchist, my journalist acquaintance in Athens told me, "one has only to read Bakunin and Dostoevsky." In fact, I think of Dostoevsky's *Demons,* in which one of the radicals proclaims:

> As soon as there is just a tiny bit of family or love, there's a desire for property. We'll extinguish [that] desire: we'll get drinking, gossip, denunciation going; we'll get unheard-of depravity going; we'll stifle every genius in infancy. Everything reduced to a common denominator.[12]

Everything reduced to a common denominator: this is where anarchism morphs into Communism, and eventually into Stalinism. Therefore, it is no accident that Greek anarchism since the middle of the twentieth century has existed right alongside the most orthodox Communist movement in Western Europe. Orthodoxy, anarchism, Communism have all been part of the same rejection of Western rationalism in the land where the West itself was in a spiritual sense invented.

And yet to talk of East and West as exclusivities in Greece is to ignore that the country is an inextricable compound of both. The East exists in the magical gold-leaf darkness of the Orthodox Church, as distant in spirit from the Protestant and Catholic West as it is from Islam. Not only was the Byzantine Empire essentially Greek, so too was the Ottoman Turkish Empire, often ruled as it was through Greek diplomats and local governors. "Greece," writes the late Philip Sherrard, a renowned translator of modern Greek poetry, echoing Father Kallistos in *The Orthodox Church,* "never had any Middle Ages, as we understand them, or any Renaissance, as we understand it, or an Age of Enlightenment. That elevation of reason over the rest of life had not taken place. Greece," Sherrard goes on, "had not gone through that debauchery of rationalism of which the modern western world is the product," and with it "the consequent paralysis of man's emotional life."

Nevertheless, approaching from the opposite geographical and civilizational direction, Greece is also where the oxygen of the West begins to diffuse the crushing totalitarian logic of ancient Mesopotamia and Egypt. This, after all, was the ultimate achievement of Periclean Athens: to breathe humanism and a sense of the individual into the tyrannies of the antique East, where the gods did not look like men at all but like half animals.[13]

YET, TO INTERPRET THIS rather grim and tragic modern history as unrelated to a brilliant and heroic ancient one is to misunderstand the message that Greece offers for our own era. For the Greek classics of antiquity were, too, very much about blood and tragedy—acted out against a landscape that, as Durrell wrote, constituted the eternal Eye. Nothing and no one teaches this lesson as powerfully as the twentieth-century Greek poetry of Nobel laureate George Seferis.

Seferis, born and brought up in Smyrna, who as a lonely twenty-two-year-old studying in Paris experienced from a distance the Asia Minor Catastrophe, employs Greek antiquity and the heart-rending voyage of Odysseus in order to deeply intuit its relevance to the appalling suffering and sheer disappointment of his own time. In his poetry the sufferings of Odysseus and his men collapse into the sufferings of the million Greek refugees from Asia Minor in 1922. To know Greece is to know its modern burden—that of an epic past within a ruptured and small, very confined present; the impossibility of living up to its reputation means it is thus crushed under a stereotype. Seferis's poetry is shorthand for this tragically misunderstood identity.

Seferis, according to Sherrard, both his translator and his interpreter, saw how men, women, and children "suffered a pattern of despair and tragedy which some years later was to become the common pattern of Europe: homes destroyed, files of refugees, forced marches down endless roads to unknown and often lethal destinations, separation of families, detention camps, boats overweighted with desperate human cargo capsizing in open seas."[14] It was the end of a world and of a civilization, a demonstrable forerunner to the horrors of World War II—and to the Syrian and Libyan crises of our own time. In a letter to his mother in December 1922, Seferis wrote about the destruction of Smyrna:

> Can the human mind find room for such a thing, in the twentieth century, the century of humanity, a city of three hundred thousand people can be made into a graveyard in just four days.[15]

And all around him as his friends and loved ones were forced into exile from Smyrna, the young Seferis saw the material legacy of greater Greece, complete with its historical echoes: in Sherrard's spare and inimitable words, "the broken statues and the Venetian forts, the white shores of the Aegean Isles and Alexander the Great, the bony mountains and the argonauts, Byzantine churches and plane-trees."[16]

In Seferis's poetry, Odysseus and the exiles from Smyrna, the exiles and refugees from any time and place—from Syria and Libya in our own day—all cohere into one:

> What are they after, our souls, traveling
> on the decks of decayed ships
> crowded in with sallow women and crying babies
> unable to forget themselves either with the flying fish
> or with the stars that the masts point out at their tips
> grated by gramophone records
> committed to non-existent pilgrimages unwillingly,
> murmuring broken thoughts from foreign languages?
>
>
> What are they after, our souls, traveling
> on rotten brine-soaked timbers
> from harbor to harbor?[17]

The words and phrases from Seferis's other poems are equally moving: "Wherever I travel Greece wounds me. . . . This road has no end, no relief. . . . Few are the moonlit nights that I've cared for. . . . The houses I had they took away from me. The times / happened to be unpropitious: war, destruction, exile. . . ."[18]

There is nothing more mythic and archetypal than the refugee experience, encompassing as it does humanity's hopes, dreams, terrors, and wanderings, all contained within the individual's daily struggle to keep himself or herself and his or her family intact despite dislocation and privation. As I write, tens of thousands of refugees from the greater Middle East live stranded in miserable conditions, scattered in camps about the Greek islands, where they have arrived from Turkey in an attempt to land inside the boundaries of the European Union. Greece offers up the burden of history still—and yet, as Sherrard tells us, a way to comprehend and deal with it. For man is not merely a link in an "endless chain" reaching back into the past; "he possesses within himself" the "microcosm" of "all historical periods." And through both myth and symbols, Seferis describes this inner life, and so reveals archetypal patterns of experience that unite us with the past and therefore with universal truth.[19]

We are back, in other words, to the literary modernism of Joyce, Eliot, and Pound, with its use of symbols to describe individual experience. Except that with Seferis, the symbolism is less abstract because Greece itself, with all of its classical, medieval, and modern historical associations, is his own personal landscape. Greece, the real Greece—not the one-dimensional postcard vision of the Acropolis, but the tragic and sumptuous fusion of the ancient world, Byzantium, and the modern age, complete with the destruction of Smyrna, something that is neither specifically Western nor Eastern—provides the final image of Europe.

INDEED, THE FAULT LINE between East and West that I have traveled along during this entire journey is actually shorthand for a category of distinctions that gets harder and harder to define. For Europe comprises a mystery of creation born of innumerable and complex political, cultural, and economic interactions among Christians, Jews, and Muslims.

And yet broad tidal waves of change and influence are undeniable. The Greek Orthodox Byzantines helped shape Europe, both in their own oriental religiosity and in the barrier they struggled to maintain for hundreds of years against Seljuk and Ottoman Turks. The Mongols helped shape Europe, by the role they played in effectively shielding Russia from the experience of the Enlightenment. The Arabs helped shape Europe, by linguistically and culturally separating (to a significant extent) North Africa from it. The Sassanid Persians helped shape Europe, by clashing with the Byzantines, thus weakening them both, so as to enable the Arab conquest of the southern shore of the Mediterranean. Both the Middle East and particularly Africa may help shape Europe, by generating millions of refugees and migrants for years and decades to come.

For Europe, with all of its difficulties, will continue to constitute the most desired and proximate location for the victims of political and economic upheaval throughout much of Afro-Eurasia. Between now and 2050, for example, Africa's population will have doubled to 2.4 billion, while the number of indigenous Europeans stagnates and declines.[20] Even without war and upheaval, and even with the growth of African middle classes and the subsequent decline of the African birthrate, we are only in the early stages of a significant population movement from south to north. (New African middle classes will actually generate more migrants, not fewer, as people will have the means to leave their homes and choose where to live, as upheavals of rising expectations take hold.) Finally, China will help shape Europe, as the Greek port of Piraeus becomes a western dagger point of China's emerging Silk Road, or the Belt and Road Initiative, as it is called. Greece is, in a very concrete geopolitical sense, very much back at the crossroads of East and West.

Europe, therefore, is only at the beginning of monumental change. It is the crucible where many of the challenges of Afro-Eurasia will play out. Europe's own present-day secularism and universalism, by-products of the need to escape from history (and specifically from the Götterdämmerung of two world wars), only leave the continent more vulnerable to civilizational upheaval. Remember that Europe's Western identity has always been more contingent than commonly realized. For long centuries, the West was a geographical accident shaped in part by the clash of empires in the Near East and North Africa. Despite the myriad of contacts and interactions that occurred between civilizations from Late Antiquity to modern times, Christendom remained cohesive enough— and for long enough—to combine with feudalism to forge the rudiments of the West as it came to be known.

Going forward, the solution may lie counterintuitively in the past: in the early modernism of an imperial world, where cosmopolitanism reigned. Empire has acquired a bad odor owing to the crimes of modern European empires in Africa and elsewhere. Yet the future could benefit from benign imperial constructions like the EU, as well as from vibrant city-states.

And as technology erodes distance, cultural and civilizational distinctions also erode. Thus, the populist nationalism that we have seen is but a cri de coeur—an epiphenomenon—before there is more gnawing away at national histories and cultures. In the digital age, it is harder than in the print-and-typewriter era to pass on histories and traditions from one generation to the next. For now everything can be deconstructed, with competing rather than common narratives, even as information floods over society and attention spans become nonexistent. Historical memory itself dissolves as one intense and all-consuming news cycle is rendered obsolete by the next. In such an environment, the maintenance of a distinctly Western identity—separate from an Eastern or Asian or African one—becomes a vestige of a bygone age.

THE ADRIATIC HAS ALWAYS been a civilizational transition zone, and so it becomes especially iconic in a world of overlapping and dissolving identities. But because of its very cultural richness—Eastern Orthodox, Roman Catholic, and Muslim; Slav, Italian, Albanian, and Greek; Mediterranean, Central European, and Balkan—the Adriatic, rather than signify incoherence, demonstrates an enlightened alternative to the debasement of losing all memory and tradition. For just as too much memory can be a prison of hatred and resentment, too little memory renders us indistinguishable from the lower forms of life, for whom existence has no context and no awareness beyond the present moment. Tradition, however particularist, provides a defense against this. It is far better to be confused about one's identity because one has several of them than to have no identity at all.

To say that Eurasia, as distinct from Europe, begins at the Adriatic is a commonplace in all of this. But the more fundamental issue is this: Can one imagine a universal civilization that is at the same time richly rooted in tradition?

Yes, one can, if, to repeat, one thinks as Pierre Manent does, in terms of cities and empires rather than exclusively in terms of states.[21] Cities and city-states throughout history have been multicultural, just as empires in the long historical sense (as opposed to strictly the European colonial sense) have been cosmopolitan and multinational. And while cities and empires are political creations rooted in antiquity, states have a less classic vintage, and are associated more with modernity. Postmodernity does not necessarily mean the passing of states. But the fact is, across Eurasia and particularly in the greater Middle East, the state model is weakening. The cratering Levant is only the most obvious example. Even in more historically well-rooted states—the legacy of venerable empires—such as Turkey and Iran, governance has become increas-

ingly fraught. Inside Europe itself the state model is continually
stressed by structural economic difficulties and a supra-state mechanism, the European Union, which does not work as it should. Thus,
political evolution tumultuously goes on. And as in the case of all
evolutions, the ground moves silently under our feet, so that we
don't notice it.

Indeed, "globalization means we are all Levantines now," writes
the British historian Philip Mansel, referring to the eclectic cities of
the Levant at the turn of the twentieth century: Alexandria, Smyrna,
and Beirut, where, as he writes, "people switched identities as easily
as they switched languages."[22] (He might also have included the
Black Sea port of Odessa in that category, for there was "nothing
national" about that cosmopolitan city, writes one scholar.)[23] Of
course, nationalism would eat away and destroy such cities. And as
with so much else, it is Greece that offers the most poignant example of this. To wit, in the port city of Salonica (now the Greek Thes-
saloniki), a relatively easygoing Ottoman imperial tolerance allowed
for the coexistence of Orthodox Christians, Muslims, and Jews.
Only later did that give way to harder national and ethnic divides
that have been a feature of the industrial and post-industrial ages.
"Muslims turned into Turks, Christians into Greeks," as monoethnic twentieth-century states took hold, explains Columbia professor
Mark Mazower.[24] And yet, as Philip Mansel suggests, we are returning, at least in a sense, to the fluid and multiple identities that prevailed in those early modern cosmopolitan cities. The difference is
that those cities flourished in an imperial world, in which, because
the Ottoman sultan was sovereign everywhere, there was little territory to dispute among the various religious and ethnic communities.
Meanwhile, we must still live for quite a while longer in a world of
nation-states in which territory is jealously guarded. Levantine-like
cosmopolitanism, moreover, is a feature less of political evolution
than of blunt economic transactions enabled by communications
technology—everything from the Internet to passenger jets.

Yes, once again, the ground is moving silently under our feet, as city- and region-states grow in importance and a neo-medievalism sets in. In the sixteenth and seventeenth centuries, as the British historian Mark Greengrass (echoing Denys Hay) explains, the concept of Christendom was gradually replaced by that of *Europe*. Though Christendom had in the course of Late Antiquity and the Middle Ages come to represent a geographical concept, it remained at root a religious identity, whereas *Europe* was at root all about geography. *Europe*'s subjugation of Christendom was complete when Christianity stopped being a political identity and became merely a private religion having to do exclusively with the soul.[25] Given that Europe replaced Christendom, are we now in a transition period in which some concept will replace Europe? And if it does, where does identity finally settle—at the national level, at the regional level, the level of the city or town? Or will Europe revert to a religious identity, a *neo-Christendom* of some sort, to psychologically wall off Muslims from the Middle East? Or might Europe itself simply fade as a concept, as it dissolves into Afro-Eurasia and identities within the continent become, as I've speculated, increasingly local? Greengrass traces the destruction of the concept of Christendom over an arc of 131 years. So it is quite likely that the real substantive changes that are occurring now will not be apparent inside the strictures of any news cycle.

The late British-American historian Tony Judt provides a somewhat alternative view; or rather, a view focused on the immediate future rather than on the middle-term and distant one. As he explains, the integration process that culminated eventually in the European Union was in part an accident born of the realpolitik of politicians who each needed a predictable economic framework for their own national aims. To wit, France needed German coal, but at the same time needed to contain German political power; and Germany needed to hide its own national interests within a larger community in order to regain legitimacy in a post-Hitler era. The context for this realpolitik was a just-ended Second World War that was "peculiar," in that countries were often divided among themselves and "almost every European participant *lost*." Thus, everybody wanted to forget about what had just happened, so that defeatism, pacifism, and ahistoricism reigned. At the same time, the Cold War had enforced unity in the western half of the continent. It was defeatism and unity that gave birth to this new *Europe*. Yet, because the combination of these and other factors (e.g., the Marshall Plan) was specific to a certain moment in history, they could never be repeated in the same way, and so the European Union could not simply go on as it had indefinitely—for other factors must eventually intrude.

What is particularly impressive is that Judt published this analysis in 1996, when few troubles loomed on the horizon and Europe was dull and happy. He then goes on to expose Europe's "foundation myth": that it must keep expanding to the east in order to improve not only Europe but the world, or else the current success would merely indicate an amoral utilitarian arrangement. Of course, as we know, Europe's eastward expansion following the end of the Cold War occurred under different historical circumstances and so the result has been complex and not altogether a triumph. Judt concludes his 1996 essay noting again, presciently, that with postmodern life hollowing out the communal functions of family, church, school, the military, and even political parties and trade unions, all that is left now is the nation. For it is the nation that embodies a common memory and a community within an "appropriately scaled frame": larger than that of the city, but smaller than that of a nebulous pan-European or global identity.[26]

Beyond the present and the immediate future, though, embracing this nationalist revival—which, because the nation itself has been partly abandoned by elites, is also a populist revival—means that something new must emerge alongside it. And probability points to multiple forms of identity.

I WALK UPHILL FROM the port to the new section of Corfu, where I find the municipal theater, a modernist rectangular affair brutally marred by graffiti. Indeed, the stone slabs look as if they were haphazardly glued together. But before this structure was built, there had been another municipal theater here, a handsome neoclassical building erected at the turn of the twentieth century and destroyed by the Luftwaffe in 1943. This was where the Serbian parliament in exile, having retreated under pressure from Austro-Hungarian and German forces on the Balkan mainland during World War I, met in 1916 to propose the creation of the Kingdom of Yugoslavia. The new Yugoslav kingdom was envisioned as a parliamentary system under the Serbian Karadjordjević dynasty, representing the national denominations of the Croats and Slovenes as well, and using both Latin and Cyrillic alphabets. The vision came into effect the following year with a declaration, also signed on Corfu, by Serbian, Croatian, and Slovenian politicians in exile. This Yugoslav kingdom, which existed between the two world wars, was violently dismantled by occupation and ethnic civil war between 1941 and 1945. The socialist republic of Yugoslavia under Tito would replace it in 1945, and last until the civil war of the 1990s. The twentieth-century history of Yugoslavia began on this site.

It is worth examining more closely, since the Yugoslav question is both a variation and summation of the European question.

Let me explain.

The dismantling of the Old World had at its core the collapse of the Austro-Hungarian Habsburg Empire, which sprawled across Central Europe from the Alps to the shadow zone of the Black Sea, providing the continent with its organizing principle. It was the Habsburg Empire that embodied the grand compromise of national groups that lay at the heart of Metternich's post-Napoleonic peace plan. And Habsburg Austria-Hungary, writes the Italian historian Leo Valiani, "declared war in 1914 in order to solve, by military victory ... the Southern Slav [or *Yugoslav*] problem." Yet, as Valiani points out, "even the victory of the Central Powers could not have solved this problem.... The Southern Slavs were there to stay," and would have remained a rebellious state-in-being inside Habsburg Europe. Moreover, even with a reformist, federalized Habsburg monarchy, there would still have been "the explosive character of the different, antagonistic nationalisms" of the western Balkans. In other words, World War I, which gave birth to the horrors of the twentieth century, had as a principal cause the vexing dilemma of the South Slavs or *Yugoslavs*.

Valiani was no armchair historian. He was born in 1909 in Fiume, later Rijeka, and died in 1999 after the Kosovo war. His masterwork, *The End of Austria-Hungary*, displays an intuitive grasp of the historical and ethnic challenges of the two Yugoslav states in the twentieth century. As he writes, the birth of Yugoslavia was not inevitable, amid the tensions among Serbs, Croats, and Slovenes and the complexities of Great Power politics as World War I drew to a conclusion.[27] And yet right here in Corfu, Yugoslavia was born, a vast and unwieldy federation that lasted, with the exception of World War II, for nearly three-quarters of the twentieth century. Tito, whom Claudio Magris calls in spirit the last of the Habsburg emperors, held it together by a mixture of benevolence and repression, in true imperial style. Tito's death in Ljubljana in 1980 led to a decade of institutional calcification and decline, with each republic in an increasing political and bureaucratic wrangle with every other, until it all ignited into violence. Alas, since the Kosovo War ended nearly a quarter century ago, the former Yugoslavia has been—even without large-scale violence—anything but stable. Perhaps the only way for the South Slavs to truly live in peace and prosperity is under the umbrella of another necessary empire: that of the European Union, by far the most benign of imperial formations. Just like many imperial formations, the European Union is infused with cosmopolitanism and universalism, something that accompanies the reality of different peoples living under a common bureaucratic regime. This is not to justify imperialism per se, but merely to point out the ambiguities of it.

The late English historian A. J. P. Taylor wrote that the "Great Powers of Europe have always" lived in a "state of nature," and generally "owed" their only periods of peace to the "Balance of Power."[28] Peace did reign in Europe throughout the Cold War and—with the exception of Yugoslavia—for decades after. That was mainly because of an American security guarantee over Europe as well as the expansion and strengthening of the European Union. But were that American security guarantee to weaken, and that necessary EU empire also to atrophy, then Europe might well be back to unstable and uncertain balance-of-power arrangements in order to keep the peace.

BUT MY ANSWER TO anyone who claims that he or she can specifically predict the future is to look at Peter Paul Rubens's painting *Fortuna*, completed in 1638 and residing in the Prado in Madrid. It depicts fate as a nude young woman, her foot resting precariously on a beach ball that is headed straight into the tumultuous waves of the sea. Her slightly playful and enigmatic expression suggests that only a fool would follow her; only a fool would think to know exactly what was going to happen to her next. Of course, we know that she might fall, but how and exactly when remains a mystery.

I offer only general outlines and alternative scenarios for Europe deeper into the twenty-first century, but go no further. The key is to be always aware of the past, for the present by itself provides no context for anything. It is the present placed alongside the past that can open a window, however small and oblique, into the future.

TOWARDS THE END OF my travels, my bibliography is becoming unwieldy, a hodgepodge of books, united only by chance and my sometimes deliberate encounters with academia and literature in the course of a journey. In Corfu, I now read Boccaccio's *Decameron*, which in my mind flows naturally from *The Arabian Nights*. While one is considered Western and the other Eastern, they both issue from the same spirit and thus make for a common culture beyond arbitrary divisions. The *Decameron*, like the *Nights*, is a feast of orality, the purest form of literature, that challenges prudery, hypocrisy, status, greed, anything false or full of pretense, and consequently celebrates the raw expression of the unconquerable life force. In it, while a plague ravages Florence, ten young men and women take refuge in a villa outside the city, tasting "delightful sweetmeats and choice wines," hearing "the song of a thousand birds," and telling one another stories that in their exuberance deliver a categorical "no" to fate.

It is the least depressing book that I know, sanctifying what makes us human. And what makes us human is an earthy material-ism. Like the *Nights*, the *Decameron* abjures the abstract and focuses instead on the most concrete elements of the human drama: sex, wealth, beauty; things that, while not of the highest moral value, are what moral values cannot but concern themselves with. And yet the flesh is celebrated. Take the humorous story of a convent where the nuns all want to lie with a dumb man. The best of the stories have the power of myth, which, being myth, unites all cultures. There is the tale of a young woman who dies of grief after she can no longer worship her dead lover's head, which she had placed in a pot of basil. The seven women and three men who have told each other such stories must return to Florence where uncertainty awaits them. The *Decameron* teaches us all to be resilient. Yes, there is a mecha-nism, a "hidden judgment," that determines our lives, but precisely because we cannot know it we have no choice but to strive and struggle.[29]

True, we are condemned to concentrate on our sins, spoiling the enjoyment of our consciousness, and to be imprisoned without peace of mind. But we also have responsibilities in this world, to friends and loved ones who depend on us, who depend on us not being distracted and being fully engaged with them. It is to them that we owe our own will to go on. To be weary of life is cowardly.

And so travel is a challenge that never ceases. It is the ultimate compression of life—in which a week on the road can be a short epic. It is not an escape or an indulgence; ethics and aesthetics fit together. Because travel advances an appreciation of the latter, it also focuses the mind relentlessly on the former—for real beauty is moral as well as material. It is my second afternoon here and time for me to further explore the town of Corfu, the synthesis of Italy and Greece, and thus the summation of the Adriatic. I hope that will always be so. Something great will be lost if Corfu Town becomes merely global. But now I must enjoy this moment in time. As Borges writes, "The evening was near, yet infinite."[30]

Author's Note

—

THIS BOOK AROSE FROM TRAVEL AND DIARIES BETWEEN 2016 and 2018. Publication was held up because of a biography that I wrote in the interim, which itself appeared late because of the effect of the coronavirus on the publishing industry. Nevertheless, the descriptions and issues raised herein, and therefore the conversations conveyed, I hope stand the test of time. Indeed, the fate of Europe is a question that is obviously with us still. And the hunt for worthy and often obscure books that assist in a journey—the other major theme of these pages—has been a lifelong pursuit of mine. Thus, I have updated the text sparingly.

I am grateful to the editors of *The New Criterion* for publishing works in progress from the book about the Greek poet George Seferis and about the poets Ezra Pound and Joseph Brodsky.

In the course of my travels around the Adriatic, people were immensely kind to me. I stand in great debt to Maurizio Molinari, editor in chief of *La Repubblica*, and his young colleague Beniamino Pagliaro, for providing me with a flood tide of contacts in Trieste, of whom particularly generous were Hedy Benvenuto, Monika Bulaj, Veit Heinichen, and Paolo Rumiz. I owe a similar debt of gratitude to my friend Reva Goujon, who opened many doors for me in Ljubljana. Very warm gratitude is also due to Sanja and Petar Bojanić for doing the same for me in Rijeka, as well as hosting me there. Sanja, with her diplomatic and organizational skills inside the hothouse of academia, is a quietly amazing person. In Zagreb, Nebojša Taraba, Ivana Ljubičić, and Mladen Bašić generously helped me with their time and contacts, and in arranging a veritable chess game of a schedule. Nebojša, full of friendship and insights, took me under his wing, after an introduction from a mutual friend of decades ago, Bruce Clark of *The Economist*. Mladen, who is Belgrade-based, also eased my path and offered me his trust and deep knowledge. Indeed, friendship was a theme of this journey. My dear old friends John and Martyna Fox introduced me to their own friends the esteemed journalists Michael Dobbs and David Ensor, who co-own a house in Korčula and generously provided contacts and all sorts of insights for my use—another debt that will be hard to repay. David also introduced me to Elez Biberaj, the chief of the Voice of America's Eurasia Division, an Albanian by family background. It was Elez who, along with his colleagues Ilirian Agolli and Predrag Milić, generously provided me the names of people to meet in Albania and Montenegro.

The following people also deserve heartfelt thanks for suggesting books to read, places to go, people to see, and so much more: Michael Auslin, Adriano Bosoni, Ivan Cerovac, Vanni D'Alessio, Charles Edel, John Felton, Vjeran Filippi, Jonathan Holslag, Bill Jones, Stavros Katsios, Spyros Katsoulas, Elias Maglinis, Damir Marusic, Alexis Papahelas, Natasha Sardzoska, Marius Stan, Vladimir Tismăneanu, and Joel Weickgenant.

Anna Pitoniak shaped this manuscript with exquisite skill. Both Anna and Kate Medina at Random House made this book possible with their relentless support. Then Molly Turpin expertly and indefatigably brought me over the finish line. Steve Messina at Random House has been for many books of mine a dependable technician in the copyediting department. Gail Hochman, Marianne Merola, and Henry Thayer at Brandt & Hochman Literary Agents have represented me with no letup in enthusiasm for decades. I am also indebted to the Center for a New American Security in Washington and the Foreign Policy Research Institute in Philadelphia for support and understanding while I wrote this book.

My wife, Maria Cabral, provides the unique framework of love and encouragement without which I could not survive. Elizabeth M. Lockyer, who handled the copyright permissions and the map, runs my professional life with unrivaled efficiency, with help from Diane and Marc Rathbun.

Finally, I must acknowledge a great debt to David Leeming, professor emeritus of English, and the late Charles Boer, translator from the ancient Greek of *The Homeric Hymns* and from Latin of Ovid's *Metamorphoses*, both of whom a half century ago at the University of Connecticut started me on a path of lifelong learning and exploration.

A FEW PAGES OF the text, dealing with the local histories of Split and Dubrovnik, are borrowed from a previous travel book of mine, *Mediterranean Winter* (2004), and are marked by endnotes.

Notes

PROLOGUE: THE GLOBE IN MINIATURE

1. Jorge Luis Borges, "Averroes' Search," in *Collected Fictions*, trans. Andrew Hurley (New York: Penguin Books, [1949] 1998), p. 238.

CHAPTER I. RIMINI: EUROPE IN LIMESTONE

1. Philip Sherrard, *The Greek East and the Latin West: A Study in the Christian Tradition* (Limni, Greece: Denise Harvey, 1959), p. 119. Steven Runciman, *Mistra: Byzantine Capital of the Peloponnese* (London: Thames and Hudson, 1980), p. 111.
2. Robert D. Kaplan, *Mediterranean Winter: The Pleasures of History and Landscape in Tunisia, Sicily, Dalmatia, and the Peloponnese* (New York: Random House, 2004), pp. 210, 213, 217–19, and 232.
3. Frederic C. Lane, *Venice: A Maritime Republic* (Baltimore: Johns Hopkins University Press, 1973), pp. 231–32. A. David Moody, *Ezra Pound: Poet; A Portrait of the Man and His Work*, vol. 2, *The Epic Years 1921–1939* (New York: Oxford University Press, 2014), p. 42 (part of which I paraphrase in my text).
4. Hugh Kenner, *The Poetry of Ezra Pound* (London: Faber and Faber, 1951), p. 318 (University of Nebraska Press edition, 1985). Humphrey Carpenter, *A Serious Character: The Life of Ezra Pound* (Boston: Houghton Mifflin, 1988), pp. 418–20. Bernard Berenson, "The Venetian Painters of the Renaissance," 1894, in *Italian Painters of the Renaissance*, vol. 1, *Venetian and North Italian Schools*, and vol. 2, *Florentine and Central Italian Schools* (London: Phaidon, [Preface 1952], 1968). Moody, *Ezra Pound: Poet*, pp. 42 and 44. Donald Davie, *Ezra Pound: Poet as Sculptor* (Oxford: Oxford University Press, [1964] 1968), pp. 85 and 126.

5. Carpenter, *A Serious Character*, pp. 418, 420, 225–26, 258–59, and 318. Charles Boer, *Charles Olson in Connecticut* (Rocky Mount: North Carolina Wesleyan College Press, 1975), p. 78. Davie, *Ezra Pound*, pp. 130–31.

6. Ezra Pound, *The Cantos of Ezra Pound* (New York: New Directions, [1934, etc.] 1993), pp. 34–35.

7. Ronald L. Bush, *The Genesis of Ezra Pound's Cantos* (Princeton, NJ: Princeton University Press, [1977] 1989), pp. 247–48.

8. Kenner, *The Poetry of Ezra Pound*, p. 7.

9. Carpenter, *A Serious Character*, p. 163.

10. Carpenter, *A Serious Character*, p. 347.

11. Pound, *The Cantos of Ezra Pound*, p. 260.

12. Pound, *The Cantos of Ezra Pound*, pp. 229–30.

13. Carroll F. Terrell, *A Companion to the Cantos of Ezra Pound* (Berkeley: University of California Press, 1980), p. 178. Carpenter, *A Serious Character*, pp. 89, 570, and 913. Kenner, *The Poetry of Ezra Pound*, p. 13.

14. Carpenter, p. 14. Langdon Hammer, *Hart Crane & Allen Tate: Janus-Faced Modernism* (Princeton, NJ: Princeton University Press, 1993), p. 14.

15. Edmund Wilson, *Axel's Castle: A Study of the Imaginative Literature of 1870–1930*, intro. by Hugh Kenner (New York: Modern Library, [1931, 1991] 1996), pp. xx–xxii and 126.

16. Catherine Seelye, ed., *Charles Olson and Ezra Pound* (New York: Grossman, 1975) (February 1948 letter).

17. Wilson, *Axel's Castle*, pp. 25–28.

18. Ezra Pound, *Selected Cantos of Ezra Pound* (New York: New Directions, 1970), pp. 3–5.

19. Robert Conquest, *The Abomination of Moab* (London: Maurice Temple Smith, 1979), p. 249.

20. Bush, *The Genesis of Ezra Pound's Cantos*, p. 129.

21. Conquest, *The Abomination of Moab*, p. 254.

22. Pierre Missac, *Walter Benjamin's Passages*, trans. Shierry Weber Nicholsen (Cambridge, MA: MIT Press, [1987] 1995), p. 61.

23. Adrian Stokes, *Stones of Rimini* (New York: Schocken Books, [1934] 1969), pp. 15, 48, 77, 89–90, 97, 105, and 149.

24. José Ortega y Gasset, *The Revolt of the Masses*, trans. Anthony Kerrigan (Notre Dame, IN: University of Notre Dame Press, [1932] 1985), p. x.

25. Denys Hay, *Europe: The Emergence of an Idea* (New York: Harper & Row, [1957] 1966), pp. viii, 25–26, 29, 85, 87, and 110–11.

26. Hay, *Europe*, pp. 100–102, 115–16, 122–23, and 125.

27. Hay, *Europe*, p. 125.

28. Henri Pirenne, *Mohammed & Charlemagne*, trans. Bernard Miall (Mineola, NY: Dover Publications, [1937 and 1954] 2001), pp. 17, 62–63, 143, 152–53, 183–84, 234, and 275.

29. Stokes, *Stones of Rimini*, p. 172.

CHAPTER 2. RAVENNA: HOW THEODORIC AND DANTE
SHAPED THE WEST

1. Elias Canetti, *Crowds and Power*, trans. Carol Stewart (New York: Penguin Books, [1960] 1973), pp. 199 and 202.
2. Albert Camus, *The Outsider*, trans. Joseph Laredo (New York: Everyman's Library, [1942] 1998), p. 73.
3. Pirenne, *Mohammed & Charlemagne*, p. 120.
4. Edward Gibbon, *The Decline and Fall of the Roman Empire*, vol. 4 (New York: Everyman's Library, [1776–1788] 1910), p. 160.
5. Anton Chekhov, "A Dreary Story," in *My Life and Other Stories*, trans. Constance Garnett (New York: Everyman's Library, [1889] 1992).
6. Miguel de Unamuno, *Tragic Sense of Life*, trans. J. E. Crawford Flitch (New York: SophiaOmni, [1912] 2014), pp. 163 and 216.
7. T. S. Eliot, *Collected Poems, 1909–1962* (New York: Harcourt Brace Jovanovich, 1991), p. 40 (translated in an online blog by Seamus Geary, November 21, 2009). Wilson, *Axel's Castle*, p. 115.
8. Jorge Luis Borges, "Story of the Warrior and the Captive Maiden," in *Collected Fictions*, trans. Andrew Hurley (New York: Penguin Books, [1949] 1998), pp. 208–11.
9. John Julius Norwich, *Byzantium: The Early Centuries* (New York: Knopf, 1989), p. 144.
10. Peter E. Knox and J. C. McKeown, eds., *The Oxford Anthology of Roman Literature* (New York: Oxford University Press, 2013), p. ix.
11. Peter Brown, *The World of Late Antiquity: AD 150–750* (London: Thames and Hudson, 1971), p. 24.
12. R. W. Southern. *The Making of the Middle Ages* (New Haven, CT: Yale University Press, 1953), pp. 12–13. Robert D. Kaplan, "Augustine's World: What Late Antiquity Says About the 21st Century and the Syrian Crisis," *Foreign Policy*, December 2013.
13. Colin McEvedy, *The New Penguin Atlas of Medieval History* (London: Penguin Books, 1961), p. 9.
14. The image appears as a frontispiece in Peter Brown's *Late Antiquity*.
15. Procopius, *History of the Wars*, book V, ix, 18–25.
16. Procopius, book VI, xviii, 11–19.
17. Procopius, book VI, xxix, 32–37.
18. Cassiodorus, *Variae*, II, 27. Deborah Mauskopf Deliyannis, *Ravenna in Late Antiquity* (New York: Cambridge University Press, 2010), p. 142. John Julius Norwich, *A History of Venice* (New York: Knopf, [1977 and 1981] 1982), p. 7.
19. Procopius, book V, pp. i, 28–35.
20. Norwich, *Byzantium*, p. 180.
21. Gibbon, *The Decline and Fall of the Roman Empire*, vol. 4, pp. 128 and 139.
22. Deliyannis, *Ravenna in Late Antiquity*, p. 187.
23. John Darwin, *After Tamerlane: The Rise and Fall of Global Empires, 1400–2000* (New York: Bloomsbury Press, 2008), p. 29.

24. George Holmes, *The Oxford History of Medieval Europe* (New York: Oxford University Press, 1988), p. 44.

25. Brown, *The World of Late Antiquity*, p. 103.

26. Bernard Berenson, *Aesthetics and History* (Garden City, NY: Doubleday, [1948] 1954), pp. 68, 93, 201, and 263–64. Bernard Berenson, *Italian Painters of the Renaissance*, vol. 1, *Venetian and North Italian Schools*, and vol. 2, *Florentine and Central Italian Schools* (London: Phaidon, [Preface 1952], 1968).

27. Deliyannis, *Ravenna in Late Antiquity*, pp. 227, 230, 232.

28. Milan Kundera, *The Unbearable Lightness of Being*, trans. Michael Henry Heim (New York: Harper & Row, 1984), p. 101.

29. Deliyannis, *Ravenna in Late Antiquity*, p. 263.

30. David Gilmour, *The Pursuit of Italy: A History of a Land, Its Regions, and Their Peoples* (New York: Farrar, Straus and Giroux, 2011), pp. 11 and 53.

31. Hugh Trevor-Roper, introduction to vols. 4–6 of Gibbon's *The Decline and Fall of the Roman Empire* (New York: Everyman's Library, 1994).

32. Dante Alighieri, *The Divine Comedy*, vol. 1, *Inferno*, trans. Mark Musa (New York: Penguin Books, [1971] 2003), Canto I, 1–9.

33. Dante, *Inferno*, Canto XX, 3.

34. Dante, *Inferno*, Canto XXXIX, 139.

35. Jacob Burckhardt, *The Civilization of the Renaissance in Italy* (New York: Modern Library, [1860] 1995), p. 149.

36. Walter Pater, *Marius the Epicurean: His Sensations and Ideas* (London: Jonathan Cape, 1885; New York: Cosimo Classics reprint, 2005), p. 294.

37. T. S. Eliot, *Dante* (London: Faber & Faber, 1929), p. 12. Richard Ellmann, *James Joyce* (New York: Oxford University Press, [1959] 1982), p. 218.

38. Dante, *Inferno*, Canto VI, 100–101; Canto IX, 31; Canto XXIX, 1; and Canto XXXII, 36.

39. Dante Alighieri, *The Divine Comedy*, vol. 2, *Purgatory*, trans. Mark Musa (New York: Penguin Books, [1981] 2003), Canto I, 1–6.

40. Dante, *Purgatory*, Canto III, 77–78, and Canto IV, 53–54.

41. Dante, *Purgatory*, Canto V, 13–15.

42. Dante, *Purgatory*, Canto XVI, 82–83, and Canto XXVI, 118–23.

43. Dante Alighieri, *The Divine Comedy*, vol. 3, *Paradise*, trans. Mark Musa (New York: Penguin Books, [1984] 2003), Canto I, 13–15.

44. Dante, *Paradise*, Canto II, 7–9.

45. Dante, *Paradise*, Canto X, 7–12, and Canto XXXIII, 91–96.

CHAPTER 3. VENICE: FRAZER'S *GOLDEN BOUGH* AND THE DEFEAT OF FATE

1. Francis Oakley, *Empty Bottles of Gentilism: Kingship and the Divine in Late Antiquity and the Early Middle Ages (to 1050)* (New Haven, CT: Yale University Press, 2010), pp. 34 and 39.

2. Oakley, *Empty Bottles of Gentilism*, pp. 58–59 and 128.

3. Oakley, *Empty Bottles of Gentilism*, pp. 172, 188, and 198.

4. Francis Oakley, *The Mortgage of the Past: Reshaping the Ancient Political Inheritance (1050–1300)* (New Haven, CT: Yale University Press, 2012), pp. 26 and 89–90. Brian Tierney, *Religion, Law, and the Growth of Constitutional Thought, 1150–1650* (Cambridge: Cambridge University Press, 1982), pp. 14–16.

5. Francis Oakley, *The Watershed of Modern Politics: Law, Virtue, Kingship, and Consent (1300–1650)* (New Haven, CT: Yale University Press, 2015), pp. 4–5, 50, and 286. Albert Camus, *The Rebel: An Essay on Man in Revolt,* trans. Anthony Bower (New York: Vintage, [1956] 1991), p. 120.

6. Thomas Mann, *Death in Venice* (New York: Knopf, [1912] 1963), pp. 29 and 53–54.

7. Jan Morris, *The World of Venice* (New York: Harcourt, [1960 by James Morris] 1993), pp. 22 and 50–51.

8. Jan Morris, *The Venetian Empire: A Sea Voyage* (New York: Penguin Books, [1980] 1990), p. 2.

9. Burckhardt, *The Civilization of the Renaissance in Italy,* p. 51.

10. Sheila Hale, *Titian: His Life* (London: HarperPress, 2012), p. 52.

11. Rachel Cohen, *Bernard Berenson: A Life in the Picture Trade* (New Haven, CT: Yale University Press, 2013), p. 67.

12. John Ruskin, *The Stones of Venice,* ed. J. G. Links (New York: Da Capo Press, [1853] 1960), pp. 164 and 173.

13. Tony Tanner, *Venice Desired* (Cambridge, MA: Harvard University Press, 1992), p. 80.

14. Henry James, *The Wings of the Dove* (New York: Penguin Books, [1902] 1986), pp. 404 and 416. Henry James, *Henry James: Letters from the Palazzo Barbaro,* ed. Rosella Mamoli Zorzi (London: Pushkin Press, 1998), p. 68.

15. Henry James, *The Aspern Papers and Other Tales,* ed. Michael Gorra (New York: Penguin Books, [1888] 2014), pp. 76–77.

16. Joseph Brodsky, *Watermark* (New York: Farrar, Straus & Giroux, 1992), pp. 5, 7–8, 13, 23, 27, 43, and 96.

17. Brodsky, *Watermark,* pp. 62 and 70.

18. Mary McCarthy, *Venice Observed* (New York: Penguin Books, [1956] 1972), pp. 177, 180–81, and 275.

19. Johann Wolfgang von Goethe, *Italian Journey [1786–1788],* trans. W. H. Auden and Elizabeth Mayer (New York: Penguin Books, [1816] 1962 and 1970), p. 77.

20. McCarthy, *Venice Observed,* pp. 190–93.

21. Roger Crowley, *City of Fortune: How Venice Ruled the Seas* (New York: Random House, [2011] 2012), pp. xxvi–xxviii and 5.

22. McCarthy, *Venice Observed,* pp. 190–93 and 196.

23. McCarthy, *Venice Observed,* pp. 205–06, 216, 219, 246, and 249. John Julius Norwich, *A History of Venice* (New York: Knopf, [1977 and 1981] 1982), p. 594.

24. McCarthy, *Venice Observed,* pp. 193, 228, and 244.

25. Norwich, *A History of Venice,* p. 280.

26. Ruskin, *The Stones of Venice*, pp. 141–42 and 191.

27. Crowley, *City of Fortune*, p. 377.

28. Norwich, *A History of Venice*, pp. xxvi, 16, and 25. Frederic C. Lane, *Venice: A Maritime Republic* (Baltimore: Johns Hopkins University Press, 1973), pp. 5 and 203.

29. Norwich, *A History of Venice*, pp. 155 and 606. Lane, *Venice*, p. 92.

30. Berenson, "The Venetian Painters of the Renaissance."

31. David Rosand, *Myths of Venice: The Figuration of a State* (Chapel Hill: University of North Carolina Press, 2001), pp. 3, 7, 26, 39–40, and 146–49.

32. McCarthy, *Venice Observed*, p. 183.

33. Norwich, *A History of Venice*, pp. 330 and 635–36.

34. Norwich, *A History of Venice*, pp. 34, 66, and 282. Lane, *Venice*, p. 101.

35. Lane, *Venice*, p. 251.

36. Burckhardt, *The Civilization of the Renaissance in Italy*, p. 55.

37. Lane, *Venice*, pp. 21, 36, 246, and 248.

38. Lane, *Venice*, pp. 225 and 427.

39. James, *The Aspern Papers and Other Tales*, pp. 141–42.

40. James George Frazer, *The Golden Bough: A Study in Magic and Religion* (New York: Macmillan, [1890] 1922), p. 1.

41. Frazer, *The Golden Bough*, pp. 1–2, 6, 9, 344, and 815.

42. Edith Hamilton, *Mythology* (Boston: Little, Brown and Company, 1942), pp. 11–12.

43. Plutarch, *Plutarch's Lives*, vol. 2, trans. John Dryden, ed. and rev. Arthur Hugh Clough (New York: Modern Library, [1683–86, 1864] 1992), p. 139.

44. Fernand Braudel, *The Mediterranean and the Mediterranean World in the Age of Philip II*, vol. 2, trans. Sian Reynolds (New York: Harper & Row, [1949] 1973), pp. 1243–44.

45. Pound, *The Cantos of Ezra Pound*, p. 78.

46. Tanner, *Venice Desired*, pp. 306–08.

47. Pound, *The Cantos of Ezra Pound*, pp. 540–41.

48. Pound, *The Cantos of Ezra Pound*, pp. 540–41.

49. Carpenter, *A Serious Character*, p. 680.

50. Pound, *The Cantos of Ezra Pound*, pp. 540–41.

51. Ruskin, *The Stones of Venice*, p. 101.

52. Tanner, *Venice Desired*, p. 342.

53. Wendy Flory, "Pound and Anti-Semitism," in *Cambridge Companion to Ezra Pound*, ed. Ira B. Nadel (New York: Cambridge University Press, 1999), p. 296.

54. Michael Dirda, introduction to *ABC of Reading*, by Ezra Pound (New York: New Directions, [1934] 2010), pp. 7–8.

55. Ezra Pound, "In a Station of the Metro," *Poetry*, April 1913.

56. Joseph Brodsky, *Collected Poems in English* (New York: Farrar, Straus & Giroux, 2000), pp. 50, 67, 87, and 44.

57. Joan Acocella, "A Ghost Story," *New York Review of Books*, January 14, 2016.

58. Charles Simic, "Working for the Dictionary," *New York Review of Books*, October 19, 2000.

59. Brodsky, *Collected Poems in English*, pp. 282–83 (1981).

60. James Smith Reid, *Encyclopaedia Britannica*, 11th ed. (New York, 1910–11). Barbara Levick, *Tiberius: The Politician* (London: Routledge, [1976] 1999), pp. 138–39, 142, and 144. Robert D. Kaplan, *Warrior Politics: Why Leadership Demands a Pagan Ethos* (New York: Random House, 2002), pp. 150–52.

61. Lawrence Durrell, *Bitter Lemons* (London: Faber and Faber, [1957] 1978 paperback), p. 15.

CHAPTER 4. TRIESTE: ITALY'S GEOGRAPHIC COMPLEXITY

1. Christopher Duggan, *A Concise History of Italy* (Cambridge: Cambridge University Press, 2014), pp. 9 and 11.

2. Adriano Bosoni, "Understanding Italian Defiance," *Stratfor*, January 26, 2016.

3. David Gilmour, *The Pursuit of Italy: A History of a Land, Its Regions, and Their Peoples* (New York: Farrar, Straus and Giroux, 2011), pp. 7–9 and 238.

4. Elsa M. Spencer, *Good-bye, Trieste* (self-pub., Xlibris, 2008), pp. 11 and 15.

5. Fernand Braudel, *The Mediterranean and the Mediterranean World in the Age of Philip II*, vol. 1, trans. Sian Reynolds (New York: Harper & Row, [1949] 1972), pp. 17, 125, and 131–33. H. M. Denham, *The Adriatic: A Sea-Guide to the Dalmatian Coast and Islands, Venice and Eastern Italy* (London: John Murray, 1967), p. 28. Larry Wolff, *Venice and the Slavs: The Discovery of Dalmatia in the Age of Enlightenment* (Stanford, CA: Stanford University Press, 2001), pp. 1–3. Edward Gibbon, *The Decline and Fall of the Roman Empire*, vol. 1 (New York: Modern Library, [1776] 1910), p. 21. Crowley, *City of Fortune*, pp. 3–4, 14, and 118. Horace, *Odes and Epodes* (Cambridge, MA: Harvard University Press, 2004), Ode III.9, "Reconciliation," pp. 170–71. Dominique Kirchner Reill, *Nationalists Who Feared the Nation: Adriatic Multi-Nationalism in Habsburg Dalmatia, Trieste, and Venice* (Stanford, CA: Stanford University Press, 2012), pp. 20–22.

6. Rainer Maria Rilke, *Duino Elegies and The Sonnets to Orpheus*, ed. and trans. Stephen Mitchell (New York: Vintage International, [1923] 1982), p. xiii. Rainer Maria Rilke, *The Notebooks of Malte Laurids Brigge*, trans. and ed. Michael Hulse (New York: Penguin Books, [1910] 2009), pp. xii, 11, 52, and 119–20.

7. Rilke, *Duino Elegies*, p. 5.

8. Rilke, *Duino Elegies*, p. 37.

9. For an explanation of why I supported the Iraq War, see Robert D. Kaplan, *In Europe's Shadow: Two Cold Wars and a Thirty-Year Journey Through Romania and Beyond* (New York: Random House, 2016), pp. 21–23.

10. Renzo S. Crivelli, *James Joyce: Triestine Itineraries* (Trieste, Italy: MGS Press, 1996), pp. 48, 126, 173, 216. *The Trieste of James Joyce*, brochure, Comune di Trieste.

11. Neil Kent, *Trieste: Adriatic Emporium and Gateway to the Heart of Europe* (London: Hurst, 2011), p. 1.

12. John Gunther, *Behind the Iron Curtain* (New York: Harper & Brothers, 1948), p. 18.

13. Pamela Ballinger, *History in Exile: Memory and Identity at the Borders of the Balkans* (Princeton, NJ: Princeton University Press, 2003), pp. 86–87.

14. Timothy Snyder, *The Red Prince: The Secret Lives of a Habsburg Archduke* (New York: Basic Books, 2008), p. 31.

15. Jan Morris, *Trieste and the Meaning of Nowhere* (New York: Da Capo Press, 2001), p. 39, 115, 121–23, and 132.

16. Claudio Magris, *Danube,* trans. Patrick Creagh (New York: Farrar, Straus & Giroux, [1986] 1989), pp. 29, 31–32, 36, and 41. Robert D. Kaplan, "A Globe-Trotting Celebration of Erudition," *Wall Street Journal,* February 21, 2015.

17. Magris, *Danube,* p. 70.

18. Magris, *Danube,* pp. 67 and 97–98.

19. Magris, *Danube,* p. 332.

20. Magris, *Danube,* p. 386.

21. Morris, *Trieste and the Meaning of Nowhere,* p. 99.

22. Richard Ellmann, *James Joyce* (New York: Oxford University Press, [1959] 1982), pp. 355 and 389.

23. Ellmann, *James Joyce,* p. 110. Wilson, *Axel's Castle,* p. 217.

24. James Joyce, *Dubliners* (Harmondsworth, UK: Penguin Books, [1914] 1976), p. 47.

25. Ellmann, *James Joyce,* p. 5.

26. James Joyce, *Ulysses* (New York: Vintage, [1934] 1990), pp. 34 and 661.

27. Italo Svevo, *Confessions of Zeno,* trans. Beryl de Zoete (New York: Knopf, [1923] 1930), p. 91.

28. Claudio Magris, *Microcosms,* trans. Iain Halliday (London: Harvill Press, [1997] 2000), pp. 12, 155, 200, and 249.

29. Robert Musil, *The Man Without Qualities,* vol. 2, trans. Sophie Wilkins and Burton Pike (New York: Vintage, [1978] 1995 and 1996), pp. 913 and 918.

30. Ballinger, *History in Exile,* p. 18.

31. Claudio Magris, *Blindly,* trans. Anne Milano Appel (New Haven, CT: Yale University Press, [2006] 2008), p. 26.

32. Paolo Rumiz, *The Fault Line: Traveling the Other Europe from Finland to Ukraine,* trans. Gregory Conti (New York: Rizzoli Ex Libris, [2012] 2015), p. 2.

33. Norman Davies, *Europe: A History* (New York: Oxford University Press, 1996), p. 25.

34. Ian Morris, *Why the West Rules—for Now: The Patterns of History, and What They Reveal About the Future* (New York: Farrar, Straus and Giroux, 2010), p. 41.

35. Harold C. Raley, *José Ortega y Gasset: Philosopher of European Unity* (Tuscaloosa: University of Alabama Press, 1971), p. 65.

36. Paul Collins, *The Birth of the West: Rome, Germany, France, and the Creation of Europe in the Tenth Century* (New York: PublicAffairs, 2013), pp. 4, 414, and 424.

37. David Gress, *From Plato to NATO: The Idea of the West and Its Opponents* (New York: The Free Press, 1998), p. 1.

38. Oswald Spengler, *The Decline of the West,* trans. Charles Francis Atkinson (New York: Knopf, [1918 and 1922] 1961), pp. 73 and 326. Robert W. Merry, "Spengler's Ominous Prophecy," *The National Interest,* January/February 2013. Alexander Herzen, *My Past and Thoughts,* trans. Constance Garnett (Berkeley: University of California Press, [1968] 1973), p. 390.

39. Edward Rice, *Captain Sir Richard Francis Burton: The Secret Agent Who Made the Pilgrimage to Mecca, Discovered the Kama Sutra, and Brought the Arabian Nights to the West* (New York: Charles Scribner's Sons, 1990), pp. 1–2, 542, 544, 567–68, 577, and 579.

40. Richard F. Burton, "Terminal Essay" to *The Thousand Nights and a Night* (New York: Heritage Press, 1934), pp. 3673, 3689–90, and 3695.

41. Richard F. Burton, *The Arabian Nights: Tales from A Thousand and One Nights,* trans. Sir Richard F. Burton (New York: Modern Library, 2001), pp. xiv and 16.

42. Burton, "Terminal Essay," p. 3722.

43. Berenson, *Aesthetics and History,* p. 128.

44. Berenson, *Aesthetics and History,* pp. 133–34.

45. Edward W. Said, *Orientalism* (New York: Pantheon, 1978), pp. 7 and 301.

46. Samuel P. Huntington, "If Not Civilizations, What?" *Foreign Affairs,* November/December 1993.

47. Burton, "Terminal Essay," p. 3653.

CHAPTER 5. PIRAN, KOPER, LJUBLJANA, AND RIJEKA: THE EARLY MODERN WORLD AWAITING US

1. Joseph Roth, *Hotel Savoy,* trans. John Hoare (London: Pan Books, [1924] 1988), pp. 157 and 183.

2. Roth, *Hotel Savoy,* p. 98.

3. Ballinger, *History in Exile,* p. 1.

4. John Rupert Martin, *Baroque* (Boulder, CO: Westview Press, 1977), p. 13.

5. Timothy Snyder, "Mapping Eastern Europe" (presentation at the World Economic Forum, Davos, Switzerland, January 25, 2018).

6. Boris Pahor, *Necropolis,* trans. Michael Biggins (Champaign, IL: Dalkey Archive Press, [1967] 2010), pp. 9–10, 22, 41, 104, and 147.

7. Pahor, *Necropolis,* pp. 83 and 109.

8. Aleksandr Solzhenitsyn, *November 1916: The Red Wheel / Knot II,* trans. H. T. Willetts (New York: Farrar, Straus and Giroux, [1984] 1999), p. 337.

9. Euan Cameron, ed., *Early Modern Europe: An Oxford History* (Oxford: Oxford University Press, 2001), pp. xvii and 374.

10. Samuel P. Huntington, *The Clash of Civilizations and the Remaking of World Order* (New York: Simon & Schuster, 1996), p. 125.

11. Noel Malcolm, *Agents of Empire: Knights, Corsairs, Jesuits and Spies in the Sixteenth-Century Mediterranean World* (New York: Oxford University Press, 2015), p. xviii.

12. Malcolm, *Agents of Empire*, p. 14.

13. Malcolm, *Agents of Empire*, pp. 138, 192, 405, and 427.

14. Malcolm, *Agents of Empire*, pp. 224 and 175.

15. Malcolm, *Agents of Empire*, p. 34.

16. Malcolm, *Agents of Empire*, p. 215.

17. Pierre Manent, *Metamorphoses of the City: On the Western Dynamic*, trans. Marc LePain (Cambridge, MA: Harvard University Press, 2013), pp. 5 and 18.

18. Robert D. Kaplan, "The Fine Facades of a Yugoslav City: Ljubljana's Buildings Are a Textbook of Architectural Styles," *New York Times*, April 1, 1990.

19. James D. Tracy, *Balkan Wars: Habsburg Croatia, Ottoman Bosnia, and Venetian Dalmatia, 1499–1617* (Lanham, MD: Rowman & Littlefield, 2016), pp. 1–28.

20. Marisa Madieri, *Aqua Green: A Childhood in Istria*, trans. Gareth Norbury (Munich: Swiss Re, [1987] 2004), pp. 143 and 167.

21. Aram Bakshian Jr., "Votaries of Power," *The National Interest*, January/February 2018. Paul Hollander, *From Benito Mussolini to Hugo Chavez: Intellectuals and a Century of Political Hero Worship* (Cambridge: Cambridge University Press, 2016), pp. 76–81.

22. Ballinger, *History in Exile*, p. 220.

23. Ballinger, *History in Exile*, pp. 129 and 144.

24. Reill, *Nationalists Who Feared the Nation*, pp. 1–3.

25. Ivan Krastev, *After Europe* (Philadelphia: University of Pennsylvania Press, 2017), p. 11.

26. Parag Khanna, "Connectivity and Strategy: A Response to Robert D. Kaplan," *CNAS Stories*, www.cnas.org, May 2017.

27. Manent, *Metamorphoses of the City*, pp. 3, 13, 18–19, and 319–20. Ian Buruma, "In the Capital of Europe," *New York Review of Books*, April 7, 2016.

28. Mark Mazower, *Governing the World: The History of an Idea, 1815 to the Present* (New York: Penguin Press, 2012), p. 49.

29. Jan Zielonka, *Is the EU Doomed?* (Cambridge, UK: Polity Press, 2014), pp. xi–xii and 81–82.

30. John Milton, *Paradise Lost*, Book XII, line 646.

31. C. M. Bowra, *From Virgil to Milton* (London: Macmillan, [1945] 1967), pp. 207 and 209–10.

32. Unamuno, *Tragic Sense of Life*, p. 37.

33. Benedict Anderson, *Imagined Communities: Reflections on the Origin and Spread of Nationalism* (New York: Verso, 1983), pp. 7, 10, 12, and 144.

34. Anthony D. Smith, *National Identity* (London: Penguin Books, 1991; Reno, NV: University of Nevada Press, 1993), pp. 160–61.

CHAPTER 6. ZAGREB, SPLIT, KORČULA, AND DUBROVNIK: "NATIONS ARE NOT INSCRIBED INTO THE NATURE OF THINGS"

1. Ivo Banac, *The National Question in Yugoslavia: Origins, History, Politics* (Ithaca, NY: Cornell University Press, 1984), pp. 35–36.
2. Robert D. Kaplan, *Balkan Ghosts: A Journey Through History* (New York: St. Martin's Press, 1993), pp. 6, 9, and 15.
3. Denham, *The Adriatic*, p. 29.
4. José Ortega y Gasset, *Man and Crisis*, trans. Mildred Adams (New York: Norton, [1942 and 1958] 1962), p. 120.
5. Giuseppe Praga, *History of Dalmatia*, trans. Edward Steinberg (Pisa, Italy: Giardini, [1954] 1993), pp. 20–21. Robert D. Kaplan, *Mediterranean Winter: The Pleasures of History and Landscape in Tunisia, Sicily, Dalmatia, and the Peloponnese* (New York: Random House, 2004), p. 159.
6. Peter Frankopan, *The Silk Roads: A New History of the World* (New York: Knopf, 2015), p. 160.
7. Braudel, *The Mediterranean and the Mediterranean World in the Age of Philip II*, vol. 1, p. 57.
8. Wolff, *Venice and the Slavs*, pp. 17, 293, 324.
9. Ernest Gellner, *Nations and Nationalism* (Ithaca, NY: Cornell University Press, 1983), pp. 39–62. Wolff, *Venice and the Slavs*, p. 331.
10. John V. A. Fine Jr., *When Ethnicity Did Not Matter in the Balkans: A Study of Identity in Pre-Nationalist Croatia, Dalmatia, and Slavonia in the Medieval and Early-Modern Periods* (Ann Arbor: University of Michigan Press, 2006), pp. 3, 7, 9, and 84–85.
11. Banac, *The National Question in Yugoslavia*, p. 69.
12. Count Louis Voinovitch, *Dalmatia and the Jugoslav Movement* (London: George Allen & Unwin, [1917] 1920), p. 96.
13. Voinovitch, *Dalmatia and the Jugoslav Movement*, pp. 101–04.
14. Praga, *History of Dalmatia*, p. 217.
15. Voinovitch, pp. 150, 238, 244–45, and 248–49. Rebecca West, *Black Lamb and Grey Falcon* (New York: Papermac [1941] 1982), pp. 105–09. Kaplan, *Balkan Ghosts*, pp. 9–10, 24–25, and 28.
16. Banac, *The National Question in Yugoslavia*, p. 64.
17. Morris, *The Venetian Empire*, p. 162.
18. West, *Black Lamb and Grey Falcon*, pp. 124–25. Malcolm, *Agents of Empire*, pp. 328 and 391.
19. Georg Wilhelm Friedrich Hegel, *Philosophy of Right*, trans. T. M. Knox (Oxford, UK: Clarendon Press, [1820] 1942 and 1952), p. 102.
20. Freya Stark, *The Southern Gates of Arabia: A Journey in the Hadhramaut*

(New York: Modern Library, [1936] 2001), p. 144. Robert D. Kaplan, "Cultivating Loneliness," *Columbia Journalism Review*, January/February 2006.

21. See the prologue and chapter 1 of my book *In Europe's Shadow: Two Cold Wars and a Thirty-Year Journey Through Romania and Beyond* (New York: Random House, 2016).

22. Robert D. Kaplan, "Europe's Third World," *The Atlantic*, July 1989.

23. Predrag Matvejević, *Mediterranean: A Cultural Landscape*, trans. Michael Henry Heim (Berkeley: University of California Press, [1987] 1999), pp. 10, 66, and 207.

24. Kaplan, *Mediterranean Winter*, pp. 154–55.

25. Kaplan, *Mediterranean Winter*, p. 155.

26. Kaplan, *Mediterranean Winter*, pp. 155–56.

27. Kaplan, *Mediterranean Winter*, p. 156.

28. West, *Black Lamb and Grey Falcon*, p. 146. Kaplan, *Mediterranean Winter*, p. 157.

29. Kaplan, *Mediterranean Winter*, p. 158.

30. Kaplan, *Mediterranean Winter*, pp. 158–59.

31. Michael Dobbs, "Where Venice Once Ruled," *Smithsonian*, Winter 2015.

32. Laurence Bergreen, *Marco Polo: From Venice to Xanadu* (New York: Knopf, 2007), pp. 27, 94, and 152.

33. Frankopan, *The Silk Roads*, pp. 1–6.

34. Marco Polo, *The Travels of Marco Polo: The Complete Yule-Cordier Edition*, vol. 1 (New York: Dover Publications, [1903] 1993), inset after p. 144.

35. Fitzroy Maclean, *Eastern Approaches* (New York: Time-Life Books, [1949] 1964), pp. xv, 313, 365, 375, 379, and 399.

36. Kaplan, *Mediterranean Winter*, p. 172. West, p. 235. Gábor Kármán and Lovro Kunčević, eds., *The European Tributary States of the Ottoman Empire in the Sixteenth and Seventeenth Centuries* (Boston: Brill, 2013), pp. 111–12. Frankopan, *The Silk Roads*, p. 190.

37. Morris, *The Venetian Empire*, p. 165. Zdenko Zlatar, *Our Kingdom Come: The Counter-Reformation, the Republic of Dubrovnik, and the Liberation of the Balkan Slavs* (Boulder, CO: East European Monographs, 1992), pp. 261–62, 334–35, and 341–43.

38. Robin Harris, *Dubrovnik: A History* (London: Saqi Books, 2003), pp. 34, 49, 50, 60–63, 80–81, 97–98, 110, and 220. Zlatar, *Our Kingdom Come*, pp. 4–5 and 179. Kármán and Kunčević, pp. 92 and 368 (see essay in this collection by Domagoj Madunić, "The Defensive System of the Ragusan Republic [C. 1580–1620]."

39. Harris, *Dubrovnik*, p. 122.

40. Harris, *Dubrovnik*, pp. 145 and 189. Kaplan, *Mediterranean Winter*, pp. 173–74.

41. Kaplan, *Mediterranean Winter*, pp. 170–71.

42. Kaplan, *Mediterranean Winter*, p. 175.

43. Kaplan, *Mediterranean Winter*, pp. 175–76.

44. Kaplan, *Mediterranean Winter,* p. 176.
45. Kaplan, *Mediterranean Winter,* p. 177.

CHAPTER 7. KOTOR, PODGORICA, TIRANA, AND DURRËS:
THE HEART OF EUROPE?

1. Robert D. Kaplan, *In Europe's Shadow: Two Cold Wars and a Thirty-Year Journey Through Romania and Beyond* (New York: Random House, 2016), p. 37.
2. Victoria Clark, *Why Angels Fall: A Journey Through Orthodox Europe from Byzantium to Kosovo* (London: Macmillan, 2000), p. 229.
3. Timothy Ware, *The Orthodox Church* (Middlesex, UK: Penguin Books, [1963] 1975), pp. 9, 15–16, and 98–100.
4. Marci Shore, *The Ukrainian Night: An Intimate History of Revolution* (New Haven, CT: Yale University Press, 2017), pp. 157–58.
5. Tim Judah, *The Serbs: History, Myth and the Destruction of Yugoslavia* (New Haven, CT: Yale University Press, [1997] 2000), pp. 17–18 and 65.
6. Joel Weickgenant, "The New NATO Outpost in the Adriatic," *RealClearWorld,* September 7, 2016. S. Frederick Starr and Svante E. Cornell, eds., *Putin's Grand Strategy: The Eurasian Union and Its Discontents* (Washington: Johns Hopkins University–SAIS, 2014), p. 25.
7. Damir Marusic, "Did Moscow Botch a Coup in Montenegro?" *American Interest,* October 30, 2016.
8. L. Todd Wood, "Haven't We Had Enough in Montenegro?" *Washington Times,* December 14, 2017.
9. Gordon Bardos, "Montenegro's Corrupt Party of Socialists Is Killing the Country," *National Interest,* January 28, 2020.
10. Michael Gorra, *The Bells in Their Silence: Travels Through Germany* (Princeton, NJ: Princeton University Press, 2004), p. xvi.
11. See Timothy Snyder's review of *In Europe's Shadow:* "A Journey Through Time and Autobiography in Search of Romania," *Washington Post,* April 8, 2016.
12. Kaplan, *Balkan Ghosts,* pp. xxv and 46.
13. Anton Logoreci, *The Albanians: Europe's Forgotten Survivors* (London: Victor Gollancz, 1977), pp. 15 and 16. Miranda Vickers, *The Albanians: A Modern History* (New York: I. B. Tauris, [1995] 2014), pp. 1–3. Nicholas Hammond, "The Relations of Illyrian Albania with the Greeks and the Romans," in *Perspectives on Albania,* ed. Tom Winnifrith (London: Palgrave Macmillan, 1992), p. 39. Tajar Zavalani, *History of Albania,* ed. Robert Elsie and Bejtullah Destani (London: Centre for Albanian Studies, [1961–1963] 2015), pp. 11, 19–20, 30, 45–47, and 52–53.
14. Vickers, *The Albanians,* pp. 7–8. Zlatar, *Our Kingdom Come,* pp. 410–11.
15. Vickers, *The Albanians,* pp. 12–14 and 29.
16. Vickers, *The Albanians,* p. 112.

17. Bernd J. Fischer, *King Zog and the Struggle for Stability in Albania* (Tirana: Albanian Institute for International Studies, [1984] 2012), pp. 237 and 305.

18. Vickers, p. 200.

19. Robert D. Kaplan, "The Thrill of Burning Bridges," *New York Times*, November 6, 1994.

20. Besart Kadia, "Can Albania Be Saved from Narco-Government?" CapX.co, June 5, 2017.

21. Edith Durham, *High Albania* (London: Phoenix Press, [1909] 2000), pp. 2, 11, 40–41, 48, 54, 62, 69, 93, 133, and 154.

22. Durham, *High Albania*, p. 60.

23. Durham, *High Albania*, pp. 40 and 71.

24. Robert Carver, *The Accursed Mountains: Journeys in Albania* (London: Flamingo, [1998] 2009), pp. 2, 148, 191, and 310.

25. Winston Churchill, *Never Give In! The Best of Winston Churchill's Speeches* (New York: Hyperion, 2003), p. 413.

CHAPTER 8. CORFU: THE ARCHETYPAL REFUGEE EXPERIENCE

1. Plutarch, *Plutarch's Lives*, vol. 2, trans. John Dryden (New York: Modern Library, [1683–1686] 1992), p. 316.

2. Braudel, *The Mediterranean and the Mediterranean World in the Age of Philip II*, vol. 1, p. 125. Henry Jervis-White-Jervis, *History of the Island of Corfu, and of the Republic of the Ionian Islands* (London: Colburn and Co., [1852] 2005), p. 113. Crowley, *City of Fortune*, p. 234.

3. Jervis-White-Jervis, *History of the Island of Corfu*, p. 124. Malcolm, *Agents of Empire*, pp. 169 and 172–73.

4. Jervis-White-Jervis, *History of the Island of Corfu*, p. 230.

5. Joanna Hodgkin, *Amateurs in Eden: The Story of a Bohemian Marriage; Nancy and Lawrence Durrell* (London: Virago Press, 2012), pp. 3, 154, 230, and 328.

6. Lawrence Durrell, *Prospero's Cell: A Guide to the Landscape and Manners of the Island of Corfu* (London: Faber and Faber, 1945), p. 11.

7. Durrell, *Prospero's Cell*, pp. 12, 34, 72, and 131.

8. Richard Clogg, *A Short History of Modern Greece* (New York: Cambridge University Press, 1979), p. vii.

9. Clogg, *A Short History of Modern Greece*, pp. 11 and 16–17.

10. Clogg, *A Short History of Modern Greece*, p. 70.

11. Bruce Clark, *Twice a Stranger: The Mass Expulsions That Forged Modern Greece and Turkey* (Cambridge, MA: Harvard University Press, [2006] 2009), p. 91.

12. Fyodor Dostoevsky, *Demons*, trans. Richard Pevear and Larissa Volokhonsky (New York: Vintage Classics, [1872] 1994), p. 418.

13. Philip Sherrard, *The Wound of Greece: Studies in Neo-Hellenism* (London: Rex Collings, 1978; New York: St. Martin's, 1979), p. 61. Kaplan, *Balkan Ghosts*, p. 241. Hamilton, *Mythology*, p. 8.

14. Philip Sherrard, *The Marble Threshing Floor: Studies in Modern Greek Poetry* (Limni, Greece: Denise Harvey, [1956] 1981), p. 190.

15. Roderick Beaton, *George Seferis: Waiting for the Angel; a Biography* (New Haven, CT: Yale University Press, 2003), p. 51.

16. Sherrard, *The Marble Threshing Floor,* p. 191.

17. George Seferis, *Collected Poems (1924–1955),* trans. and ed. Edmund Keeley and Philip Sherrard (Princeton, NJ: Princeton University Press, 1967), p. 12 ("Mythistorema").

18. Seferis, *Collected Poems (1924–1955),* pp. 58, 92, 158, and 165.

19. Sherrard, *The Marble Threshing Floor,* pp. 198–99 and 241–42.

20. Joseph J. Bish, "Population Growth in Africa: Grasping the Scale of the Challenge," *Guardian,* January 11, 2016. "Eurostat Statistics Explained," www.europa.eu, March 2016.

21. Manent, *Metamorphoses of the City,* pp. 5 and 18.

22. Philip Mansel, *Levant: Splendour and Catastrophe on the Mediterranean* (New Haven, CT: Yale University Press, 2010 and 2011), pp. 2 and 356.

23. Charles King, *Odessa: Genius and Death in a City of Dreams* (New York, Norton, 2011), p. 108.

24. Mark Mazower, *Salonica, City of Ghosts: Christians, Muslims and Jews, 1430–1950* (New York: Knopf, 2005), p. 13.

25. Mark Greengrass, *Christendom Destroyed: Europe 1517–1648* (New York: Viking, 2014), pp. xxviii–xxix and 680.

26. Tony Judt, *A Grand Illusion? An Essay on Europe* (New York: New York University Press, [1996] 2011), pp. 10–11, 15, 17, 26–29, 41, and 119–20.

27. Leo Valiani, *The End of Austria-Hungary* (New York: Knopf, [1966] 1973), pp. xii and 195–97.

28. A. J. P. Taylor, *The Struggle for Mastery in Europe: 1848–1918* (Oxford: Oxford University Press, 1954), p. xix.

29. Giovanni Boccaccio, *Decameron,* trans. J. G. Nichols (New York: Knopf, [1350] 2008), pp. 69, 157–59, 268, and 447.

30. Borges, "The Garden of Forking Paths," in *Collected Fictions,* p. 122.

Bibliography

Acocella, Joan. "A Ghost Story." *New York Review of Books,* January 14, 2016.

Anderson, Benedict. *Imagined Communities: Reflections on the Origin and Spread of Nationalism.* New York: Verso, 1983.

Arendt, Hannah. *The Origins of Totalitarianism.* New York: Benediction Classics, (1951) 2009.

Augustine. *The Confessions of St. Augustine.* Translated from the Latin with an Introduction and Notes by John K. Ryan. New York: Doubleday, (A.D. 397–400) 1960.

Augustine. *The City of God.* Translated by Marcus Dods, with an Introduction by Thomas Merton. New York: Modern Library, (A.D. 413) 1950, 1993.

Bakshian, Aram, Jr. "Votaries of Power." *The National Interest,* January/February 2018.

Ballinger, Pamela. *History in Exile: Memory and Identity at the Borders of the Balkans.* Princeton, NJ: Princeton University Press, 2003.

Banac, Ivo. *The National Question in Yugoslavia: Origins, History, Politics.* Ithaca, NY: Cornell University Press, 1984.

Bardos, Gordon N. "Montenegro's Corrupt Party of Socialists Is Killing the Country." *National Interest,* January 28, 2020.

Beaton, Roderick. *George Seferis: Waiting for the Angel; a Biography.* New Haven, CT: Yale University Press, 2003.

Belloc, Hilaire. *The Path to Rome.* San Francisco: Ignatius Press, (1902) 2003.

Berenson, Bernard. *Italian Painters of the Renaissance,* Vol. 1, *Venetian and North Italian Schools,* and Vol. 2, *Florentine and Central Italian Schools.* London: Phaidon, (Preface 1952) 1968.

Berenson, Bernard. *Aesthetics and History*. Garden City, NY: Doubleday, (1948) 1954.

Bergreen, Laurence. *Marco Polo: From Venice to Xanadu*. New York: Knopf, 2007.

Blamires, Harry. *The Bloomsday Book: A Guide Through Joyce's "Ulysses."* London: Methuen & Co., 1966.

Boccaccio, Giovanni. *Decameron*. Translated by J. G. Nichols. New York: Knopf, (1350) 2008.

Boer, Charles. *The Homeric Hymns*. Chicago: Swallow Press, 1970.

Boer, Charles. *Charles Olson in Connecticut*. Rocky Mount: North Carolina Wesleyan College Press, 1975.

Borges, Jorge Luis. *Collected Fictions*. Translated by Andrew Hurley. New York: Penguin Books, (1941 and 1949) 1998.

Bosoni, Adriano. "Understanding Italian Defiance." *Stratfor,* January 26, 2016.

Bowra, C. M. *Sophoclean Tragedy*. Oxford: Oxford University Press, 1944.

Bowra, C. M. *From Virgil to Milton*. London: Macmillan, (1945) 1967.

Bradbury, Malcolm. Introduction to *A Farewell to Arms,* by Ernest Hemingway. New York: Everyman Library, 1993.

Braudel, Fernand. *The Mediterranean and the Mediterranean World in the Age of Philip II*. Vol. 1. Translated from the French by Sian Reynolds. New York: Harper & Row, (1949) 1972.

Braudel, Fernand. *The Mediterranean and the Mediterranean World in the Age of Philip II*. Vol. 2. Translated from the French by Sian Reynolds. New York: Harper & Row, (1949) 1973.

Brodsky, Joseph. *Watermark*. New York: Farrar, Straus & Giroux, 1992.

Brodsky, Joseph. *Collected Poems in English*. New York: Farrar, Straus & Giroux, 2000.

Brown, Peter. *The World of Late Antiquity: AD 150–750*. London: Thames and Hudson, 1971.

Burckhardt, Jacob. *The Civilization of the Renaissance in Italy*. New York: Modern Library, (1860) 1995.

Burns, Thomas. *A History of the Ostrogoths*. Bloomington: Indiana University Press, 1984.

Burton, Richard F. *The Arabian Nights: Tales from A Thousand and One Nights*. Translated, with a Preface and Notes, by Sir Richard F. Burton. Introduction by A. S. Byatt. New York: Modern Library, 2001.

Burton, Richard F. "Terminal Essay" to *The Thousand Nights and a Night*. New York: Heritage Press, 1934.

Buruma, Ian. "In the Capital of Europe." *New York Review of Books,* April 7, 2016.

Bush, Ronald L. *The Genesis of Ezra Pound's Cantos*. Princeton, NJ: Princeton University Press, (1977) 1989.

Byron, Robert. *The Byzantine Achievement: An Historical Perspective CE 330–1453*. London: Routledge, 1929.

Calvino, Italo. *If on a Winter's Night a Traveler*. Translated from the Italian by William Weaver. New York: Knopf, (1979) 1993.

Calvino, Italo. *Mr. Palomar*. Translated from the Italian by William Weaver. New York: Harcourt, (1983) 1985.

Cameron, Euan, ed. *Early Modern Europe: An Oxford History*. Oxford: Oxford University Press, 2001.

Camus, Albert. *The Outsider*. Translated from the French by Joseph Laredo. With an Introduction by Peter Dunwoodie. New York: Everyman's Library, (1942) 1998.

Camus, Albert. *The Rebel: An Essay on Man in Revolt*. Translated from the French by Anthony Bower. New York: Vintage, (1956) 1991.

Canetti, Elias. *Crowds and Power*. Translated from the German by Carol Stewart. New York: Penguin Books, (1960) 1973.

Canetti, Elias. *The Voices of Marrakesh*. Translated from the German by J. A. Underwood. London: Marion Boyars, (1967) 1982.

Carpenter, Humphrey. *A Serious Character: The Life of Ezra Pound*. Boston: Houghton Mifflin, 1988.

Carver, Robert. *The Accursed Mountains: Journeys in Albania*. London: Flamingo, (1998) 2009.

Cavarnos, Constantine. *Orthodox Iconography*. Belmont, MA: Institute for Byzantine and Modern Greek Studies, 1977.

Chekhov, Anton. "A Dreary Story." In *My Life and Other Stories*. Translated from the Russian by Constance Garnett. New York: Everyman's Library, (1889) 1992.

Churchill, Winston. *Never Give In! The Best of Winston Churchill's Speeches*. New York: Hyperion, 2003.

Clark, Bruce. *Twice a Stranger: The Mass Expulsions That Forged Modern Greece and Turkey*. Cambridge, MA: Harvard University Press, (2006) 2009.

Clark, Victoria. *Why Angels Fall: A Journey Through Orthodox Europe from Byzantium to Kosovo*. London: Macmillan, 2000.

Clogg, Richard. *A Short History of Modern Greece*. New York: Cambridge University Press, 1979.

Cohen, Rachel. *Bernard Berenson: A Life in the Picture Trade*. New Haven, CT: Yale University Press, 2013.

Collins, Paul. *The Birth of the West: Rome, Germany, France, and the Creation of Europe in the Tenth Century*. New York: PublicAffairs, 2013.

Conquest, Robert. *The Abomination of Moab*. London: Maurice Temple Smith, 1979.

Crivelli, Renzo S. *James Joyce: Triestine Itineraries*. Trieste, Italy: MGS Press, 1996.

Crowley, Roger. *City of Fortune: How Venice Ruled the Seas*. New York: Random House, (2011) 2012.

Dante Alighieri. *The Divine Comedy*. Vol. 1, *Inferno*. Translated with an Introduction, Notes, and Commentary by Mark Musa. New York: Penguin Books, (1971) 2003.

Dante Alighieri. *The Divine Comedy*. Vol. 2, *Purgatory*. Translated with an Introduction, Notes, and Commentary by Mark Musa. New York: Penguin Books, (1981) 2003.

Dante Alighieri. *The Divine Comedy*. Vol. 3, *Paradise*. Translated with an Introduction, Notes, and Commentary by Mark Musa. New York: Penguin Books, (1984) 2003.

Darwin, John. *After Tamerlane: The Rise and Fall of Global Empires, 1400–2000*. New York: Bloomsbury Press, 2008.

Davie, Donald. *Ezra Pound: Poet as Sculptor*. Oxford: Oxford University Press, (1964) 1968.

Davies, Norman. *Europe: A History*. New York: Oxford University Press, 1996.

Deliyannis, Deborah Mauskopf. *Ravenna in Late Antiquity*. New York: Cambridge University Press, 2010.

Denham, H. M. *The Adriatic: A Sea-Guide to the Dalmatian Coast and Islands, Venice and Eastern Italy*. London: John Murray, 1967.

Dirda, Michael. Introduction to *ABC of Reading*, by Ezra Pound. New York: New Directions, (1934) 2010.

Dobbs, Michael. "Where Venice Once Ruled." *Smithsonian*, Winter 2015.

Donatich, John. "Trieste Elegies." *The Atlantic*, June 2002.

Dostoevsky, Fyodor. *Demons*. Translated from the Russian by Richard Pevear and Larissa Volokhonsky. New York: Vintage Classics, (1872) 1994.

Dreher, Rod. *How Dante Can Save Your Life: The Life-Changing Wisdom of History's Greatest Poem*. New York: Regan Arts, 2015.

Duggan, Christopher. *A Concise History of Italy*. Cambridge: Cambridge University Press, 2014.

Durham, Edith. *High Albania*. Introduction by John Hodgson. London: Phoenix Press, (1909) 2000.

Durrell, Lawrence. *Bitter Lemons*. London: Faber and Faber, 1957.

Durrell, Lawrence. *Prospero's Cell: A Guide to the Landscape and Manners of the Island of Corfu*. London: Faber and Faber, 1945.

Eliot, T. S. *Collected Poems, 1909–1962*. New York: Harcourt Brace Jovanovich, 1991.

Eliot, T. S. *Dante*. London: Faber & Faber, 1929.

Ellmann, Richard. *James Joyce*. New York: Oxford University Press, (1959) 1982.

Fine, John V. A., Jr. *When Ethnicity Did Not Matter in the Balkans: A Study of Identity in Pre-Nationalist Croatia, Dalmatia, and Slavonia in the Medieval and Early-Modern Periods*. Ann Arbor: University of Michigan Press, 2006.

Finlay, Victoria. *Color: A Natural History of the Palette*. New York: Ballantine, 2002.

Fischer, Bernd J. *King Zog and the Struggle for Stability in Albania*. Tirana: Albanian Institute for International Studies, (1984) 2012.

Flory, Wendy. "Pound and Anti-Semitism." In *Cambridge Companion to Ezra Pound*. Edited by Ira B. Nadel. New York: Cambridge University Press, 1999.

Fox, Robert. *The Inner Sea: The Mediterranean and Its People*. New York: Knopf, (1991) 1993.

Frankopan, Peter. *The Silk Roads: A New History of the World*. New York: Knopf, 2015.

Frazer, James George. *The Golden Bough: A Study in Magic and Religion*. New York: Macmillan, (1890) 1922.

Gaddis, John Lewis. *On Grand Strategy*. New York: Penguin Press, 2018.

Gellner, Ernest. *Nations and Nationalism*. Ithaca, NY: Cornell University Press, 1983.

Gibbon, Edward. *The Decline and Fall of the Roman Empire*. Vols. 4, 5, and 6. New York: Everyman's Library, (1776–1788) 1910.

Gilmour, David. *The Pursuit of Italy: A History of a Land, Its Regions, and Their Peoples*. New York: Farrar, Straus and Giroux, 2011.

Goethe, Johann Wolfgang von. *Italian Journey [1786–1788]*. Translated from the German by W. H. Auden and Elizabeth Mayer. New York: Penguin Books, (1816) 1962 and 1970.

Gorra, Michael. *The Bells in Their Silence: Travels Through Germany*. Princeton, NJ: Princeton University Press, 2004.

Graves, Robert. *The Greek Myths*. Vol. 1. New York: Penguin Books, 1955.

Graves, Robert. *The Greek Myths*. Vol. 2. New York: Penguin Books, 1955.

Greengrass, Mark. *Christendom Destroyed: Europe 1517–1648*. New York: Viking, 2014.

Gress, David. *From Plato to NATO: The Idea of the West and Its Opponents*. New York: The Free Press, 1998.

Gunther, John. *Behind the Iron Curtain*. New York: Harper & Brothers, 1948.

Hale, Sheila. *Titian: His Life*. London: HarperPress, 2012.

Hamilton, Edith. *Mythology*. Boston: Little, Brown and Company, 1942.

Hammer, Langdon. *Hart Crane & Allen Tate: Janus-Faced Modernism*. Princeton, NJ: Princeton University Press, 1993.

Hammond, Nicholas. "The Relations of Illyrian Albania with the Greeks and the Romans." In *Perspectives on Albania*. Edited by Tom Winnifrith. London: Palgrave Macmillan, 1992.

Harris, Robin. *Dubrovnik: A History*. London: Saqi Books, 2003.

Hay, Denys. *Europe: The Emergence of an Idea*. New York: Harper & Row, (1957) 1966.

Hegel, Georg Wilhelm Friedrich. *Philosophy of Right*. Translated by T. M. Knox. Oxford, UK: Clarendon Press, (1820) 1942 and 1952.

Herodotus. *The History*. Translated by David Grene. Chicago: University of Chicago Press, 1987.

Herrin, Judith. *Ravenna: Capital of Empire, Crucible of Europe*. Princeton, NJ: Princeton University Press, 2020.

Herzen, Alexander. *My Past and Thoughts*. Translated by Constance Garnett. Berkeley: University of California Press, (1968) 1973.

Hesiod. "Ode to Work." Translated by A. E. Stallings. *New Criterion*, April 2015.

Hodgkin, Joanna. *Amateurs in Eden: The Story of a Bohemian Marriage; Nancy and Lawrence Durrell*. London: Virago Press, 2012.

Hollander, Paul. *From Benito Mussolini to Hugo Chavez: Intellectuals and a Century of Political Hero Worship*. Cambridge: Cambridge University Press, 2016.

Holmes, George. *The Oxford History of Medieval Europe*. New York: Oxford University Press, 1988.

Horace, *Odes and Epodes*. Edited and translated by Niall Rudd. Cambridge, MA: Harvard University Press, Loeb Classical Library, 2004.

Huntington, Samuel P. *The Clash of Civilizations and the Remaking of World Order*. New York: Simon & Schuster, 1996.

Huntington, Samuel P. "If Not Civilizations, What?" *Foreign Affairs*, November/December 1993.

Jackson, Thomas Graham. *Recollections: The Life and Travels of a Victorian Architect*. London: Unicorn Press, (1915) 2003.

James, Henry. *The Aspern Papers and Other Tales*. Edited and with an Introduction and Notes by Michael Gorra. New York: Penguin Books, (1888) 2014.

James, Henry. *The Wings of the Dove*. Introduction by John Bayley. New York: Penguin Books, (1902) 1986.

James, Henry. *Henry James: Letters from the Palazzo Barbaro*. Edited by Rosella Mamoli Zorzi. London: Pushkin Press, 1998.

Jervis-White-Jervis, Henry. *History of the Island of Corfu, and of the Republic of the Ionian Islands*. London: Colburn and Co., 1852 (2005).

Joyce, James. *Dubliners*. Harmondsworth, UK: Penguin Books, (1914) 1976.

Joyce, James. *A Portrait of the Artist as a Young Man*. New York: Viking, (1916) 1970.

Joyce, James. *Ulysses*. New York: Vintage, (1934) 1990.

Judah, Tim. *The Serbs: History, Myth and the Destruction of Yugoslavia*. New Haven, CT: Yale University Press, (1997) 2000.

Judt, Tony. *A Grand Illusion? An Essay on Europe*. New York: New York University Press, (1996) 2011.

Kadare, Ismail. *The Concert*. New York: William Morrow, (1988) 1994.

Kadia, Besart. "Can Albania Be Saved from Narco-Government?" CapX.co, June 5, 2017.

Kagan, Robert. *Of Paradise and Power: America and Europe in the New World Order*. New York: Knopf, 2003.

Kaplan, Robert D. *Balkan Ghosts: A Journey Through History*. New York: St. Martin's Press, 1993.

Kaplan, Robert D. *Mediterranean Winter: The Pleasures of History and Landscape in Tunisia, Sicily, Dalmatia, and the Peloponnese*. New York: Random House, 2004.

Kaplan, Robert D. "A Globe-Trotting Celebration of Erudition." *Wall Street Journal*, February 21, 2015.

Kármán, Gábor, and Lovro Kunčević, eds. *The European Tributary States of the Ottoman Empire in the Sixteenth and Seventeenth Centuries*. Boston: Brill, 2013.

Keats, John. *Keats: Poems*. Selection by Peter Washington. New York: Knopf, 1994.

Kenner, Hugh. *The Poetry of Ezra Pound*. Lincoln: University of Nebraska Press, 1985. First published 1951 by Faber and Faber (London).

Kent, Neil. *Trieste: Adriatic Emporium and Gateway to the Heart of Europe*. London: Hurst, 2011.

Khanna, Parag. *Connectography: Mapping the Future of Global Civilization*. New York: Random House, 2016.

King, Charles. *Odessa: Genius and Death in a City of Dreams*. New York, Norton, 2011.

Knox, Peter E. and J. C. McKeown, eds. *The Oxford Anthology of Roman Literature*. New York: Oxford University Press, 2013.

Krastev, Ivan. *After Europe*. Philadelphia: University of Pennsylvania Press, 2017.

Kundera, Milan. *The Unbearable Lightness of Being*. Translated from the Czech by Michael Henry Heim. New York: Harper & Row, 1984.

Lane, Frederic C. *Venice: A Maritime Republic*. Baltimore: Johns Hopkins University Press, 1973.

Leigh Fermor, Patrick. *Mani: Travels in the Southern Peloponnese*. London: John Murray, 1958.

Levick, Barbara. *Tiberius: The Politician*. London: Routledge, (1976) 1999.

Lewis, Bernard. *What Went Wrong? The Clash Between Islam and Modernity in the Middle East*. New York: Oxford University Press, 2002.

Lewis, David Levering. *God's Crucible: Islam and the Making of Europe, 570–1215*. New York: W. W. Norton, 2008.

Logoreci, Anton. *The Albanians: Europe's Forgotten Survivors*. London: Victor Gollancz, 1977.

Luttwak, Edward N. *The Grand Strategy of the Byzantine Empire*. Cambridge, MA: Harvard University Press, 2009.

McCarthy, Mary. *Venice Observed*. New York: Penguin Books, (1956) 1972.

McEvedy, Colin. *The New Penguin Atlas of Medieval History*. London: Penguin Books, 1961.

McNeill, William H. *The Rise of the West: A History of the Human Community*. Chicago: University of Chicago Press, 1963.

Machiavelli, Niccolò. *History of Florence: And of the Affairs of Italy*. Introduction by Hugo Albert Rennert. Seattle: CreateSpace Independent Publishing Platform, (1520–1525) 2014.

Machiavelli, Niccolo. *The Prince*. New York: Everyman's Library Classics, (1532) 1992.

Maclean, Fitzroy. *Eastern Approaches*. New York: Time-Life Books, (1949) 1964.

Madieri, Marisa. *Aqua Green: A Childhood in Istria*. Translated from the Italian by Gareth Norbury. Munich: Swiss Re, (1987) 2004.

Magris, Claudio. *Blindly*. Translated from the Italian by Anne Milano Appel. New Haven, CT: Yale University Press, (2006) 2008.

Magris, Claudio. *Danube*. Translated from the Italian by Patrick Creagh. New York: Farrar, Straus & Giroux, (1986) 1989.

Magris, Claudio. *Microcosms*. Translated from the Italian by Iain Halliday. London: Harvill Press, (1997) 2000.

Malcolm, Noel. *Agents of Empire: Knights, Corsairs, Jesuits and Spies in the Sixteenth-Century Mediterranean World*. New York: Oxford University Press, 2015.

Manent, Pierre. *Metamorphoses of the City: On the Western Dynamic*. Translated from the French by Marc LePain. Cambridge, MA: Harvard University Press, 2013.

Mann, Thomas. *Death in Venice*. New York: Knopf, (1912) 1963.

Mansel, Philip. *Levant: Splendour and Catastrophe on the Mediterranean*. New Haven, CT: Yale University Press, 2010 and 2011.

Martin, Benjamin G. "'European Culture' Is an Invented Tradition." *Aeon*, March 2017.

Martin, John Rupert. *Baroque*. Boulder, CO: Westview Press, 1977.

Marusic, Damir. "Did Moscow Botch a Coup in Montenegro?" *American Interest*, October 30, 2016.

Matvejević, Predrag. *Mediterranean: A Cultural Landscape*. Translated from the Croatian by Michael Henry Heim. Berkeley: University of California Press, (1987) 1999.

Mazower, Mark. *Salonica, City of Ghosts: Christians, Muslims and Jews, 1430–1950*. New York: Knopf, 2005.

Mazower, Mark. *Governing the World: The History of an Idea, 1815 to the Present*. New York: Penguin Press, 2012.

Merry, Robert. "Spengler's Ominous Prophecy." *National Interest*, January/February 2013.

Milton, Giles. *Paradise Lost: Smyrna 1922; The Destruction of a Christian City in the Islamic World*. New York: Basic Books, 2008.

Milton, John. *Paradise Lost*. New York: Penguin Books, (1667) 2003.

Missac, Pierre. *Walter Benjamin's Passages*. Translated by Shierry Weber Nicholsen. Cambridge, MA: MIT Press, (1987) 1995.

Moody, A. David. *Ezra Pound: Poet; A Portrait of the Man and His Work*. Vol. 1, *The Young Genius, 1885–1920*. New York: Oxford University Press, 2007.

Moody, A. David. *Ezra Pound: Poet; A Portrait of the Man and His Work*. Vol. 2, *The Epic Years, 1921–1939*. New York: Oxford University Press, 2014.

Morris, Ian. *Why the West Rules—for Now: The Patterns of History, and What They Reveal About the Future*. New York: Farrar, Straus and Giroux, 2010.

Morris, Jan. *The Venetian Empire: A Sea Voyage*. New York: Penguin Books, (1980) 1990.

Morris, Jan. *The World of Venice*. With a New Foreword by the Author. New York: Harcourt, (1960 by James Morris) 1993.

Morris, Jan. *Trieste and the Meaning of Nowhere*. New York: Da Capo Press, 2001.

Moyle, Franny. *Turner: The Extraordinary Life & Momentous Times of J. M. W. Turner*. New York: Penguin Press, 2016.

Musil, Robert. *The Man Without Qualities*. Vols. 1 and 2. Translated by Sophie Wilkins and Burton Pike. New York: Vintage, (1978) 1995 and 1996.

Nightingale, Steven. *Granada: A Pomegranate in the Hand of God.* Berkeley, CA: Counterpoint Press, 2015.

Njegoš, Petar II Petrović, *The Mountain Wreath.* Translated and edited by Vasa D. Mihailovich. Irvine, CA: Charles Schlacks Jr., 1986.

Norwich, John Julius. *A History of Venice.* New York: Knopf, (1977 and 1981) 1982.

Norwich, John Julius. *Byzantium: The Early Centuries.* New York: Knopf, 1989.

Oakley, Francis. *Empty Bottles of Gentilism: Kingship and the Divine in Late Antiquity and the Early Middle Ages (to 1050).* The Emergence of Western Political Thought in the Latin Middle Ages. New Haven, CT: Yale University Press, 2010.

Oakley, Francis. *The Mortgage of the Past: Reshaping the Ancient Political Inheritance (1050–1300).* The Emergence of Western Political Thought in the Latin Middle Ages. New Haven, CT: Yale University Press, 2012.

Oakley, Francis. *The Watershed of Modern Politics: Law, Virtue, Kingship, and Consent (1300–1650).* The Emergence of Western Political Thought in the Latin Middle Ages. New Haven, CT: Yale University Press, 2015.

Ormsby, Eric. "Pound's Confucian Confusions." *New Criterion,* February 2016.

Ortega y Gasset, José. *The Revolt of the Masses.* Translated from the Spanish by Anthony Kerrigan. Foreword by Saul Bellow. Notre Dame, IN: University of Notre Dame Press, (1932) 1985.

Ortega y Gasset, José. *Man and Crisis.* Translated from the Spanish by Mildred Adams. New York: Norton, (1942 and 1958) 1962.

Ostrogorsky, George. *History of the Byzantine State.* Translated from the German by Joan Hussey. Oxford, UK: Basil Blackwell, 1956.

Pahor, Boris. *Necropolis.* Translated from the Slovenian by Michael Biggins. Champaign, IL: Dalkey Archive Press, (1967) 2010.

Pater, Walter. *Marius the Epicurean: His Sensations and Ideas.* New York: Cosimo Classics reprint, 2005. First published 1885 by Jonathan Cape (London).

Pirenne, Henri. *Mohammed & Charlemagne.* Translated from the French by Bernard Miall. Mineola, NY: Dover Publications, (1937 and 1954) 2001.

Plutarch. *Plutarch's Lives.* Vol. 2. Translated by John Dryden, edited and revised by Arthur Hugh Clough. New York: Modern Library, (1683–86, 1864) 1992.

Polo, Marco. *The Travels of Marco Polo: The Complete Yule-Cordier Edition.* Vols. 1 and 2. New York: Dover Publications, (1903) 1993.

Pound, Ezra. "In a Station of the Metro." *Poetry,* April 1913.

Pound, Ezra. *The Cantos of Ezra Pound.* New York: New Directions, (1934) 1993.

Pound, Ezra. *Selected Cantos of Ezra Pound.* New York: New Directions, 1970.

Pound, Ezra. *Guide to Kulchur.* New York: New Directions, 1970.

Praga, Giuseppe. *History of Dalmatia*. Translated from the Italian by Edward Steinberg. Pisa, Italy: Giardini, (1954) 1993.

Procopius. *History of the Wars: Books V–VI.15, Books VI.16–VII.35, Books VII.36–VIII*. Translated by H. B. Dewing. Cambridge, MA: Harvard University Press, Loeb Classical Library, 1919, 1924, and 1928.

Quigley, Carroll. *The Evolution of Civilizations: An Introduction to Historical Analysis*. Indianapolis, Liberty Fund, (1961) 1979.

Raley, Harold C. *José Ortega y Gasset: Philosopher of European Unity*. Tuscaloosa: University of Alabama Press, 1971.

Reill, Dominique Kirchner. *Nationalists Who Feared the Nation: Adriatic Multi-Nationalism in Habsburg Dalmatia, Trieste, and Venice*. Stanford, CA: Stanford University Press, 2012.

Rice, Edward. *Captain Sir Richard Francis Burton: The Secret Agent Who Made the Pilgrimage to Mecca, Discovered the Kama Sutra, and Brought the Arabian Nights to the West*. New York: Charles Scribner's Sons, 1990.

Rilke, Rainer Maria. *The Notebooks of Malte Laurids Brigge*. Translated from the German, edited, and introduced by Michael Hulse. New York: Penguin Books, (1910) 2009.

Rilke, Rainer Maria. *Duino Elegies and The Sonnets to Orpheus*. Edited and translated from the German by Stephen Mitchell. New York: Vintage International, (1923) 1982.

Roberts, Andrew. *Napoleon: A Life*. New York: Viking, 2014.

Rodogno, Davide. *Fascism's European Empire: Italian Occupation During the Second World War*. Translated from the Italian by Adrian Belton. New York: Cambridge University Press, (2003) 2006.

Rosand, David. *Myths of Venice: The Figuration of a State*. Chapel Hill: University of North Carolina Press, 2001.

Roth, Joseph. *Hotel Savoy*. Translated from the German by John Hoare. London: Pan Books, (1924) 1988.

Roth, Joseph. *The Radetzky March*. Translated from the German by Eva Tucker, based on an earlier translation by Geoffrey Dunlop. New York: Penguin Books, (1932) 1984.

Rothman, E. Natalie. *Brokering Empire: Trans-Imperial Subjects Between Venice and Istanbul*. Ithaca, NY: Cornell University Press, 2012.

Rumiz, Paolo. *The Fault Line: Traveling the Other Europe from Finland to Ukraine*. Translated from the Italian by Gregory Conti. New York: Rizzoli Ex Libris, (2012) 2015.

Runciman, Steven. *Mistra: Byzantine Capital of the Peloponnese*. London: Thames and Hudson, 1980.

Ruskin, John. *The Stones of Venice*. Edited and abridged by J. G. Links. New York: Da Capo Press, (1853) 1960.

Said, Edward W. *Orientalism*. New York: Pantheon, 1978.

Savic, Domen. "Slovenia's Prime Minister Is a Far-Right Conspiracy Theorist and Twitter Addict Who Won't Admit Trump Lost." *Foreign Policy*, November 11, 2020.

Scott, Emmet. *Mohammed & Charlemagne Revisited: The History of a Controversy*. London: New English Review Press, 2012.

Seelye, Catherine, ed. *Charles Olson and Ezra Pound*. New York: Grossman, 1975.

Seferis, George. *Collected Poems (1924–1955)*. Translated, edited, and introduced by Edmund Keeley and Philip Sherrard. Princeton, NJ: Princeton University Press, 1967.

Segalen, Victor. *Essay on Exoticism: An Aesthetics of Diversity*. Translated and edited by Yael Rachel Schlick. Foreword by Harry Harootunian. Durham, NC: Duke University Press, (1918) 2002.

Shaw, Prue. *Reading Dante: From Here to Eternity*. New York: Liveright, 2014.

Sherrard, Philip. *The Marble Threshing Floor: Studies in Modern Greek Poetry*. Limni, Greece: Denise Harvey, (1956) 1981.

Sherrard, Philip. *The Greek East and the Latin West: A Study in the Christian Tradition*. Limni, Greece: Denise Harvey, 1959.

Sherrard, Philip. *The Wound of Greece: Studies in Neo-Hellenism*. New York: St. Martin's, 1979. First published 1978 by Rex Collings (London).

Shore, Marci. *The Ukrainian Night: An Intimate History of Revolution*. New Haven, CT: Yale University Press, 2017.

Simic, Charles. "Working for the Dictionary." *New York Review of Books*, October 19, 2000.

Smith, Anthony D. *National Identity*. Reno, NV: University of Nevada Press, 1993. First published 1991 by Penguin (London).

Smith, Stephen. *The Scramble for Europe: Young Africa on Its Way to the Old Continent*. Cambridge, UK: Polity, 2019.

Snyder, Timothy. *The Red Prince: The Secret Lives of a Habsburg Archduke*. New York: Basic Books, 2008.

Snyder, Timothy. "Mapping Eastern Europe." Presentation at the World Economic Forum, Davos, Switzerland, January 25, 2018.

Solzhenitsyn, Aleksandr. *November 1916: The Red Wheel / Knot II*. Translated from the Russian by H. T. Willetts. New York: Farrar, Straus & Giroux, (1984) 1999.

Southern, R. W. *The Making of the Middle Ages*. New Haven, CT: Yale University Press, 1953.

Spencer, Elsa M. *Good-bye, Trieste*. Self-published, Xlibris, 2008.

Spengler, Oswald. *The Decline of the West.* Translated from the German by Charles Francis Atkinson. Abridged by Helmut Werner. New York: Knopf, (1918 and 1922) 1961.

Stark, Freya. *The Southern Gates of Arabia: A Journey in the Hadhramaut.* New York: Modern Library, (1936) 2001.

Starr, S. Frederick, and Svante E. Cornell, eds. *Putin's Grand Strategy: The Eurasian Union and Its Discontents.* Central Asia–Caucasus Institute & Silk Road Studies Program of the Johns Hopkins University–SAIS, 2014.

Stokes, Adrian. *Stones of Rimini.* New York: Schocken Books, (1934) 1969.

Svevo, Italo. *Confessions of Zeno.* Translated from the Italian by Beryl de Zoete. New York: Knopf, (1923) 1930.

Tanner, Marcus. *Croatia: A Nation Forged in War.* New Haven, CT: Yale University Press, (1997) 2010.

Tanner, Tony. *Venice Desired.* Cambridge, MA: Harvard University Press, 1992.

Taylor, A. J. P. *The Struggle for Mastery in Europe: 1848–1918.* Oxford: Oxford University Press, 1954.

Terrell, Carroll F. *A Companion to the Cantos of Ezra Pound.* Berkeley: University of California Press, 1980.

Theroux, Paul. *The Pillars of Hercules: A Grand Tour of the Mediterranean.* New York: Ballantine Books, 1995.

Thompson, Mark. *The White War: Life and Death on the Italian Front, 1915–1919.* New York: Basic Books, (2008) 2009.

Thucydides. *The Peloponnesian War.* Translated by Thomas Hobbes. Ann Arbor: University of Michigan Press, (1629) 1959.

Tierney, Brian. *Religion, Law, and the Growth of Constitutional Thought, 1150–1650.* Cambridge: Cambridge University Press, 1982.

Tracy, James D. *Balkan Wars: Habsburg Croatia, Ottoman Bosnia, and Venetian Dalmatia, 1499–1617.* Lanham, MD: Rowman & Littlefield, 2016.

Unamuno, Miguel de. *Tragic Sense of Life.* Translated from the Spanish by J. E. Crawford Flitch. New York: SophiaOmni, (1912) 2014.

Valéry, Paul. "The Crisis of the Mind." *Athenaeum,* April and May 1919.

Valiani, Leo. *The End of Austria-Hungary.* New York: Knopf, (1966) 1973.

Vickers, Miranda. *The Albanians: A Modern History.* New York: I. B. Tauris, (1995) 2014.

Voinovitch, Count Louis. *Dalmatia and the Jugoslav Movement.* With a preface by Sir Arthur Evans. London: George Allen & Unwin, (1917) 1920.

Ware, Timothy. *The Orthodox Church.* Middlesex, UK: Penguin Books, (1963) 1975.

Weickgenant, Joel. "The New NATO Outpost in the Adriatic." *RealClearWorld,* September 7, 2016.

West, Rebecca. *Black Lamb and Grey Falcon*. New York: Papermac, (1941) 1983.

Wickham, Chris. *Early Medieval Italy: Central Power and Local Society, 400–1000*. London: Macmillan, 1981.

Wilson, Edmund. *Axel's Castle: A Study of the Imaginative Literature of 1870–1930*. Introduction by Hugh Kenner. New York: Modern Library, (1931, 1991) 1996.

Wolff, Larry. *Venice and the Slavs: The Discovery of Dalmatia in the Age of Enlightenment*. Stanford, CA: Stanford University Press, 2001.

Wood, L. Todd. "Haven't We Had Enough in Montenegro?" *Washington Times*, December 14, 2017.

Woodhouse, C. M. *George Gemistos Plethon: The Last of the Hellenes*. New York: Oxford University Press, 1986.

Woodward, Anthony. *Ezra Pound and the Pisan Cantos*. London: Routledge, 1980.

Yeats, William Butler. "Sailing to Byzantium," 1926.

Zavalani, Tajar. *History of Albania*. Edited by Robert Elsie and Bejtullah Destani. London: Centre for Albanian Studies, (1961–1963) 2015.

Zielonka, Jan. *Is the EU Doomed?* Cambridge, UK: Polity Press, 2014.

Žitko, Salvator, et al. *Koper: The Town and Its Heritage*. Koper, Slovenia: Libris, 2011.

Zlatar, Zdenko. *Our Kingdom Come: The Counter-Reformation, the Republic of Dubrovnik, and the Liberation of the Balkan Slavs*. Boulder, CO: East European Monographs, 1992.

Index

—

ROBERT D. KAPLAN is the bestselling and widely acclaimed author of twenty books on foreign affairs and travel translated into many languages, including *The Good American*, *The Revenge of Geography*, *Asia's Cauldron*, *The Coming Anarchy*, and *Balkan Ghosts*. He holds the Robert Strausz-Hupé Chair in Geopolitics at the Foreign Policy Research Institute. For three decades he reported on foreign affairs for *The Atlantic*. He was a member of the Pentagon's Defense Policy Board and the Chief of Naval Operations' Executive Panel. *Foreign Policy* magazine twice named him one of the world's Top 100 Global Thinkers.

robertdkaplan.com

ABOUT THE TYPE

This book was set in Caslon, a typeface first designed in 1722 by William Caslon (1692–1766). Its widespread use by most English printers in the early eighteenth century soon supplanted the Dutch typefaces that had formerly prevailed. The roman is considered a "workhorse" typeface due to its pleasant, open appearance, while the italic is exceedingly decorative.